ISBN 3−89356−130−7

© 1991
**Tetra-Press**
TetraWerke Dr. rer nat. Ulrich Baensch GmbH
P.O.Box 1580, D-4520 Melle, Germany
All rights reserved, incl. film, broadcasting, television as well as the reprinting
1st edition 1−10.000, 1991
Printed in Spain
Egedsa - Sabadell D.L.B. 7715-91
Distributed in U.S.A. by
Tetra Sales (Division of Warner-Lambert)
Morris Plains, N.J. 07950
Distributed in UK by
Tetra Sales, Lambert Court
Chestnut Avenue, Eastleigh
Hampshire SO5 3ZQ
WL-Code: 16031

Hans A. Baensch / Dr. Paul V. Loiselle

# Marine Aquarist's Manual

## Comprehension Edition

# Contents

The goal of the marine aquarists: to reproduce the marvels of the coral reef in his home.

# THE MARINE AQUARIUM

# Introduction

The unquestioned beauty and often bizzare form of marine organisms have long fascinated mankind and excited a lively curiosity about their way of life. The Greek philosopher Aristotle, while doubtless not the first person to take a more than casual interest in what would today be considered marine biology, was the first to publish his observations. We can deduce the degree of his enthusiasm for the subject from the fact that he spent his honeymoon wading through the tidepools of the Hellespont in search of specimens! His bride's reaction to her husband's activities remain a matter for speculation, but it seems safe to assume the poor girl was the first of a long line of spouses totally bemused by their partner's seemingly inexplicable obsession with things aquatic. Interestingly enough, mediaeval Persian romances detailing the adventures of Alexander the Great recount that the great conquerer ordered the construction of a glass diving bell to observe the wonders of the deep in comfort. Assuming a kernel of truth underlies this admittedly fanciful piece of versification, might it be possible that Aristotle passed his lively interest in the marine realm to his most famous pupil? In keeping with their relentlessly practical bent, the Romans were chiefly concerned with aquaculture as a source of food. To that end, they pioneered many technologies taken for granted today, such as the warming of pond water to accelerate the growth of fish and invertebrates to marketable size. However, Cicero's caustic comments about *piscinarii* who wept over the death of a prized fish suggest that at least of few members of the Roman aristocracy would have found common ground with contemporary marine aquarists.

The contemporary interest in marine aquaria has its roots in the mid-nineteenth century's fashionable involvement in nature study of all sorts. The scope of these Victorian aquarists was essentially restricted to the fish and invertebrates native to the North Atlantic and Baltic coasts. Their efforts were both valiant and well intentioned. However, their unsatisfactory outcome was predetermined by both an incomplete understanding of basic aquaristic principles and a hopelessly rudimentary technology. The opening decades of the twentieth century saw the first efforts to maintain coral reef fishes and invertebrates in closed systems, with equally disappointing results. By the mid-1950's, pioneering marine aquarists had, through the painful process of trial and error, defined the basic problems entailed in salt-water fish keeping and worked out partial solutions. However, the difficulties inherent in protecting both tanks and equipment from the corrosive effects of sea water continued to bedevil the development of the marine hobby.

The technological bottleneck that had so long frustrated marine aquarists was broken by the successful introduction of the silicone-bonded all-glass aquarium and the development of magnetic impeller-driven, plastic power filters in the 1960's. Equally important was the development of reliable synthetic salt mixes, whose proper use opened a window to the sea for aquarists living thousands of miles away from the nearest coastline. As interest in marine aquaristics grew, so did the demand for colorful fishes and invertebrates. Throughout the Caribbean and Indo-Pacific regions, enterprising exporters sprang up to satisfy this rapidly expanding market. Today, thanks to their efforts and the availability of reliable, globe-girdling air links, marine aquarists routinely enjoy access to the inshore faunas of such exotic locales as the Florida Keys, Belize, Hawaii, Fiji, the Gilbert Islands, the Philippines, Australia's Great Barrier Reef and the Red Sea.

Marine aquaristics has now evolved to the point where hobbyists whose principal preoccupation was keeping their pets alive for more than a few weeks can now debate the merits of such diverse styles of aquarium management as the Dutch mini-reef and the natural marine system. Tank-bred clownfish and neon gobies are routinely available through commercial channels, a state of affairs undreamed of as recently as a decade ago. As pioneering aquaculturists discover the reproductive secrets of yet other popular reef denizens, it is only a matter of time before domestically bred fish assume the same commercial importance in the marine as they do in freshwater hobby.

Notwithstanding these remarkable advances in the theory and practice of marine aquaristics, the sad fact remains that most initial efforts to set up a salt water tank end badly. It is a testimony to the potent attraction marine organisms exert on most hobbyists that so many neophytes bother to repeat their efforts however many times it takes them to learn good technique by trial and error! Nevertheless, many aquarists, disappointed in their initial failure and detered by the high cost of replacing dead fish, consign coral and gravel to the garage or basement and put their tank to other uses. These failures are all the sadder in that a marine aquarium is no more inherently difficult to set up and maintain than a freshwater system. Aquarists who take the trouble to learn a few basic principles and practice good aquarium technique rarely have cause to complain of the fragility of marine organisms in captivity.

Our aim in this book is to provide a primer of marine aquarium keeping. It is written for the hobbyist with some prior experience with freshwater aquaristics who desires to expand into the marine hobby or has already made initial efforts to set up a saltwater tank in his home. We assume that the reader is familiar with the basic rules of aquarium maintenance and knows something of the biology of fishes. The first chapter contrasts the freshwater and marine environments and explores the ways in which the differences between the two influence the husbandry of marine organisms in captivity. The second discusses the basic equipment necessary to keep marine organisms alive and well in captivity, placing special emphasis om alternative approaches to filtration, while the third is concerned with how to furnish the tank in an appropriate manner. The fourth takes the reader step by step through the procedure of setting up the marine aquarium and running in a biological filter. The fifth considers the factors that determine how many and what kinds of organisms can be successfully housed in a saltwater aquarium and suggests guidelines for selecting healthy specimens and introducing them without incident to either a new or an established tank. The sixth is devoted to the nutrition of marine organisms, the seventh to proper maintenance practices, the eighth to corrective measures to be taken when events take an untoward turn, as they sometimes will even in the tanks of experienced aquarists! Chapter nine is devoted to the diagnosis and treatment of the most commonly encountered diseases of marine fish. Chapters ten and eleven discusse the selection and care of macroalgae and invertebrates that can be expected to prosper under home aquarium conditions, while chapter twelve is devoted to a similar treatment of saltwater fishes. The final chapter outlines approaches to learning more about marine aquaristics and includes a list of recommended readings.

It is our hope that this book will increase the number of successful first marine aquaria and thus contribute to the positive development of the saltwater hobby.

Hans A. Baensch, Melle, 1991
Dr. Paul V. Loiselle, Jersey City, 1991

# CHAPTER 1.

# The Challenge of the Marine Aquarium

The conventional wisdom has it that keeping marine organisms is difficult. As it stands, this aphorism is less a statement of absolute fact than a comparison of two different types of fish keeping. What is really meant is that marine aquaria are more difficult to manage succesfully than are freshwater aquaria. While accuracy of even this position is questionable, one must concede the premise that there are major differences between the marine and freshwater environments. Failure to appreciate these differences and how they bear on the husbandry of aquatic organisms will almost certainly bear adversely upon initial attempts at marine aquarium keeping. Hence it is well worth the effort to to understand the degree to which the two major aquatic environments differ from one another.

If pressed for a single way in which freshwater and marine environments differ from one another, most aquarists would immediately reply that the latter are salty, while the former are not. This observation is true enough, but it lacks precision. The ammount of dissolved material varies considerably from one locality to the next in both marine and freshwater habitats, and while common table salt, **sodium chloride**, is the most abundant chemical species dissolved in sea water, it is by no means its only constituent. It is more accurate to describe marine as those aquatic habitats in which the concentration of dissolved salts, dominated by sodium chloride, exceeds that found within the cells of living organisms. The concentration of dissolved salts in freshwater habitats, by way of contrast, is always less.

The processes defined as life can occur only within a relatively narrow range of chemical concentrations. Living organisms must therefore take great care to maintain the internal chemical composition of their bodies' cells within quite precise limits. Because cell membranes are selectively permeable, water ends to migrate from areas of low salinity to those of high salinity, a process known as **osmosis**. Thus, both freshwater and marine organisms are faced with a major survival challenge by the very nature of the media they inhabit. Freshwater organisms must counter the risk of water moving into their cells until the concentration of dissolved salts on both sides of the cell membranes is equal. Marine organisms, on the other hand, live in constant risk of dehydration because of water's tendency to move from the interior of their cells into the surrounding environment. Because living cells must be able to transport the raw materials of chemical synthesis and waste products across cell membranes, organisms cannot resolve this problem by simply developing impermeable barriers. Such mechanisms as they do evolve must necessarily be active, rather than passive.

Freshwater fishes deal with the problem of surplus water by "waterproofing" as much of their internal and external body surfaces as physiologically possible and swallowing very little water, thus reducing the ammount inevitably absorbed through the intestinal walls. Obviously, significant ammounts of water are unavoidably absorbed across the surface of the gills. However, highly efficient kidneys allow them to compensate for this by excreting copious ammounts of very dilute urine. Such a strategy entails a risk of depleting the body's reserve of ions essential to normal cellular function, such as potassium and calcium. However, the wall of the urinary bladder in freshwater fishes can selectively reabsorb these substances into the body, thus minimizing the extent of such losses to the point where they can easily be made good from dietary sources.

Marine fish, on the other hand, have evolved several options to the problem of managing excessive external salt concentrations. Sharks, rays and the coelecanth osmoregulate by allowing the concentration of dissolved solids in their body fluids to slightly exceed that of the surrounding environment by retaining urea and other metabolic wastes. This puts them in much the same position with regard to absorbing excess water faced by freshwater fishes. Not surprisingly, they also cope with it in much the same way. However, cartilaginous fishes also have to cope with more elevated salt concentrations in their body fluids than do freshwater fishes, so they have not evolved the highly efficient salt recycling system of the latter and thus excrete a rather concentrated urine.

Bony fishes, on the other hand, drink constantly to compensate for water loss across their gills, taking in as much as 35% of their body weight **daily**. Most of the heavier ions with a double elctrical charge, such as calcium, magnesium and sulfate remain in the gut, but sodium, potassium and chloride ions pass freely into the body fluids. These excess ions are excreted by specialized "chloride cells" located in the gills. The precise nature of this excretory mechanism is not known, but it requires both the presence of appropriate concentrations of potassium ion and a great deal of energy to "pump" these substances against the prevailing gradient in concentration. As marine fishes face the problem of retaining rather than eliminating water from their bodies, their kidneys are relatively inefficient and they excrete only small volumes of rather concentrated urine.

**The speed with which many marine fishes learn to take food from their keeper's fingers is largely driven by their active metabolism.**

The aquaristic implications of this aspect of marine fish physiology are profound. First of all, it should now be perfectly clear why neon tetras will not prosper in a marine aquarium, nor neon gobies in a freshwater tank! Secondly, the mechanism of salt excretion requires expenditure of a great deal of energy to function. This fact accounts in great part for the voracious appetites of marine fishes as well as for the repeated observation that such fish do better when maintained under a regime of frequent, small feedings in captivity. Secondly, such a mechanism is necessarily quite finely tuned to external conditions and can be very easily upset by abrupt changes in salinity. Hence the constant need to monitor salinity levels in a marine aquarium closely and the frequent admonition to acclimate marine organisms very slowly to a new set of living conditions.

Salinities in the open ocean range from 33.0 to 37.0 parts per thousand (ppt). It is deemed prudent to maintain marine organisms in captivity at salinities of 30.0 to 32.0 ppt. These slightly lower salt concentrations reduce the burden of salt excretion somewhat. Furthermore, small volumes of sea water tend to become markedly saltier due to evaporation. Starting out at a slightly lower salinity minimizes the chance that a marine tank's residents will be exposed to seriously stressful salinities over the passage of time.

The salinity of sea water introduces a further complication to the husbandry of marine organisms. Because of the quantities of dissolved solids it contains, the ability of sea water to retain oxygen is notably less than that of fresh water. Given the constant agitation of the ocean surface, the habitats from which the great majority of marine aquarium residents are always very thoroughly aerated, so this fact has little if any impact upon the lives of their inhabitants. Consequently, few marine organisms have evolved the capacity to cope with reduced oxygen levels that occur quite widely among freshwater animals. This can lead to problems in captivity. It is not that difficult to create conditions conditions that favor efficient gas exchange. A well-placed airstone usually serves this purpose admirably. Problems rather arise when summer heat waves push water temperatures above those normally encountered even in shallow tropical reef habitats. Elevated temperatures also reduce water's ability to dissolve gases such as oxygen, while increasing the respiratory demands of fish and other organisms. When this factor interacts with the already limited capacity of sea water to hold this essential gas in solution, even highly efficient aeration may not suffice to prevent the loss of some or all of a tank's inhabitants. This is one reason why experienced marine aquarists prefer to work with the largest possible tanks and sometimes seem quite tiresome in their insistance upon very conservative stocking rates.

Finally, it should be remembered that salt water exerts a far more powerful corrosive effect upon metals than does fresh water. While the chemical products of such activity are in both cases toxic to aquatic organisms to a greater or lesser degree, their impact upon marine animals seems to be substantially greater. Many marine invertebrates in particular are acutely sensitive to even trace concentrations of such heavy metals as iron or zinc. Salt water mist also has a more devestating effect upon electrical circuitry than does simple water vapor. Hence it is essential to keep salt water and metal completely apart. This task has been rendered relatively simple by progress in aquarium technology over the past two decades. Thanks to the avilability of all glass aquaria, sealed unit heaters and magnetic impeller driven filters, it is only necessary to provide the marine aquarium with a tight glass cover and to choose non-metallic tank accessories to totally avoid problems of this sort.

Other environmental factors also underlie the preference for larger aquaria shown by marine aquarists. Marine organisms as a group display very little tolerance for abrupt fluctuations in any biologically relevant environmental parameters. This is due largely to the fact that their natural habitats are so effectively buffered against sudden changes in temperature or water chemistry that they have either never developed or else lost the sort of physiological plasticity that characterizes many of their freshwater counterparts. Many freshwater habitats are characterized by significant seasonal changes with regard to such factors as pH, hardness, dissolved oxygen, temperature and nitrogen cycle byproducts. Those organisms that have successfully colonized such habitats have necessarily evolved means of coping with such changes. This gives them an edge in coping with the vicissitudes of life in captivity that aquarists collectively refer to as "hardiness". Because they lack this sort of physiological plasticity, successful management of marine organisms in captivity affords the aquarist less of a margin for error than is the case with freshwater animals. One way to widen that margin somewhat is to house marine organisms under conditions that tend to buffer environmental fluctuations to a degree. Large volumes of water are less apt to manifest abrupt changes in temperature or water chemistry than are small. Hence the advantage of investing in the largest tank practical when setting up a marine aquarium.

Without question, the single most challenging problem facing the marine aquarist is successful management of the nitrogen cycle in captivity. As I pointed out in the Introduction, failure to appreciate the extreme sensitivity of marine organisms to ammonia and, to a lesser degree, nitrite poisoning doomed Victorian efforts at marine aquaristics from the start. The inability of marine animals to cope with even very low concentrations of these substances again reflects the fact that in nature, they never encounter them. The sheer volume of water contained in the world ocean, local patterns of water circulation and a highly efficient system of nutrient recycling in coral reef habitats interact to keep even local concentrations of ammonia and nitrite at subcritical levels. Marine organisms lack tolerance for these toxic substances because they have never been exposed to situations were natural selection would favor its evolution.

Again, a comparison with freshwater habitats is instructive. Particularly in the tropics, many such habitats are characterized by extreme

Many freshwater habitats, such as the Rio Ciruelas in Costa Rica, are characterized by dramatic seasonal variation in flow, water chemistry and temperature.

variability in total volume and rate of water flow. During the dry season, conditions frequently arise that permit a significant buildup of nitrogen cycle by-products in swamps, oxbows, small streams and even in the main channel of sizeable rivers. The flushing action of the rains puts an end to such eutrophic conditions quickly enough, but their effect notwithstanding, the animals that live in such habitats are still exposed to selection pressures that favor the evolution of limited resistance to ammonia and nitrite intoxication.

It is the greater robustness of freshwater fishes in the face of exposure to these substances that usually alows them to survive the trauma of their first 10 to 14 days of life in a newly set-up aquarium.

Like many freshwater species native to seasonally variable habitats, the cichlid, *Heros nigrofasciatus* possesses the physiological mechanisms to cope with short-term exposure to elevated metabolite concentrations.

Even very hardy marine fishes, like this Beau Gregory, *Stegastes leucostictus,* are lethally susceptible to even very low ammonia levels.

Marine aquarists, on the other hand, have learned by the painful process of trial and error that a newly set-up tank must be "run in" according to a very specific protocol if massive losses due to "new tank syndrome", a euphemism for ammonia poisoning, are to be avoided. Because of this one peculiarity of marine organisms, successful marine enthusiasts are necessarily more punctilious aquarists than their freshwater counterparts! It is also no conicidence that the major breathtroughs in filtration technique since the 1950's have come from the marine side of the aquarium hobby. Aquarists who have come to automatically weigh all maintenance decisions in terms of their effects on nitrogen cycle management are not unreasonably alert to inovations apt to simplify the task keeping ammonia and nitrite concentrations at acceptable levels!

Finally, the behavior of marine fishes also dictates the use of the largest possible tanks when setting up marine aquaria. Territorial behavior is hardly unknown in freshwater fishes. However, many groups of popular freshwater aquarium fishes do not display territorial behavior at any point in their life cycles. In the remainder, its expression is ephemeral, usually a function of reproductive activity. Persistant territorial behavior occurs much more rarely among freshwater fishes. When it does, it is usually tied to defense of a shelter. In either case, it can be managed in a relatively straightfoward manner. Regretably, persistant territorial behavior characterizes the most popular groups of coral reef fishes. The resource being defended in the great majority of cases is a secure food supply. Thus the territories held by most coral reef fishes are very large in proportion to the size of their occupants. Furthermore, while territorial species are understandably most intolerant of other individuals of their own species, they will often exclude other species

Many marine fishes, such as these wimplefish, *Heniochus intermedius*, and yellow butterfly fish, *Chaetodon semilarvatus*, are quite social in nature but behave less tolerantly towards others of their own species in the confines of an aquarium.

Some of the most popular marine fishes, such as the magnificent emperor angelfish, *Pomacanthus imperator*, are extremely territorial in nature. This behavior carries over in captivity and complicates their management to a degree.

with similar feeding patterns from their domains as well. This obviously dictates that the residents of a marine tank must be selected with behavioral compatibility in mind. However, the absolute area available for territorial fish to colonize also has a marked influence on how aggressively they will behave towards their tankmates. Once again, the larger the tank, the less the liklihood of encountering serious problems in its management.

In conclusion, it is essential for the beginning marine aquarist to fix in his mind the fact that conditions in the marine environment have not favored the evolution of the sort of physiological plasticity on the part of its inhabitants

that he may have come to take for granted in most freshwater organisms. Simply put, he cannot count on "one free mistake" when setting up a marine tank. This is not to say that it is any more difficult to establish or maintain a marine aquarium than it is a freshwater tank. What it does mean is that the marine aquarist must be aware from the very start that successful husbandry of marine organisms requires careful adherence to certain guidelines that have been formulated with their peculiarities clearly in mind. Once he has accepted this premise, he can next proceed to the next step in setting up a marine aquarium, the selection of appropriate equipment.

# CHAPTER 2.

# Selecting Equipment for the Marine Aquarium

## Choosing a Location for a Marine Aquarium

A marine aquarium can be placed just about anywhere in the house with minimal difficulty. Because most hobbyists are attracted to marine aquaria because of the brilliant color of its inhabitants, it is hardly surprising that most such tanks wind up in the living room or den, where their aesthetic impact will be greatest. Many neophyte aquarists succumb to the temptation to place the tank as close as possible to the television set, on the grounds that this is the most visible spot in the room. As noted in the previous chapter, it is best to keep salt water as far away as possible from any sort of electrical equipment. Hence in such cases, the most visible spot in the room is not always the best location for a marine tank.

Some authors recommend a mixture of natural and artificial light for the marine aquarium. Recent advances in lighting technology have obviated the necessity of the former even for the culture of macroalgae, while in many instances, a window location can lead

A properly placed marine aquarium contributes to the decor of any room.

However pleasing it may be to the eye, a marine aquarium should never be placed above or adjacent to books or any sort of electronic equipment.

to problems that would otherwise never make an appearance. If one selects a window location, it should afford the tank no more than two hours of **morning or afternoon sun**, but not more and not both. Avoid south facing windows. Tanks placed in such locations can receive too much sunlight. This can cause overheating during the summer months and may well lead to a year-around algae control problem. Locations dependant upon artificial light afford the aquarist much tighter control over the duration and intensity of the tank's illumination and are preferable for that reason.

The availability of such water changing devices as Python Products' No Spill Clean and Fill makes it unnecessary to site the tank in the immediate vicinity of a sink or tub. It is essential that an electric socket be near at hand. Three-pronged, grounded outlets should be used whenever available for the aquarium equipment.

Because a certain ammount of splashing is

inevitable when servicing a marine tank, it is best to locate it in a room with a plastic tile floor or synthetic carpeting. If the tank is to be located in a room with a bare wood floor or natural fiber carpeting, it is prudent to place the tank stand on a length of plastic carpet runner. In any event, when filling the tank or making large-scale water changes, it is best to cover the floor in the immediate vicinity of the tank with a plastic drip sheet of the sort used by professional house painters.

It is sometimes tempting to make use of existing furniture as a tank stand. For obvious reasons, this is not a wise idea if the tank is to rest **above** either electronic equipment of any sort or books. Given the unavoidability of splashes and drips in the tank's vicinity, it might also be wise to think twice before setting a marine tank up on a piece of expensive hardwood furniture. If neither consideration prevails, than any piece of furniture strong enough to bear its weight can serve as a tank stand. **Remember, however, that water is** very heavy! A 200 l aquarium (c. 55 US gallons) holds 200 kg (c. 450 lbs) of water. When the weight of the tank itself, gravel and furnishings is added, the total to be supported can come close to 400 kg (c. 675 lbs). A stand strong enough to support such a weight should be capable of holding up five adults at once!

Built-in wall installations are easthetically pleasing, but unless they are incorporated into a house's initial design, setting them up can be more trouble than they are worth. If such wall niches are contemplated in the design of a house, make it clear to the builder that they are intended to house an aquarium and be certain that he uses wood of the appropriate thickness in constructing the support work. If retrofitting such a niche, use 2″ by 4″ stock to support the tank platform. When designing such wall niches, allow sufficient space in back of and above the tank to allow the installation of equipment and facilitate routine maintenance. If possible, incoporate a cupboard beneath the tank platform to accomodate essential equipment.

It is usually a simple matter to purchase an aquarium stand that will fit in harmoniously with a room's existing furniture. Both wood and all metal stands are readily available for all of the commercially available tank sizes. Such units are designed to support the considerable weight of a fully furnished aquarium, reason enough to give them priority of choice as a tank base. Metal stands concentrate a great deal of weight over a very narrow cross-sectional area. It is therefore prudent to set such a stand up on casters or similar supports to prevent its feet from sinking into vinyl tiles or carpets and leaving an ineradicable impression. Any sort of contact with sea water leaves wrought iron stands vulnerable to severe rusting. Such stands should be treated with a clear protective primer before being used to support a marine tank.

## Choosing a Suitable Tank

Two types of aquarium are suitable for use with saltwater fish and invertebrates. The most generally available are all glass tanks bonded together with silicone elastic sealant. These are available in a variety of shapes from the basic "glass box" to hexagonal or trapezoidal. These "decorator tanks" tend to have a relatively unfavorable surface area/volume ratio, but as long as this is taken into account when stocking them, there is no reason why they cannot be used to house a marine display. These tanks are usually offered with either solid black or wood toned

**All glass aquaria such as this are ideal for housing marine organisms. Tanks with a rated capacity in excess of 30 gallons (114 l) are best mounted on stands constructed to bear their weight rather than on pieces of furniture, whose ability to do so is often questionable.**

*Anthias squamipinnis* in a beautiful aquarium

ornamental plastic molding, which simplifies the task of integrating the tank into a room's existing decor. Tanks of the second type are made of acrylic, or more rarely, polycarbonate plastic. Both panel type and single piece molded plastic aquaria in a wide variety of shapes are available, ranging from rounded "bubbles" to transparent coffee tables.

Each type of tank has its unique advantages and disadvantages. Glass tanks are available in a wider range of sizes, are relatively inexpensive, and are resistant to scratching. On the debit side of the ledger, they are heavier than plastic tanks and more easily broken. Plastic aquaria are lighter than those made of glass. Single-piece units are also totally leak-proof, and regardless of type, plastic tanks are very difficult to crack. However, they are easily scratched. It is usually a

simple matter to polish out a scratch on the outside of such a tank, but eliminating one from its interior surface is another matter altogether. Finally, the geometry of some single-piece plastic tank designs unavoidably distorts the appearance of their inhabitants.

If intended as a highlight of a room's interior decor, a tank should obviously be in scale with its other furnishings. This caveat aside, make a point of purchasing the largest tank compatible with available space and funding. Beginners are not adivsed to try setting up a marine aquarium in tanks of less than 100 l (c. 29 US gallons) capacity. A 200 l tank offers a much better liklihood of success, while larger tanks are better still for this purpose. The greater ease of managing the nitrogen cycle in a larger tank has already been given as a primary reason for purchasing the largest tank practical, while the behavioral idiosyncrasies of many marine fishes in captivity furnish yet another.

A tight lid is absolutely necessary for marine aquaria. While some marine animals, eels of all sorts and octopi notable among them, suffer from the wanderlust, the real reason for keeping such tanks as tightly covered as possible is to minimize evaporative water loss. Evaporation results in a slow increase in the salinity of the tank's water, a process that can prove stressful to its inhabitants. The plastic hoods usually sold as adjuncts to a freshwater aquarium are not as effective in keeping evaporation at a minimum as are simple glass covers. The hinged cover glasses generally available from retailers are equipped with a plastic rear strip in which openings for air lines, heaters and other appliances can easily be made. This eliminates the only possible objection to their use.

In most plastic tanks, the top is an integral part of the tank structure, with openings cut to accomadate lights and other equipment. Such an arrangement does cut down on evaporation, but the dimensions of the openings may limit the size of the rockwork or coral used to aquascape the tank. While the cover panes of all glass aquaria are not as efficient in preventing water loss, they can be removed *in toto* from the tank. This affords the aquarist free access to its interior, which simplifies the placement of tank furnishings.

Make a point of purchasing a smaller tank – 60 l to 80 l (c. 15 to 20 US gallons) is ideal – to use as a quarantine/hospital tank. Much future grief can be avoided by isolating new arrivals for several days to a week in an envrinoment that facilitates effective treatment before introducing them to an established community, while the aggressive nature of many popular marine species makes a hospital tank a very useful adjunct to the successful husbandry of coral reef fishes.

It is a simple matter to convert an all glass or plastic aquarium that has been used for freshwater fish keeping to a marine tank. Simply soak it overnight in a solution of 1 cup of chlorine laundry bleach/40 l of tank water, then rinse it thoroughly with hot water of about 60° C. (c. 140° F.). The tank can then be allowed to dry naturally, or else dried with a soft towel. Newly purchased aquaria need only be rinsed thoroughly with warm water and allowed to dry before being put to use.

The plastic molding along the upper rim of most glass aquaria is attached to the side panels by only a few dabs of silicone elastic sealant. The gaps between patches of sealant can allow a capillary flow to develop that will draw water out of the tank. The resultant saline drip is both an eyesore and a focus for evaporative water loss that can and should be eliminated. Fortunately, it is a simple matter to ensure a water tight seal along the upper rim of the tank.

First lift off the plastic molding. Usually only a firm upward pressure is required to lift it free from the side panels of the tank. Depending upon the brand of tank, the molding will come off either as a single piece or as four discrete sections. Set the molding aside, and using a single-edged razor blade, scrape all the old silicone sealant from the now exposed rim and sides. Next remove any traces of the old sealant from the inside of the molding. A cuticle pusher or watchmaker's screwdriver often proves helpful in removing patches from tight corners. As silicone elastic sealant will not adhere to dirty or greasy surfaces, clean the exposed rim and sides of the tank with rubbing alcohol, acetone, or a commercial glass cleaning product, then wipe the cleaned surface dry with a paper towel.

Now run a thin **continuous** bead of sealant around the entire rim of the tank. Replace the plastic molding, making certain to press it firmly down against the glass to assure a watertight seal. It usually takes 24 hours for the sealant to cure fully. During this interval, the molding should not be disturbed. Once the sealant has hardened, any overlap can be removed with a sharp razor blade.

# Choosing a Heater for the Marine Aquarium

Most aquarists set up marine aquaria in order to enjoy the grace and beauty of tropical reef fishes and invertebrates. In their native habi-

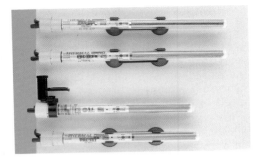

Heaters intended for use in a marine aquarium must be completely sealed to prevent corrosion of their components by salt mist.

tat, these organisms are exposed to minimal variations in water temperature over a 24 hour period, although a seasonal variation of 22°–30° C. (c. 72°–86° F.) is not unusual. **Temperatures below 20° C. (68° F.) and above 30° C. (86° F.) must be avoided.** The water temperature in a marine aquarium should reflect this pattern. Note that at the lower end of this temperature range, fish are less aggressive and organisms of all sorts tend to have depressed appetites. At its upper end, both appetite and aggression are stimulated, but the life span of many smaller species may be shortened by prolonged exposure to these elevated temperatures. A good compromise is a temperature range of 24°–27° C. (75°–80° F.)

Tropical marine aquaria thus require a reliable heater with an adjustable thermostat. Regretably, an ideal unit for use in marine aquaria has yet to be developed. Sealed unit heaters come the closest. However, their thermostat control is difficult to manipulate, and the rubber sealing material has a tendency to become brittle with age and exposure to sea water. Less expensive unsealed units are not recommended for use in marine tanks. Because their working parts are exposed to salt water mist, they are extremely vulnerable to corrosion. In the case of heaters that rely upon bimetallic strip thermostats, the inevitable result of such exposure is a control circuit welded into the "On" position and a tank of extremely expensive *bouilla-*

*baise.* Heaters that rely upon a solid state thermistor to regulate the temperature are less vulnerable to such damage, but eventually, their heating coils will eventually suffer sufficient corrosive damage to impair their function.

When selecting a heater, a good rule of thumb is 2 watts/3.5 l (c. 1 US gallon) of water for tanks set up in centrally heated rooms, double that for those set up in unheated rooms. The accompanying table should simplify the task of selecting a heater of the correct wattage. Remember that the actual volume of water held by a tank can be reduced by as much as 25% by the substratum and decorations in contains. This factor should be taken into account when assessing the actual, as opposed to the rated, volume of an aquarium.

# Choosing a Filteration-System for the Marine Aquarium

The key to successful management of the nitrogen cycle in the aquarium is the selection of an appropriate filtration system. The freshwater aquarist usually finds nitrogen cycle management a relatively simple matter, because a major water change is no farther away than the hearest tap. Marine aquarists do not enjoy this option. Mixing and storing large volumes of sea water is a major project and can be expensive in the bargain. It is thus in all respects advantageous to keep water changes in the marine aquarium to a minimum. Marine hobbyists are thus committed to maintaining the highest level of quality possible for the volume of water already present in their tanks. This dictates reliance on efficient biological filtration.

The operation of the nitrogen cycle will be discussed in greater detail in Chapter 4. The accompanying diagram presents its main elements. Aquarists are primarily concerned with the **catabolic** phase of the cycle, in which proteins and metabolic wastes are sequentially broken down to nitrate ion and ultimately, nitrogen gas. Each stage of this

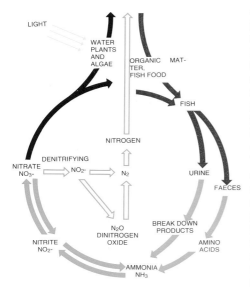

LIGHT

WATER PLANTS AND ALGAE

ORGANIC MATTER, FISH FOOD

FISH

NITROGEN

DENITRIFYING

NITRATE NO₃⁻  →  NO₂⁻  →  N₂

URINE

FAECES

N₂O DINITROGEN OXIDE

BREAK DOWN PRODUCTS

NITRITE NO₂⁻

AMINO ACIDS

AMMONIA NH₃

**Nitrogen cycle**
**The nitrogen cycle in the marine aquarium. It is very important to maintain good aeration, thus encouraging the *aerobic* bacteria which convert toxic ammonia and nitrite into much less toxic nitrate. Nitrate levels are prevented from building up by regular, partial water changes.**

An efficient biological filter should thus (1) provide an ample area for useful bacteria to colonize (2) an oxygen-rich environment that (3) allows them maximum access to the dissolved wastes upon which they feed. Fortunately for the aquarist, there are several alternative approaches to biological filtration that meet these requirements satisfactorily. The final choice of filter should thus be influenced by the both the size and setting of the tank as well as by financial considerations.

The operation of a biological filter can be enhanced by the judicious use of both **mechanical** and **chemical** filtration. An efficient, easily serviced mechanical filter traps particulate waste where it can be removed from the system before undergoing nitrification. It thus works to reduce the waste load the resident bacterial flora must process, which is in itself a significant contribution to the maintenance of high water quality in the marine aquarium. Chemical filtration, which relies chiefly upon the use of **activated carbon**, serves the same end by removing soluble organic compounds that tend to accumulate in a closed system as a result of the metabolic processes of its inhabitants. It is these substances that give a the water in a marine aquarium a characteristic yellow tint with the passage of time. These substances are not broken down by bacterial activity in the biological filter. They thus must be removed from the system by other means.

Note that activated carbon does not remove nitrogen cycle by-products from solution. There are chemically active media that can perform this function in a marine aquarium. The most useful of these is PolyFilter, a material similar to the medium used in kidney dialysis machines. PolyFilter also removes a broad selection of other dissolved contaminants from solution, changing color from ivory white to black as it reaches the limits of its absorbtive capacity. This material is particularly useful as a means of eliminating residual traces of copper or other medications from a marine aquarium. On the debit side, it will also efficiently scavenge an equally wide range of trace elements and water soluble vitamins. This fact, as much as its consider-

process is accomplished by the activity of specific bacteria. Biological filtration is nothing more than the creation of circumstances that facilitate such activity under aquarium conditions. The object is to reduce metabolic wastes to relatively harmless nitrate as quickly as possible and with minimal accumulation of toxic ammonia and nitrite ion along the way. Note that all the stages of this process through the synthesis of nitrate from nitrite, known collectively as **nitrification**, require the presence of abundant oxygen, while **denitrification**, the breakdown of nitrate ion to free nitrogen gas, occurs only in the absence of oxygen. As customarily understood, biological filtration comprises the process of nitrification exclusively. However, recent advances in filtration technology offer the promise of incorporating denitrification into nitrogen cycle management.

able cost, tends to restrict its use to crisis management rather than ongoing maintenance in a marine aquarium

## Internal Filters
As their name implies, these units operate within the tank itself. Such an arrangement reduces the clutter of equipment in the vicinity of the tank, but has the unavoidable disadvantage of taking up space within the aquarium and thus reducing the actual volume of water in contains. Two filters of this sort are generally available for use in the marine aquarium.

## The Undergravel Filter
In the minds of many hobbyists, such units are virtually synonymous with the term "biological filtration". An undergravel filter consists of a perforated plastic bottom plate with one or more return tubes along one end. The unit is placed within a tank, then covered with a layer of some particulate substratum. Water flow up the return tubes, provided by either a strong column of air bubbles or a small rotary impeller driven pump, or power head, mounted on its summit, draws the tank water through the particulate layer. After a reasonably brief interval, nitrifying bacteria will colonize the filter bed, where they will metabolize both trapped particulate and dissolved nitrogenous wastes.

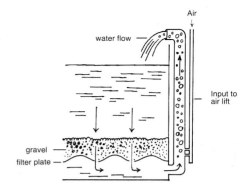

**Bottom filter**
**An undergravel filter plate in place an awaiting its overlay of washed substratum.**

Solid wastes eventually accumulate in sufficient quantity in the bed of an undergravel filter to require its periodic purging. This process is significantly hindered in the so-called "reverse flow" under-gravel filter units. These filters pass detritus-laden water through a mechanical prefilter, then return in to the filter bed. Coarse particles are thus trapped where they can be easily removed from the system. Reverse flow units are substantially more expensive than unmodified undergravel filters. It is thus up to the individual aquarist to decide whether the savings in labor entailed in filter maintenance is reason enough to pay their higher purchase price. Using an outside power filter in conjunction with an undergravel filter will also slow down the rate at which waste accumulates in its bed.

The greater the water flow through an undergravel filter, the greater the concentration of dissolved oxygen and the more efficiently the bacteria can metabolize nitrogenous waste. Thus it is advantageous to choose a unit with a rippled bottom plate. This increases the number of perforations possible, thus serving to maximize water flow through the overlying medium. Water flow is also influenced by the volume of water moved through the return tubes. This is a function of both the force of the pumping action that drives the water and the diameter of the return tube itself. Thus it is always advantageous to select a unit with the widest available return tubes.

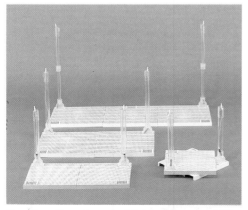

**Cross-section of an air-driven undergravel filter.**

**Rotary impeller driven power heads such as this can greatly augment the waste processing capacity of an undergravel filter.**

The use of a power head will also greatly accelerate the movement of water through the filter bed. However, such units do not adequately aerate the tank water. There is thus a tendency for tightly covered marine aquaria that rely exclusively upon pump-driven undergravel filters to suffer from chronic low pH conditions. This is apparently due to the fact that dissolved carbon dioxide tends to be retained in the system, thus pushing the pH downwards. This problem is easily corrected by running one or more supplementary airstones in the tank.

Because such units depend upon a free flow of water throughout the gravel bed to function effectively, it is very important to select a substratum with uniform particle size. There is otherwise a continual risk that fine particles will sift down to the bottom plate and block enough of the perforations to create local "dead spots". Wastes trapped in such oxygen poor pockets undergo anaerobic decay, producing decomposition products that can prove very toxic to marine organisms if inadvertedly released into the water. For much the same reason, it is necessary to select a substratum whose particles will not pack too tightly over the course of normal filter operation. The question of suitable substrata for the marine aquarium will be considered in the next chapter.

Undergravel filters represent an inconspicuous, relatively efficient and quite cost-effective approach to biological filtration. They do suffer from several drawbacks, however. First of all, anything that blocks water flow through the substratum reduces their effectiveness. Rockwork or large pieces of coral unavoidably obstruct water movement through the filter bed, thus reducing the overall efficiency of the filtration process. Secondly, the vulnerability of its bacterial flora to the effects of a wide range of medications seriously limits the therapuetic options available to the marine aquarist faced with an outbreak of disease. The aquarist who elects to rely upon an undergravel filter is well advised to invest in an isolation tank and practice the stringent quarantine of new arrivals before introducing them to an established marine community.

## Sponge Filters

Such filters, exemplified by the Tetra Brillant series, represent the second alternative to internally sited biological filtration. As their name implies, they utilize a synthetic sponge as a substratum for nitrifying bacteria to colonize. Smaller units rely upon the airlift principle to draw waste-laden water through the sponge. Larger units can be successfully mated to a power head, while a wide selection of internal power filters that make use of a sponge cylinder as their medium is also available. The extreme porosity of the sponge affords nitrifying bacteria an enormous surface to colonize. Taken with the efficiency with which waste laden water is drawn through the sponge, this factor makes for very efficient biological filtration indeed.

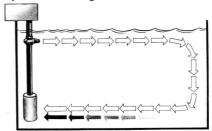

**A power head mated to a sponge filter likewise increases the effeiciency dramatically. Such augmented sponge filters are weel suited for use in quarantine tanks.**

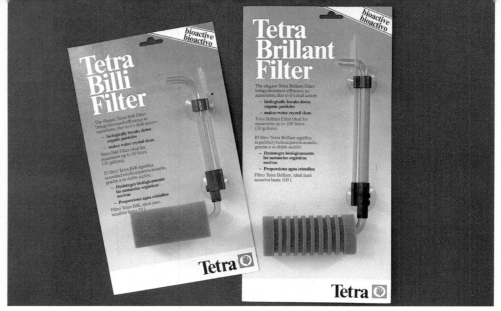

The Tetra Brillant line of sponge filters are well suited for use in a marine aquarium.

Sponge filters have the further advantage of mobility. They can be removed to another marine tank and continued in operation while a tank is under treatment for an outbreak of disease. A mature sponge filter can also be moved easily to a newly set-up marine tank, immediately providing it with a fully functional biological filter. This makes them particularly useful when setting up a quarantine tank.

Sponge filters do suffer from a number of drawbacks, however. No sponge filter could be said to contribute significantly to the decor of an aquarium, and the larger units in particular are extremely difficult to camouflage effectively. This is unlikely to endear them to marine aquarists who view their tanks as an opportunity to exercise their aquascaping skill! Secondly, sponge filter surfaces are easily clogged by large waste particles or overgrown by algae. Either eventuality seriously compromises their effectiveness. Hence they require more frequent maintenance than do undergravel units. Weekly rinsing with **clean sea water** is recommended to keep them working at peak efficiency. Finally, the sponges themselves will eventually deteriorate due to bacterial action and must be replaced.

**Protein Skimmers**

A protein skimmer exploits the tendency shown by many molecules in solution to cling to the surface of an air-water interface. Such units consist at their simplest of a plastic tube into which a large airstone is inserted. Sufficient air is bled into the unit to release a stream of bubbles. This produces extensive foaming and dumps the resulting froth into a cup set at the top of the tube. The toxic residue in the cup is then emptied on a regular basis. The finer the bubbles produced by the airstone, the greater the surface with which these large organic molecules can interact and the more efficiently the skimmer will function. By removing such nitrogenous substances as dissolved protein fragments and amino acids from the aquarium before they can undergo more extensive breakdown, a protein skimmer reduces the waste load that must be processed by the biological filter.

Contact or countercurrent skimmers are clearly more effective than the simple cup type units initially described, although they do require a powerful air pump as a motive source. The Tetra Luftpump serves this purpose admirably. Regardless of their design, protein skimmers require careful attention to

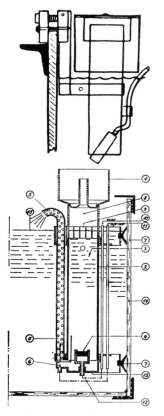

**Both simple (above) and countercurrent (below) protein skimmers can play a useful ancillary role in managing the nitrogen cycle in a marine aquarium.**

their airstones to keep them operating at peak capacity. Their surfaces should be scrubbed under running water regularly to prevent blockage. Do not hesitate to replace an airstone whose output of bubbles has become irregular or seems to be falling off.

Protein skimmers are unfortunately obtrusive. This factor as much as any other seems to militate against their wider use by marine aquarists. There is also some evidence that they remove trace elements and medications from solution as well. However, this caveat would seem to argue more for the exercise of common sense in their use rather than for complete abandonment of an otherwise useful adjunct to biological filtration.

German marine aquarists are the strongest advocates of protein skimmers. They elicit considerably less enthusiasm elsewhere. The concensus seems to be that in very lightly stocked tanks or those supporting a vigorous growth of green algae, protein skimmers are largely irrelevant to successful nitrogen cycle management. In heavily stocked tanks, particularly those containing invertebrates with a tendency to slough off substantial quantities of body slime on a regular basis or larger fish with messy feeding habits, on the other hand, protein skimmers appear to serve a useful purpose.

The use of ozone in conjunction with protein skimmers is sometimes advocated to increase their operating efficiency. Ozone is an extremely dangerous substance, toxic not only to pathogens but also to higher organisms and to nitrifying bacteria. Given the problems that ozone introduces to the maintenance of a fully functional biological filter, it is highly questionable whether the advantages of its use can ever outweigh its disadvantages in a display aquarium.

### External Filters

These units, as their name implies, are situated outside the aquarium. As the intake and return tubes are the only elements of an externally placed filter that enter the aquarium, such units take up less valuable tank space than do their internally placed analogs. However, the problems entailed in camouflaging the tubing that carries water to and from the filter unit as well as the unit itself constitute a valid aesthetic objection to outside filters. This difficulty can be more easily managed if the aquarist selects a cabinet-style stand for a marine aquarium, for the filter unit can be easily convealed within its enclosed lower compartment.

### Outside Power Filters

These filters are designed to hang from the rim of the tank. They primarily provide effective mechanical filtration by drawing detritus-laden water through a retentive medium and returning it to the aquarium free of suspended particles. These units differ among them-

Passive intake outside power units such as this rely upon siphon to draw waste-laden water into the filter chamber.

Active intake units employ a rotary impeller driven pump to pull waste-laden water into the filter chamber and upon gravity to return clean water to the tank.

selves in their mode of operation. Passive intake units rely upon siphon action to draw water into the filter box, whence it is pumped back into the aquarium. Active intake units make use of a pump to pull dirty water into the unit and push it through the filter media. The design of the filter box then allows clean water to flow passively back into the aquarium.

Active intake units are somewhat more convenient to use. One is spared the bother of starting siphons and maintaining their flow. Passive intake filters are very sensitive to the tank's water level. If it drops below a certain point, siphon action is broken off and the filter no longer functions. Siphons are also vulnerable to disruption by large fish. Interruption of water flow through the filter can, in some instances, this can result in the pump burning out unless prompt action is taken to either shut it off or restart the siphons. The one advantage passive intake power filters enjoy over their rivals is greater water-moving ability, confered by the greater diameter of their intake siphons and the ability to multiply the number of such siphons serving a single unit.

Outside power filters serve two useful auxiliary functions in managing the nitrogen cycle in the marine aquarium. First of all, charged with a suitable medium and frequently cleaned, such a unit can ease the load of the tank's biological filter by trapping much organic matter where it can be easily removed from the system. Secondly, an outside power filter can be charged with activated carbon or some other chemically active medium. Its operation thus complements that of an undergravel or sponge filter in maintaining water quality in a marine aquarium.

To function adequately in this role, a power filter should move the tank's volume through the unit at least once but no more than four times an hour. There is such a wide selection of outside power filters available to aquarists that it is a relatively simple matter to select one that meets this requirement. It is a good idea to select a unit with a capacious filter box, as most marine aquarists find it necessary to use a considerably greater volume of activated carbon in their efforts to maintain suitable water quality in their tanks than do their freshwater counterparts. It is also prudent to select a power filter with ease of cleaning in mind. A filter's ability to function effectively in removing waste from the system before it can undergo biological degradation is essentially a function of how frequently its media are purged. Experience shows that a mechanical filter that cannot be easily cleaned will not be frequently cleaned.

### Canister Filters
Such units operate by drawing water from the aquarium through a plastic canister charged with a selection of appropriate filter media, then returning it to the tank. For maximum effectiveness, a canister filter should circulate

**Outside canister filters represent a portable and highly efficient approach to biological filtration.**

the entire volume of the tank to which it is attached through the filter media at least once but no more than four times an hour. If the flow of water through the filter is any more rapid than this, waste-laden water does not remain in contact with its bacterial flora long enough to be effectively treated. Given the geometry of a canister filter, the inegrity of the connections that secure intake and return tubes to the canister proper must be maintained at all times if disaster is to be avoided. Do not scrimp on the purchase of adequate hose clamps!

**Ceramic rings are readily colonized by useful nitrifying bacteria. Their durability makes them an ideal medium for use in a canister filter.**

The effectiveness of such units is largely a function of the media with which they are charged. It is important to select a medium sufficiently porous to permit the establishment of a rich and vigorous bacterial flora. Ceramic rings are the medium of choice by virtue of their durability and permeability to water flow. The growing selection of plastic rings and highly sculpted plastic spheroids currently sold for this purpose offer an adequate alternative. A layer of coarser material is sometimes recommended as a prefilter to protect the biologically active medium from mechanical blockage by large waste particles, and it is a good idea to cap the ensemble of media with a dacron pad to trap very fine particles that would otherwise be returned to the tank. A further advantage of such units is that they can also accomadate chemically active media such as activated carbon or PolyFilterà. This eliminates the need to run an auxilliary outside power filter to provide chemical filtration of the tank water.

Canister, like sponge filters, are essentially portable. It is a relatively simple matter to connect a canister filter to a vessel of sea water, where it can continue to function while its original venue is treated for parasites or disease. However, such units also suffer from a number of drawbacks. Because an external filter's intake is localized, there is the risk that detritus will accumulate in various "dead spots" within a tank. To prevent this from happening, it is best to run such filters in conjunction with one or more strategically placed air stones. Such supplementary aeration will also compensate for the fact that the unmodified return flow of most canister filters does not do a very satisfactory job of aerating the water. Canister filters also require regular maintenance to function properly. The interval between cleaning typically ranges from one to four months, depending upon the number and nature of the fish present in the tank. Correct maintenance procedures are discussed in Chapter 6. Canister filters can also suffer serious degradation of their capacity if water flow through their media is interrupted for more than an hour or two. They must thus be checked carefully after power failures, a procedure outlined in Chapter 7.

## Dry Bed or Trickle Filters

Such filters in effect unpackage the processes that take place in a canister filter and spread them out over a greater area in a manner that maximizes the efficiency of the nitrification process. Such systems are installed beneath the aquarium, usually in the lower chamber of a cabinet stand built specifically for this purpose. Water from the tank is passed through an efficient, easily cleaned mechanical prefilter, then allowed to trickle slowly over a series of shallow trays containing barely moistened, biologically active filter medium. Because of the abundance of available oxygen, bacterial activity is greatly enhanced under such conditions, while the slow passage of waste laden water over the medium affords the bacteria maximal opportunity to complete the process of degradation. The treated water collects in a separate container, whence it is returned to the tank.

Such systems are essential components of the so-called Dutch mini-reef approach to marine aquarium keeping. Their ability to maintain high standards of water quality with minimal water changes is inarguable. By moving the entire filtration apparatus outside of the tank, they also greatly increase the actual volume of water present in the system. However, they are every bit as immobile as the more traditional undergravel filters, with all the disadvantages implied thereby. They necessarily take up a great deal of space and their design faciliates rather then discourages evaporation. This in turn obliges the aquarist to monitor the salinity in his system very closely. Finally, such filters are quite expensive. This in turn suggests that they are truly cost-effective only for very large aquaria.

## Denitrifying Filters

These units represent a relatively recent addition to the technology of aquarium filtration. The denitrifying process is more difficult to manage on a small scale because the bacteria upon which it depends require anaerobic living conditions and must be "fed" a lactose solution in precise quantities in order to function. A denitrification filter is essentially a closed vessel containing a medium inno-culated with the appropriate bacteria. An automatic flow meter feeds measured amounts of lactose solution into the reactor vessel, through which nitrate laden water is slowly passed. A properly functioning denitrifying filter will reduce dissolved nitrate ion to nitrogen gas and return completely purified water to the aquarium.

The denitrifying units marketed to date are designed to be inserted between the nitrifying bed and collection tank of of a dry bed filter. With due provision to reduce the flow of water through the reactor chamber, there seems no reason why such units could not be successfully mated to a canister filter. However, while such units offer the promise of setting up entirely self-contained marine systems, the neophyte marine aquarist would do well to restrain his enthusiasm until they have accumulated a longer record of satisfactory performance than is presently available. Keeping a denitrifying filter in operation is essentially an exercise in industrial microbiology. Complaints have already surfaced about the difficulty of keeping the denitrifying bacteria alive. Indeed, a widely encountered problem is that of obtaining lactose of sufficient purity to feed the cultures successfully. None of these problems are insoluble, but the process of working them out will take a while. In the interim, the novice marine aquarist is less likely to be disappointed if he concentrates upon more traditional approaches to nitrogen cycle management.

# Lighting
# the Marine Aquarium

A marine aquarium needs a lot of light. Precisely how much depends upon the depth of the tank and the sort of organisms to be housed in it. If one wishes nothing more than a vigorous growth of attached green algae, 12 hours of illumination from 2 150 watt incandescent spotlights or 2 40 watt mirror-coated flourescent tubes are needed for a 208 l (55 US gallon) tank 50 cm (20″) deep. Shallower tanks require proportionately less lighting. A tank 35 cm (14″) deep, for example, would need only 200 watts of spotlighting to produce the same degree of algal growth. The precise wattage required for any given tank can be calculated easily using the accompanying table. In tanks where no algal growth is desired, the aquarist can illuminate them as he wishes. However, it does not pay to stint on lighting equipment. A flourishing algal garden greatly simplifies nitrogen cycle management.

Most anemones and reef corals require even more intense illumination. These animals enjoy a symbiotic relationship with algae known as **zooxanthellae** that live within their bodies. The carbohydrates produced by the photosynthesis of these algae are an important source of food for the animals, while their waste products serve to nourish the algae. This relationship can function only if the zooxanthellae have sufficient light to carry out normal photosynthesis. It is thus hardly surprising that many anemones fail to thrive in the light of standard incandescent lamps or low intensity illumination from flourescent tubes. Macroalgae such as the numerous *Caulerpa* species also require intense illumination to prosper. The aquarist who wishes to keep these organisms successfully will have to increase the intensity of his tank illumination by 50% to 100% over the figures previously suggested.

Light quality is as important as light quantity. Mercury vapor spotlights seem to give the most satisfactory results of any of the generally available incandescent light sources. **Such bulbs generate a great deal of heat and must never be placed closer than 30 cm (12″) from the water surface.** Spotlights will shatter explosively if splashed with water, so position them with care. These bulbs are relatively short-lived, so it is a good idea to always keep a couple of spares on hand.

Flourescent tubes generate much less waste heat than do incandescent spotlights. They can thus be placed much closer to the cover glass. They also consume significantly less

**Carefull attention to both the quality and quantity of light received by a marine aquarium is an absolute precondition for the culture of macroalgae and many sessile invertebrates.**

electricity for the ammount of useful light produced than do spotlights. Full spectrum
flourescent tubes are designed to emit a
spectrum that corresponds to that of sunlight.
Standard Gro-Lux tubes do not emit a
balanced light spectrum. Used by themselves, they will not sustain the growth of
either green algae or most invertebrates. Of
the four brands of full spectrum flurescent
tubes available (Vita-Lite, Colortone 50,
Chromaline 50 and Verilux), Vita-Lite tubes
have the highest outpur of the near ultraviolet
wavelengths that seem particularly important
to the well-being or marine invertebrates and
macroalgae. If full spectrum tubes are not
available, acceptable lighting conditions can
be provided by using a Gro-Lux bulb in conjunction with a warm white bulb.

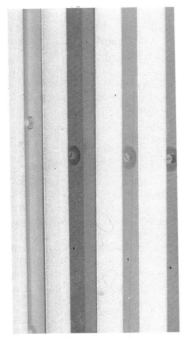

The different spectra emitted by flourescent
tubes are evident even to the naked eye.

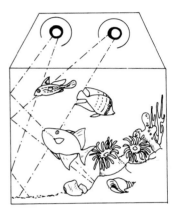

**Marine fish do not look their best when back-lit.
To enjoy their full beauty, mount any lighting
fixtures to the front of their tank.**

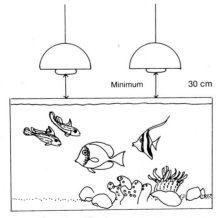

Minimum    30 cm

**Because they generate so much waste heat,
spotlights must be mounted at least 30.0 cm (1′)
above the surface of the aquarium they are
intended to illuminate.**

Remember to always use mirror-backed
flourescent tubes. If these are not available,
increase the total light wattage by 50%. Most
flourescent tubes have a rated life of 20,000
hours. However, their light output tends to
drop off with time. It is therefore necessary to
renew them regularly. Most tubes need replacement every 6–12 months. However, the
condition of the tank's inhabitants should
dictate the replacement schedule. If
previously thriving macroalgae or invertebrates begin to decline, replace flourescent
tubes immediately.

# Incidental Accesories

## Hydrometer

Because marine organisms will prosper only within a relatively narrow range of salinities, it is essential to have a means of measuring just how salty the water in an aquarium actually is. This is done indirectly by ascertaining the **specific gravity**, a measure of the density of the water. The higher the specific gravity, the greater the ammount of salt in solution. Specific gravity is measured with an instrument known as a **hydrometer**. This instrument is a weighted bulb with a narrow calibrated stem. To determine specific gravity, one merely places the hydrometer into the solution to be tested and reads off the value from the calibrated stem, as indicated in the accompanying figure. The farther the bulb sinks in the solution, the lower the specific gravity. Thus, the longer the calibrated stem, the more accurate the instrument.

Specific gravity is influenced by water temperature (see the table in Chapter 4, page 42, for the precise relationship). The marine organisms customarily maintained in aquaria prosper over a range of 1.020 to 1.024 measured at 25° C. (77° F.). These values correspond to an absolute salinity of c. 30 parts/thousand (ppt). In order to obtain the most accurate possible values, be certain to purchase a hydrometer that has been standardized for 25° C. **It does not pay to pinch pennies when purchasing a hydro-**

**An accurate hydrometer, calibrated by the National Bureau of Standards (NBS) is an absolutely essential adjunct to successful marine aquarium husbandry.**

**meter.** Invest in the most accurate instrument available and keep it in a secure place when not in use. The most accurate units are calibrated to NBS standards. As a rule, these must be purchased from a scientific supply house, as even retailers specializing in marine fishes rarely take the trouble to stock what they perceive to be an excesively costly item. Combination hydrometer/thermometer units are often offered for sale. Their thermometers are invariably too inaccurate to be used in a marine tank, so there is little point in wasting money on such combined units.

## Thermometer

A reliable thermometer is as important an adjunct to tropical marine aquarium keeping as it is to the successful husbandry of tropical freshwater fishes. Standard floating or ballasted aquarium thermometers are not entirely suitable for the marine aquarium. They have a tendency to get jammed in thoroughly inaccessible corners, which does nothing to facilitate reading them. Furthermore, many large fish, triggerfish and angelfish notable among them, derive a perverse satisfaction out of biting them to pieces. If the thermometer contains mercury, this can result in a mini-environmental crisis of major proportions, as this metal is extremely toxic to marine organisms of all types and is very difficult to completely eradicate from an aquarium once released.

The best way to keep track of the temperature in the marine aquarium is to invest in both an accurate darkroom thermometer **and** a liquid crystal display (LCD) thermometers. Mount the LCD thermometers on the outside of the aquarium, well away from the heater and in a location where sunlight will not fall directly upon it. Note the reading it gives, then take the temperature of the aquarium water with the darkroom thermometer and compare the two values. The difference that must be added to or subtracted from the value given by the LCD thermometer to equal the reading of the darkroom thermometer is the correction factor that must be applied to the LCD reading to obtain the correct water temperature. This correction factor can be consider-

Calibrated against a darkroom thermometer, liquid crystal (LCD) units such as this suffice to monitor the water temperature in a marine aquarium.

clearly as for aquarium use only. A plastic vessel whose volume is equal to half that of the hobbyist's largest tank is essential to mix fresh sea water for water changes. Plastic garbage pails serve this purpose admirably.

Mixing up any reasonable quantity of sea water from a concentrated mix can be time consuming and tends to be messy. In an emergency, time may be lacking to prepare sufficient sea water to perform an urgently needed water change. To avoid being caught in such bind, it is a good idea to keep enough premixed water on hand to carry out a 50% replacement of the volume of the largest marine tank in the house. Twenty-two liter (5 gallon) plastic water bottles are available from most hardware stores at a reasonable price. They suffice to store premixed sea water for considerable periods of time and represent a prudent investment for the marine aquarist. These containers may loose water through evaporation over long periods of time, so it is best to check the specific gravity of their contents before using them in a water change.

able in the case of plastic tanks because of the thickness of their wall panels. The accuracy of LCD units tends to degrade with the passage of time, so it is prudent to recalibrate them in the manner initially described every six months or thereabouts and consider replacing them every few years.

### Buckets and Storage Vessels

A plastic bucket comes in handy to rinse gravel, mix up small quantities of sea water and to hold specimens for short periods of time. **Plastic buckets intended for aquarium use must never be allowed to come into contact with soaps, detergents or other cleaning solutions!** Label them

Gravel cleaners allow the marine aquarist to purge a tank's substratum of wastes while carrying out a partial water change.

## Gravel Cleaner and Siphon Tubing

A gravel cleaner such as the Tetra Hydro Clean enormously simplifies the task of properly maintaining the bed of an undergravel filter by allowing necessary purging of trapped wastes to be done as an integral part of making water changes. The length of the plastic tubing sold with such units is really too short to allow of their convenient use. Hence it is a good idea to purchase an addtional length of tubing sufficient to reach from the tank to the nearest drain. A length of unmodified tubing will also prove convenient is the need arises to simply siphon or pump water from one container to another. Take care not to employ a garden hose for this purpose. Garden hoses are chemically treated to keep them flexible with a material that can prove toxic to fishes.

## Test Kits

Accurate pH, ammonia, nitrite, nitrate and copper test kits are essential adjuncts to marine fish keeping. Their use will be considered in subsequent chapters. The reagents in such kits do not have an indefinate life, so make certain that the kit in question has not been sitting on the dealer's shelf for a year before purchasing it. It is not a bad idea to insist on having kits ordered directly from the manufacturer as a condition of purchase. The longevity of all reagents is increased if the test kits are stored in the refirgerator after they have been taken home.

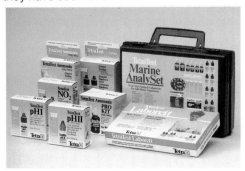

**Reliable test kits permit the marine aquarist to easily monitor the chemical make-up of his tank's water. This is essential to the successful management of a marine aquarium.**

Most ammonia test kits on the market make use of Nessler's reagent, a formulation that can prove extremely toxic is swallowed. **It is therefore essential to keep such kits well away from small children!** The Tetra ammonia test kit uses an alternative non-toxic reagent for this purpose. It takes somewhat longer to obtain an accurate reading from this particular test, but this minor inconvenience is more than compensated by the non-toxic character of its reagents.

## Nets and Probes

Several nets of various sizes are required equipment for any aquarium. Choose fine-meshed, soft nets with plastic coated frames. Deep nets are better than shallow, as the tendency of many marine fish to struggle when netted is reduced if the bag forms a pocket around them after it is lifted from the water. If only uncoated metal-framed nets are available, take care they they are not in prolonged contact with the tank water and rinse them thoroughly in fresh water immediately after each use to keep corrosion at a minimum.

A plastic probe often comes in handy to rearrange furnishings, move macroalgae clumps or sessile invertebrates from undesired locations, stir the filter bed or push items such as uneated pieces of food or dead fish into locations where they can be easily netted or siphoned out. A wide selection of such probes are commercially available. Alternatively, one can use a wooden kitchen spoon just as effectively. Choose a probe with the longest handle even if its length exceeds the depth of the tank. The extra length will come in handy when attempting to manipulate obects at the rear of the tank.

## Miscellania

A ceramic magnet algae scraper and a pad of soft abrasive are useful tools in the battle to keep the tank's viewing panels free of algae. A kitchen baster comes in handy when offering the fish live and frozen foods. It is useful to have a set of plastic measuring spoons and a glass or plastic measuring cup on hand when dispensing medications or water conditioners. There is no reason why such imple-

**Regular use of a magnetized soft abrasive pad prevents the build-up of algal encrustations on the front glass of a marine aquarium whose removal requires an aquarist's more drastic intervention.**

the correct proportions of marine salt mix to tap water to produce a known volume of sea water of proper specific gravity, the correct dosages of medications and water conditioners needed to treat each tank or the correction factor for a tank's LDC thermometer. A notebook is useful in tracking the establishment of a functional biological filter and should be used to record relevant observations about the behavior of a tank's inhabitants. Quite apart from its value as a fail-safe for fallible human memory, keeping regular track of events in a notebook promotes the systematic habit of mind so essential to implement the sort of regular maintenance routine necessary for successful marine aquarium keeping.

## Water

The easiest and safest means of obtaining suitable water for the marine aquarium is to mix synthetic sea water. This is true even for aquarists who live along the sea cost. Inshore waters are often badly polluted and even water drawn from several miles offshore must be allowed to sit long enough for the infective stages of marine parasites to die off before it can be safely used in a marine aquarium. Fortunately, good synthetic salt mixes are readily available. If used according to the manufacturer's instructions, they can be depended upon to give perfectly satisfactory results.

It does not pay to pinch pennies when purchasing synthetic salt mixes. Less expensive brands frequently leave out trace elements that are essential to the successful husbandry of marine invertebrates or may contain impurities that complicate working in a tank's biological filter. It pays to read the list of ingredients on the outside of the box very carefully before making a final choice. Regardless of the brand finally chosen, shake the box of salt before choosing. The contents should shift about freely from one side to the other. If the box feels lumpy or no movement of the contents can be detected, try another box. Salt mix that does not flow freely within the box has usually absorbed

ments cannot be borrowed from the kitchen, but domestic peace is better served if the aquarist has his own set!

A small centrifugal water pump is an investment whose value becomes painfully evident after the hobbyst has made his first water change by hand! The volumes of water involved in this operation are so great that it is virtually impossible to lift the vessels containing them high enough to siphon their contents into the tank. Hence the desirability of pumping fresh salt water to its ultimate destination. High flow capacity is not essential in such a pump. Corrosion resistance is. Buy only pumps certified suitable for use in both salt and fresh water.

Keep a box of baking soda (sodium bicarbonate) on hand to use in adjusting the tank's pH. It is also prudent to keep a few pads of PolyFilter and a supply of fresh activated carbon in reserve against possible emergencies.

Last but not least, invest in a bound notebook. It is essential to have a single reference for such things as the actual volume of a tank, water from its surroudings. Such hydrated salts are more difficult to put accurately into solution than are perfectly dry mixes.

While tap water can vary considerably in hardness from one locality to the next, these differences have no significant bearing on the final composition of the synthetic sea water made from them. Trace contamination of zinc or copper from new water pipes or the boiler of a water heater are another matter altogether. To avoid problems of this sort, run the tapwater for several minutes before using it to mix sea water. This should flush any accumulated metal salts out of the system. For safety's sake, it is also prudent to limit the use of hot tap water to an absolute minimum.

If the resulting sea water is intended for immediate use, as in a water change, it is important to remove any of the chemicals that might have been added as disinfectants before adding the salt mix. Chlorine can be easily dissipated using propietary dechlorinating agents such as Tetra's AquaSafe Chloramines are more persistant. It usually requires a doubled dosage of dechlorinating agent to dispose of the bonded chlorine in this compound. The residual ammonia can be a potential source of problems. However, as long as a marine tank has a fully functional biological filter and the total volume of water changed ammounts to no more than 10% of the tank's volume, it should not unnecessary to take additional measures to dispose of it. If larger water changes are contemplated, it would be wise to make use of one of several commercial preparations formulated to neutralize this substance before adding salt mix to the freshly drawn tap water.

Tap water should be treated to remove chlorine and dissolved metals with the appropriate agents before it is used to mix a batch of synthetic sea water.

The presence of chloramine as a disinfecting agent in many municipal water supplies requires the use of special products to eliminate it from water drawn for aquarium use.

# CHAPTER 3.

# Furnishing
# the Marine Aquarium

## Choosing a suitable Substratum

There is considerably more to be considered in selecting the substratum of a marine aquarium than selecting a material whose color sets off that of the tank's decorations and inhabitants. Any bottom material selected must be chemically compatible with a marine system. Furthermore, if the aquarist intends to employ an undergravel filter, the material chosen must also satisfy the requirements of a suitable medium. These constraints rather severely limit the choice of substrata for a marine tank.

The first factor to be considered in selecting suitable bottom material is its chemical make-up. Marine organisms require alkaline conditions to prosper. **Therefore no material that tends to lower the pH of the water should EVER be introduced into a marine aquarium!** This restricts the list of suitable materials to the following:

1. coarse quartz gravel, with particles at least 2.0–3.0 mm in size. (Fine quartz gravel is not suitable as a substratum in tanks with an undergravel filter.);
2. crushed dolomite;
3. crushed oyster shell;
4. crushed coral;
5. Philippine coral gravel.

Volcanic, basaltic and lateritic gravels are not suited for use in a marine aquarium, attractive appearance notwithstanding, as they tend to acidify the water. Of the remaining materials, quartz gravel is chemically neutral, while the others are alkaline in their reaction with water.

Philippine coral gravel is the substratum of choice for the marine aquarium. Its individual particles are fairly uniform in size, so it is unlikely to clog the bottom plate of an undergravel filter. Its surface structure is highly porous, affording numerous attachment sites for nitrifying bacteria. Finally, its rounded particles minimize the risk of injury to organisms that normally burrow of sift through the tank bottom. It is probably the most expensive of the five, but the concensus is that the results it gives fully justify its additional cost.

Of the remaining media, crushed dolomite and coarse quartz gravel are the most suitable from the standpoint of providing a suitable medium for an undergravel filter, although the former tends to display less uniformity with regard to particle size than does the latter. Crushed oyster shell tends to pack solid, behavior that severely limits its suitability as a filter bed. Crushed coral, sometimes sold as coral sand, is extremely abrasive and displays great heterogeneity of particle size. It thus poses a danger to burrowing or digging organisms and is likely to compromise the operation of an undergravel filter.

The depth of a marine aquarium's substratum is at least as important as its chemical make-up. An undergravel filter requires a bed 5.0 cm (2″) to 7.6 cm (3″) deep to function properly. This is usually taken to mean covering the bottom plate with sufficient substratum to assure such a depth. However, it is equally possible to cover the filter plate with a 2.5 cm (1″) thick sheet of synthetic sponge overlain with a piece of plastic egg crate diffuser grating cut to size. The grating serves to hold the sponge in place. The ensemble then can be covered with up to 2.5 cm (1″) of gravel. This alternative approach to undergravel filtration works as well as traditional method and has the advantage of adding much less weight to the finished tank set-up.

On the other hand, tanks equipped with sponge, canister or dry bed filters do not require a deep substratum. Indeed, a deep bed of gravel can actually complicate nitrogen cycle management by providing a place where fecal matter and uneaten food can lodge out of reach of the biological filter. Tanks equipped with such filters only need a layer of substratum deep enough to completely cover their reflective bottom panel. Equally important, both absolute particle size and homgeneity are a less critical considerations in selecting a substratum for such tanks. Fine quartz gravel, for example, is perfectly acceptable in such a set-up.

Regardless of the substratum chosen, rinse it thoroughly under running water until it is completely free of dust or grosser contaminants before adding it to the tank. Crushed coral, and to a lesser degree, crushed oyster shell, may contain sufficient dried organic material to complicate the running in of a tank's biological filter. To test for the presence of such contaminants, place a few handfuls of the substratum in a plastic bucket and cover it with sea water. Leave the bucket for several days, then check the water in the bucket with a nitrite test kit. No nitrite should be present. A simpler, albeit less sensitive test is to take a handful of substratum from the bottom of the bucket and smell it. A foul odor also betrays the presence of decomposing organic matter.

To clean such contaminated material, soak it for a week in a solution of 2 cups of chlorine bleach/4.5 l (1 gallon) of tap water. This treatment should be followed by another week's soaking in tap water. During this period of soaking, the water should be replaced daily. This approach also works well on suspect pieces of coral or large shells.

# Infrastructure for the Marine Aquarium

Essentially the same limitations apply to the selection of decorative infrastructure for a marine aquarium as do to that of a suitable substratum. Only materials that give a neutral or alkaline reaction in contact with water can be safely used to decorate a marine aquarium. This excludes driftwood and any rocks with an acidic chemical makeup. Needless to say, any metal objects or rocks containing metallic ores are totally unsuitable for use in salt water tanks. Fortunately, this still leaves a wide selection of rockwork for the marine hobbyist to choose from, not to mention dead coral, without a doubt the most popular decorative material for marine aquascaping.

It does not pay to stint on infrastructure in the marine aquarium. The level of aggression displayed by many territorial species increases dramatically when shelter is in short supply. A well furnished aquarium thus often makes the difference between an angelfish or damsel whose behavior towards other residents is totally unacceptable and one whose aggressiveness remains at tolerable levels.

### Rockwork
Quartz, granites, limestones and most basalts and lavas are well suited for use in the marine aquarium. Sandstones are problematical. Many contain traces of iron oxide, present as rusty streaks in their grain. Others have a tendency to crumble after a relatively brief exposure to water. Withal, they are best avoided. Some limestones are rich in naturally occurring holes and caves. These are particularly suitable for use in a marine tank because of the shelter they afford its residents. The softer volcanic rocks, such as pumice, can be drilled fairly easily and thus offer the aquarist the opportunity to place caves were they are needed in the rockwork.

These rocks offer a wide range of colors and textures that can be employed to good effect in decorating a tank. Most aquarists find it more convenient to use a number of medium-sized rocks to create a decorative formation rather than a few very large pieces, if for no other reason that they are easier to remove should the necessity to do so arise. Remember that many marine fishes are enthusiastic and efficient diggers. **It is therefore essential that the bases of all rockwork rest securely on the filter plate or on the tank bottom!** Remember too that the area covered by rockwork represents a "dead spot" in an undergravel filter's bed. The fewer such present in a marine tank, the better. When placing rockwork in the tank, try to create the largest possible number of caves and hiding places. Paradoxically, the more shelter available to fishes, the more secure they feel and thus the more likely they are to display themselves where they can be seen and appreciated by their keeper.

An excellent example of how dead coral and dolomitic limestone can be used to create an attractive and functional infrastructure for a marine aquarium.

## Dead coral

The calcareous skeletons of reef-building corals are far and away the most popular choice of decorative infrastructure for a marine aquarium. Large pieces of highly branched staghorn and fan coral are usually employed to provide a backdrop for more compact clumps of brain, mushroom or finger coral. The intense red color of organ pipe coral (*Tubipora* spp.) and the pastel tint of blue coral stand in dramatic contrast to the otherwise unrelieved white of most dead coral. The lovely pastel shades evident in photographs of the coral reef are a function of the presence of living coral polyps and do not survive their death.

Highly branched corals, such as this staghorn thicket, afford considerable shelter to small reef-dwelling fishes.

The more highly branched types of coral are serve both a decorative and a utilitarian function by affording cover for a marine aquarium's shyer inhabitants. Organ pipe coral is extremely soft and can be easily worked with a stout knife or an electric drill. Thus though its unmodified structure is too compact for it to provide much shelter for timid fish, it is a simple matter to carve caves wherever their presence is desired in a large chunk of this coral. Brain, mushroom and star coral afford a tank's residents no shelter and are generally used to provide a visual focal point in the foreground of the tank.

Pieces of coral sold by aquarium retailers are typically pre-bleached and ready for immediate use in a marine tank. Coral obtained from other sources should be treated in the manner previously prescribed for organically

Compact corals, such as this specimen of brain coral, are pleasing to the eye but afford little cover to fishes.

tainted substrata. A week's soaking in chlorine bleach usually suffices to purge the more highly branched corals, but the denser brain and mushroom corals may requires up to three weeks of bleaching followed by a week in fresh water before they can be safely added to a marine aquarium.

Under aquarium conditions, dead coral is quickly overgrown with algae. A vigorous growth of attached green algae does simplify nitrogen cycle management, but in the final analysis the decision to let it remain or try and remove it hinges chiefly on aesthetic considerations. A few day's soaking in a chlorine bleach solution followed by several rinses under hot fresh water will restore the coral to its original candid hue. Some aquarists keep two sets of coral for their marine tank, one for display, the other held in reserve to replace individual pieces as they are pulled out of the tank for bleaching. Given the high prices asked and paid for well-formed pieces of coral, this can prove a rather expensive solution to the problem of algal encrustation!

Sea fans or gorgonians are sometimes offered for sale along with dead coral. It is virtually impossible to render gorgonians safe for use in a marine aquarium, as their underlying structure is organic rather than calcareous.

The pleasing dark red color of organpipe coral affords a striking counterpoint to the white of most other dead coral varieties.

Sea fans can be incorporated into a background diorama outside of the tank to excellent effect, but they should never be added to the tank proper. On the other hand, large shells, either of molluscs or of barnacles, are perfectly suitable for use in the marine aquarium. Apart from being a pleasure to the eye, they provide much appreciated shelter for a wide variety of marine organisms. Large gastropod shells in particular should be bleached and soaked thoroughly before being used in the manner, as their internal structure promotes retention of traces of organic matter whose subsequent decompo-

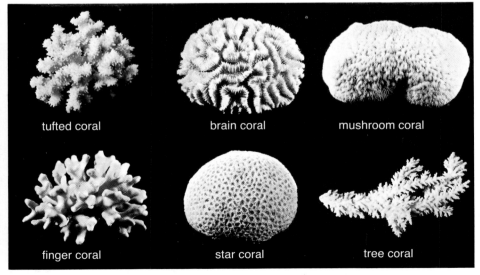

tufted coral     brain coral     mushroom coral

finger coral     star coral     tree coral

Six of the coral varieties commonly used to decorate a marine aquarium.

In a well decorated marine aquarium, the infrastructure contributes as much to its overall esthetic appeal as do its living residents.

sition can cause problems even in well established tanks.

## Plastic replicas of corals and other reef animals

Molded plastic replicas of a number of reef invertebrates have recently become available. The molds from which they are cast are based upon actual specimens of hard corals, soft corals and gorgonians, so their degree of realism is quite high. The manufacturers have also attempted, with tolerable success, to capture the life colors of the organisms in question. Bear in mind that while algae will grow as readily upon the synthetic replicas of coral as it will on their models, the end result is usually less appealing to the eye. Tank decor based primarily upon such plastic replicas may thus require more effort to keep presentable than one that relies upon the genuine articles. While the variety of size and form characteristic of any of these natural materials is clearly not to be had in their simulacra, both the color and the consider-

ably reduced weight of these plastic replicas have earned them a place in the marine aquarium.

Choice pieces of coral are not inexpensive. Neither are their plastic replicas, and in some areas, even suitable rockwork for a marine tank can represent a respectable investment. It thus pays to sit down with a pad of quadrille ruled paper, a ruler and a pen and sketch a series of possible aquascapes before going out in search of infrastructure for a marine tank. As a rule, it is easiest to construct an attractive aquascape around one or two large pieces of branched coral or well-formed rocks than it is to work successfully with a large number of smaller pieces. In any event, when shopping for decorative materials such as coral, it helps to remember that while individual fish and invertebrates will come and go, its infrastructure is a far more permanent feature of any marine aquarium. Furthermore, large pieces of coral represent a good investment, as they tend to appreciate in value with the passage of time.

# Chapter 4.

# Setting up the Marine Aquarium

## Preparing synthetic Sea water

The first step in setting up a marine aquarium is to prepare an appropriate volume of sea water. This entails calculating the exact volume of the aquarium to be filled. It is unwise to accept the rated volume of an aquarium at face value. Manufacturers are not above using using the outside measurements of a tank when calculating volume or rounding the resulting figures upwards to the nearest whole number in the interest of persuading potential purchasers that they are getting a larger tank for their money. Fortunately, it is a simple matter to calculate the volume of a standard, four-sided aquarium:

(1) measure the **inside** length and width of the aquarium, as well as the **inside** depth from bottom to the lower edge of the upper strip of ornamental plastic molding, in inches;

(2) next, calculate the tank's capacity using the formula

$$\text{Volume (US gals.)} = \frac{\text{length x width x depth}}{231}$$

(3) to convert this figure to liters, multiply the resulting value by 3.79; to convert to Imperial gallons, multiply by 0.83.

While formulae exist to calculate the volumes of hexagonal and other less traditionally configured aquaria, it is actually easier to ascertain their capacity empirically by filling them up using containers of known capacity. Needless to say, by whatever method it is obtained, the actual volume of the tank should be promptly logged in the aquarist's notebook for future reference!

Once the tank volume is known, fill it to the calculated capacity with **cold** tap water. This greatly reduces the liklihood of accidentally introducing toxic metals to the tank from the plumbing. If necessary, use a dechlorinating or dechloraminating agent agent to treat the resulting volume of water. Add the tank heater and warm the water to 25° C. (77° F.). This should take no more than 24 hours to accomplish.

Once the tank has been filled, calculate how much salt mix will be required to produce the volume of salt water in question. As a rule, marine salt mixes are sold in premeasured packages that will produce a given volume of sea water. Thus if a full box will produce 10 gallons of sea water, half that volume will produce 5 gallons, a quarter will produce 2.5 gallons, *et seq.*. This relationship is worth stressing, as calculated tank volumes rarely work out to an even value. Adding sufficient salt mix to produce 30 gallons of sea water to a drawn volume of 28.5 gallons will result in a higher than optimal salinity. As it is more bother to reduce than increase the salinity of a batch of synthetic sea water, it is clearly worth the trouble to determine precisely how much salt mix should be added to the drawn volume of warm water before the fact.

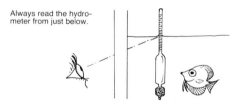

Always read the hydro-
meter from just below.

**The correct way to read a hydrometer.**

With several airstones in full play, add the salt mix to the tank a cup at a time, stirring constantly with a large wood or plastic spoon. Wait until all of the salt previously added is dissolved or suspended before adding more. When entire precalculated quantity of salt mix has been added to the tank and gone into solution, check the resulting water with the hydrometer. Remove the instrument from its case and wipe it down carefully with a paper towel. Even slight traces of grease or body oil

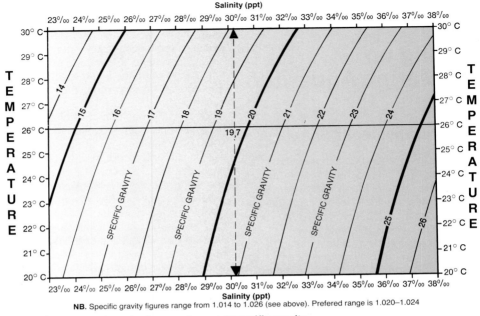

**Salinity (ppt)**

NB. Specific gravity figures range from 1.014 to 1.026 (see above). Prefered range is 1.020–1.024

**The relationship between water temperature and specific gravity.**

on the surface of the instrument can effect how it rides in the water and thus compromise the final reading. Place the instrument carefully in the tank. Never just drop a hydrometer into the water, as it may strike the bottom of the tank with sufficient force to shatter the bulb. Wait until the instrument stops bobbing, then take the reading on the calibrated scale. The accompanying figure shows exactly how to read the specific gravity from a hydrometer. It may be that the tank is too shallow to allow the instrument to float without its base resting on the bottom. Some dealers carry hydrometer cylinders, tall glass vessels sufficiently deep to permit an accurate reading to be taken. These can always be purchased from any scientific supply house that stocks NBS calibrated hydrometers. Remember that it is best to take salinity readings at the temperature for which the hydrometer has been calibrated. The accompanying table shows how the specific gravity of sea water with a salinity of 30.0 to 32.0 ppt varies over the range of temperatures acceptable for a marine aquarium.

If the specific gravity is too high, remove half a cup of water and replace it with tap water, stirring briskly all the while. Then check the specific gravity again. Continue to adjust the salinity downwards in this manner until the a value in the desired range of 1.020–1.024 is obtained. If the initial specific gravity reading is too low, dissolve a cup of salt mix in 2 cups of warm water and add a quarter of a cup of the resulting concentrated solution to the tank. Remember to stir the water briskly while adding the concentrate. Now check the specific gravity. Continue to add concentrate until a specific gravity reading in the desired range is obtained. As salinity will increase through evaporation, a value at the low end of the safe range is perfectly acceptable at this point. This same procedure should be used when mixing synthetic sea water for future water changes.

## Furnishing the Tank

Before adding any appliances or furnishings to the tank, draw off a quarter of its volume into plastic buckets, or, preferably, plastic carboys. The substratum and and decorative materials take up space and sufficient water must be removed to compensate for this fact. If an undergravel filter is to be installed, emplace the bottom plate or plates, plug in the return stems and add any large pieces of coral or rockwork to the tank. Make certain their bases rest securely on the filter plate. This may be easier to accomplish with large pieces of tall branching corals such as elkhorn and staghorn if they have been attached beforehand to a glass base plate with silicone elastic sealant.

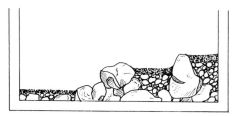

**It is customary to build up the substratum towards the rear of the tank.**

Now add sufficient precleaned substratum to provide an adequate filter bed. For both decorative reasons and to simplify tank maintenance, it is accepted practice to grade the substratum so that it rises gradually towards the rear of the tank. Smaller pieces of coral, rockwork or shells can then be placed on the surface of the substratum.

If an undergravel filter is not to be used, major items of decor should be placed directly on the tank bottom, then a thin later of substratum can be added to the tank. Lesser furnishings can then be added to complete the intended aquascape. Once the tank infrastructure has been installed, intake siphons and any other pieces of apparatus should be put in place. If the water level requires it, top off the tank using the water intially removed. Any surplus water should be held in reserve in a tightly closed container and used for making water changes.

The next step is to connect the filter. It is a good idea to poke the bed of an undergravel filter to release trapped air pockets after the unit has been in operation for an hour or so. If

**It is a good idea to briskly stir the substratum overlaying a newly installed undergravel filter to release any pockets of trapped air that may impede its operation.**

a large volume of bubbles ensues, check the filter stems to see that they have been properly inserted into the base plate and make certain that the air releasers have not been pushed too far down the length of the tubes. Volumes of air can also become trapped neneath the base plate if the aquarist attempts to run a power head and an air stone concurrently in the same lift tube. To avoid this problem, remove the airstone from the lift tube and run it elsewhere in the aquarium.

Check all hose connections on a canister filter to make certain that they are absolutely air tight. Loose connections will admit sufficient fine gas bubbles to result in an air block of the filter action in a remarkably short time. Now replace the tank cover, clean up any traces of salt from dripped or splashed sea water, set up the tank's lighting system and illuminate it. The water temperature should be checked periodically over the next 24 hours to ascertain if the heater is functioning properly. If the water temperature holds constant at 25° C., the aquarium is now ready for the seasoning process required to make it a suitable home for marine organisms.

# Running in the Biological Filter

Mention has already been made of the nitrogen cycle and the necessity to manage it properly in order to succeed with a marine aquarium. Recall that **nitrification**, the portion of the cycle of most relevance to marine aquarists, is a **stepwise** process in which complex nitrogen-containing substances are broken down into simpler compounds. Each step in the process is carried out by a specfic bacterium, which produces as a result of its metabolic activities the substance required as food by the microorganism that serves as the next link in the chain. What this means is that newly set up aquarium will go through a series of episodes characterized by very high levels of ammonia, nitrite and nitrate as the bacteria responsible for each stage of the nitrification process colonize the filter bed, undergo an explosive increase in numbers as they encounter the superabundance of food present in the environment, then drop to more a more moderate population level after having produced a superabundance of metabolic wastes that will fuel the next stage of the process. After the nitrate concentration peaks, it will drop off somewhat and remain at that level with minor oscillations for a considerable time to come. Once this level has been reached, the filter is fully functional and the tank can be stocked in earnest.

Of the three by-products produced by the degradation of nitrogen-bearing organic compounds, ammonia is far and away the most dangerous to marine organisms. This substance exists in a state of dynamic equilibrium with the positively charged – and biologically harmless – ammonium ion. As the pH rises, the ammount of ammonia present in the system increases significantly. This fact, no less than the inherent toxicity of ammonia to marine organisms, accounts for the importance attached to minimizing its concentration in closed systems. The alkaline pH that must be maintained in a salt water aquarium means that the dynamic equilibrium between ammonium and ammonia will always favor the later substance. This is the reverse of the situation prevailing in most freshwater aquaria, where the usual pH range encountered favors ammonium over ammonia.

Pleasing appearance notwithstanding, this marine aquarium will not be ready for stocking until its biological filter is fully run in.

Nitrite, on the other hand, is considerably less toxic to marine than it is to fresh water organisms. This is because sodium chloride in some manner mitigates the toxicity of nitrite to aquatic animals. Thus while nitrite concentrations of less than 1.0 ppm can prove acutely toxic to freshwater fishes, concentrations from ten to a hundred times as great pose no risk to marine fishes over the short term. While there are no hard experimental data on the effects of long-term exposure to elevated nitrite concentrations on marine organisms, the practical experience accumulated by two generations of aquarists suggests that it is prudent to keep these values as low as possible over the long haul.

Even less is known about the long-term effects of exposure to elevated nitrate concentrations on marine fish. It does seem clear that reef-building corals, many soft corals and a number of anemones do not appreciate high nitrate levels. These invertebrates seem to prosper only when nitrate concentrations can be kept below 10.0 ppm on a long-term basis. Elevated nitrate levels also promote the vigorous growth of blue-green and other undesirable algae, reason enough to avoid them in a closed system. A fully functional biological filter will keep ammonia and nitrite levels under control, but for most marine aquarists, regular partial water changes are the only means of keeping the nitrate concentration at an acceptable level.

If a marine aquarium is stocked prior to the establishment of a mature biological filter, the result is an unmitigated disaster. The elevated ammonia levels that inevitably occur as the filter establishes itself will kill off the tank's residents with apalling rapidity. The temptation to stock a newly set-up marine aquarium with its full complement of residents at once is strong, but it must be resisted at all cost. Impatience kills more marine organisms – and terminates the careers of more aspiring marine aquarists – than all other factors combined!

The usual procedure for running in a biological filter is to add one or two hardy organisms to the newly set-up tank. Their waste provides the initial source of nitrogenous wastes needed to feed the nitrifying bacteria and start the process of bacterial proliferation, while their tolerance of temporarily elevated ammonia levels will usually see them through the process safely. Hermit crabs and the hardier damselfish are usually recommended as starter organisms. Far more satisfactory are a number of readily available brackish-water fishes. The green sailfin molly, *Poecilia latipinna*, in all of its color varieties, and the Mozambique mouthbrooder, *Sarotherodon mossambicus*, adapt readily to straight sea water. Both species are widely available and quite inexpensive. The waste output of a pair of mollies or a single 10.0 cm (c. 4″) long Mozambique mouthbrooder exceeds that of any of the usually recommended marine starter organisms, while their ability to tolerate elevated ammonia and nitrate concentrations is most unlikely to be severely tested by the levels their metabolism will generate in the marine aquarium. Finally, once the filter bed is fully functional, both species can be returned to a more mundane existance in the freshwater aquarium. Almost equally satisfactory from the standpoint of both hardiness and ability to feed the filter in its earlier stages of development is the spotted scat (*Scatophagus argus*). Scats make appealing marine aquarium residents, and many aquarists wind up including their "expendable" starter fish in their tank's final complement!

An alternative approach is to dispense with starter organisms altogether and simply add premeasured ammount of ammonium chloride to the newly set-up aquarium. This provides the necessary food for the incipient *Nitrosomonas* colony and thus serves to prime the entire engine of nitrification. This approach works best if the new filter is liberally seeded with innoculated medium from an established tank and virtually mandates daily monitoring of ammonia, nitrite and nitrate levels throughout the running-in period to ascertain that all is proceeding as it should. Such stringent attention to the changes in nitrogen cycle by-products, while it can be a useful learning exercise, is not absolutely essential when starter organisms are employed to provide the filter bed with its initial source of food. Recall that such testing allows the aquarist to follow each metabolic product as it peaks, then falls off, up to the point where a stable nitrate level is attained. Under normal cicrumstances, it takes about a month to build up the *Nitrosomonas* population to a level where it can keep ammonia concentrations under toxic levels. It usually takes from four to six weeks longer before the *Nitrobacter* population can manage the task

A brackish-water species at home in both fresh and salt water, the scat, Scatophagus argus, *can also be used as a starter fish in a marine tank.*

**Inexpensive damselfish such as the domino,** Dascyllus trimaculatus, *are often recommended as starter fish for a newly set-up marine aquarium.*

A pair of sailfin mollies will live happily in a newly setup marine aquarium and can be counted upon to provide plenty of food for developing colonies of nitrifying bacteria.

Hermit crabs of the genus Dardanus also make good starter organisms.

Its justly proclaimed hardiness guarantees that Mozambique mouthbrooder, Sarotherodon mossambicus, will survive the running in of a marine aquarium's biological filter.

of keeping nitrite at trace levels. Testing can thus be postponed until the third week after adding the starter organism(s) to the tank. At this point, test for ammonia, nitrite and nitrate. If the value obtained for the first substances is lower than 0.01 parts per million (ppm), it is safe to assume that well-established colonies of *Nitrosomonas* and *Nitrobacter* are present in the filter. Repeat the tests daily for several days. If ammonia remains at trace levels while nitrite and nitrate values remain constant or else declines somewhat, the filter is running well enough to make it safe to start stocking the tank. Once the nitrite level drops into the trace range, the filter is fully run-in.

Several firms market bacterial starter cultures that are supposed to greatly speed up the process of running in a biological filter. The few controlled studies that have been made on the effectiveness of these products indicate that they do not perform as claimed. A few aquarists who have tried these cultures under less rigorously controlled conditions have reported some shortening of the running-in period, but most of those with whom I have spoken have also found that no detectable benefit resulted from their use. While the theory behind these products is sound, one suspects that problems of quality control keep them from fulfilling their promise. As with denitrifying filters, the beginning marine aquarist is best advised to allow this technology to attain a somewhat greater level of maturity – and reliability – before relying upon it as an indispensable adjunct to his fish keeping efforts.

As already noted, it is possible to speed up the running-in process by "seeding" the filter with a quantity of medium already inocculated with a full complement of nitrifying bacteria. The greater the proportion of inocculated to virgin medium, the more quickly the filter will attain full operating capacity. Allowing for a cup of inocculated medium per square foot of tank bottom, it is possible to shave a week to 10 days from the usual interval required to establish a minimallly functional undergravel filter in a newly set-up marine tank. The seeding process is most likely to be successful if the inocculated medium comes from a tank whose water temperature and specific gravity are identical to those present in the target tank, though many aquarists have reported a degree of success using dry gravel from a formerly active marine undergravel filter bed. Take care not to allow the inocculated medium to dry out in transit if it has been taken from an operating filter bed and try to get it to its destination as quickly as possible. **Never rinse inocculated medium under fresh water!** Such treatment will seriously traumatize or kill the marine-adapted nitrifying bacteria outright, thus vitiating the object of the exercise. Spread the inocculated medium as widely as possible through the superficial layer of the new filter bed, or in the case of a canister filter, mix it thoroughly with the virgin medium. As a rule, retail dealers will happily supply a few cups of gravel from a "mature" marine aquarium to help a new customer run his filter bed in. Fellow marine enthusiasts are also usually willing to give a newcomer to the hobby this sort of helping hand.

This process works equally well if one introduces a cartridge from an established sponge filter to a newly set-up filtration system. By employ a mature sponge filter as an adjunct to the tank's primary filtration system during the running in period, it may prove safe to begin adding the tank's permanent residents several weeks sooner than might otherwise be the case. However, it is best to proceed slowly in this regard and to keep the auxilliary unit in place for at least as long as the interval normally required to establish a viable bacterial flora in the primary filter bed. It is also prudent to monitor ammonia, nitrite and nitrate levels for a few days after removing the auxilliary filter. If the first two consistently register trace levels and the third remains stable, one can safely continue the process of stocking the tank.

# CHAPTER 5.

# Stocking the Marine Aquarium

## The concept of carrying capacity

Any aquarium, be it fresh or salt water, can only support a finite number of organisms in good health over an extended period of time. This value is known as the **carrying capacity** of the tank. Many environmental and behavioral considerations interact to determine the carrying capacity of an aquarium. In the early days of the hobby, before inexpensive and reliable air pumps were readily available, the ability of carbon dioxide to leave the water imposed dramatic limits on how many fish could be kept in a given tank. Hence many older aquarium references were wont to express the carrying capacity of a tank as so many centimeters (or inches) of fish per square centimeter (or inch) of surface area. The now universal reliance on some sort of aeration for aquaria has effectively removed limitations on stocking imposed by the respiratory requirements of aquatic organisms. Today, the two factors that effectively limit an aquarium's carrying capacity are the ability to manage the nitrogen cycle and the behavioral idiosyncracies of its intended inhabitants.

Leaving the question of behavioral compatibility aside for the moment, a quick review of the mechanics of biological filttration will provide some insight into the way in which nitrogen cycle management and carrying capacity interact. Recall that a biological filter depends upon the activity of a complex community of bacteria to function. The size of these bacterial populations is limited by the ammount of suitable substratum for them to colonize, while the ammount of nitrogenous waste that the filter can degrade is limited by both the availability of oxygen and the size of its associated bacterial flora. Unless the aquarist exercises prudence when stocking his tank and feeding its inhabitants, the end result can be a waste load that exceeds the capacity of the biological filter to degrade. Under these conditions, toxic by-products of the nitrification process can accumulate in the aquarium and eventually reach harmful levels.

A newly run in biological filter has considerable capacity for expansion. Assuming a well designed filter system and continuous aeration, the availability of sufficient oxygen is not likely to prove a limiting factor in its operation. Thus, as the ammount of food in the system increases, individual bacteria can accelerate their metabolisms to cope with such abundance, as well as multiply rapidly. However, a point will eventually be reached where further increases in either metabolic efficiency or numbers are no longer possible. Once this point has been reached, the tank has attained its maximum carrying capacity. The addition of further residents inevitably leads to serious losses because the rate at which toxic ammonia is produced exceeds the filter's ability to break it down to less toxic nitrite. Phrased in a somewhat homlier manner, in the marine aquarium there is **NOT** always room for one more!

Complex formulas for calculating carrying capacity have been developed by commercial mariculturists that take into account surface area of the filter bed, rate of water flow through the filter medium, water temperature, oxygen availability and weight of waste produced over a given interval of time. It makes more sense – and is a good deal easier in the bargain – for the neophyte marine aquarist to make use of a set of less complicated guidelines. **Simply put, in a newly set-up tank, stock no more than 2.5 cm (c. 1″) total length of fish per 20 l (c. 5 US gallons) of tank water, or 2.5 cm of fish per 375 square centimeters (60 square inches) of filter surface area.** Once the filter has attained its full capacity to process waste, some 2 to 3 months after the conclusion of the initial running in period, a stocking rate of 2.5 cm (1″) of fish per 13 l (3.5 US gallons) of water is permissible.

The population densities encountered on the reef are impossible to sustain in a home aquarium, due both to the limitations of existing filtration systems and the spatial requirements of the fish themselves.

Only elaborate, behind-the-scenes filtration systems allow public aquaria to duplicate the fish densities encounintered to a coral reef.

The demands an adult Koran angel, *Pomacanthus semicirculatus* (above), makes on a marine aquarium's life support system are much greater than those of a juvenile specimen. Always take the adult size of its intended residents into account when deciding a marine community's population size.

Remember when calculating stocking rate by tank volume to subtract the volume of water displaced by the filter bed and infrastructure. Calculating carring capacity by filter surface area is obviously easier if the tank is equipped with a standard undergravel filter or a trickle filter that comprises a series of discrete trays. Determining the effective surface area of the bed of a canister or sponge filter is considerably more difficult. Thus is is easier to fall back on guidelines based on tank volume if the aquarium is equipped with a filter of either sort.

Bear in mind when calculating the stocking rate for a marine aquarium that many coral reef fishes are sold as juveniles. If properly cared for, they grow quite rapidly. It is not unusual for many of the more common damselfishes to double their size in a matter of three or four months. Not all marine fishes grow this quickly, but prudence still dictates using the **adult length** of a tank's intended residents rather than their size at the moment of purchase when estimating how many fish a tank can safely support.

Determining the number of invertebrates that can be housed in a tank of given volume is a bit more complicated. Organisms that possess symbiotic zooxanthellae behave more like plants in a well lit aquarium than like animals. Their symbiotic algal partners act as an extremely efficient internal waste processing

These disk anemones, *Actinodiscus* sp., (*Discosoma* sp.) live in symbiotic association with colonies of intracellular algae, or *Zooxanthellae*. Marine invertebrates so endowed contribute much less to a tank's waste load than do residents lacking such partners.

system. Thus their contribution to the waste load is greatly reduced. A conservative approach would suggest stocking one hand-sized piece of live coral (hard or soft) or one anemone with an expanded disk diameter of 10.0 cm (4″) per 20 l of water. However, invertebrates that do not possess zooxanthellae, such as tubeworms, molluscs, arthropods, and echinoderms must be treated in the same manner as fish when the stocking rate of a tank is calculated.

It may be argued that such stocking rates are extremely conservative when compared with those prevalent in freshwater aquaria, or, for that matter, those encountered in the marine display tanks of a retailer. As previously noted, ammonia concentrations are generally much lower at the pH ranges present in most freshwater aquaria, while many freshwater fishes are less sensitive to short-term exposure to nitrite than are their marine counterparts are to comparable ammonia levels. Furthermore, a major water change for a freshwater aquarium is no further away than the nearest tap. This allows freshwater aquarists to rely extensively upon a program of regular partial water changes as a means of keeping toxic metabolite concentrations at sublethal levels even under conditions of serious crowding.

The greater fish or invertebrate densities present in a retailer's tanks are another matter altogether. First of all, a retailer turns over his stock quite rapidly. Thus he is not faced with the problem of maintaining fish and invertebrates over the long haul. Secondly, many retailers specializing in marine organisms have central filtration systems whose extensive surface areas are quite disproportionate to the volume of water actually devoted to displaying animals intended for sale. Unless the amateur marine aquarist wishes to invest in a comparable system, there is no way he can expect to successfully emulate the sort of stocking rates he is likely to encounter in a retailer's tanks.

## Compatibility

The other factor that influences how many organisms a marine aquarium can support, as well as the mix of different species ultimately chosen as its inhabitants, is their ability to coexist over an extended period of time in captivity. Freshwater aquarists must also take the compatibility of prospective tankmates into account. Their task is complicated by the necessity to consider the environmental requirements of each prospective addition to a community tank as well as its behavioral peculiarities. Fortunately for the marine aquarist, coral reef organisms, regardless of their geographic provenance, share the same temperature and pH preferences. While differences in salinity do exist between the waters of the Caribbean, the Great Barier Reef and the Red Sea, they do not seem to be as important to the long-term well-being of their respective inhabitants as differences in water hardness are to that of many freshwater fishes.

Of far greater importance to the selection of residents for a marine community is the sensitivity of its intended inhabitants to the medications commonly used to treat parasitic diseases. As a group, invertebrates are extremely intolerant of both dissolved copper and formalin, two of the most common – and effective – antiparasitical agents. This factor, as much as any other, explains why marine aquarists tend to regard the husbandry of fish and invertebrates as an either/or proposition.

With careful management, it is possible to keep both fish and invertebrates in the same aquarium. However, the neophyte marine aquarist should defer efforts to set up such a mixed community tank until he has completely mastered the fundamentals of salt water aquarium management.

The marine aquarist thus finds that the behavioral idiosyncracies of coral reef fish are the chief determinants of their compatibility with other animals in a community setting. The first, and most obvious, factor to take into consideration is the liklihood that a given species will prey upon a tank's other residents. Groupers, snappers and scorpionfishes are highly predatory fishes that will unhesitatingly make a meal of any other fish small enough to fit in their capacious gullets. Attempts to house them with small damsels or butterfly fish are thus no more likely to succeed in the long run than efforts to keep guppies and oscars together in a freshwater community tank. Nor are fishes the only

The sensitivity of many marine invertebrates to some of the medications most commonly used to treat the diseases of marine fishes complicates efforts to house the two together. Such endeavors are more apt to succeed if undertaken by experienced rather than novice marine aquarists.

Specialized piscivores, such as the common lionfish, *Pterois volitans,* must be kept only with companions too large to make a convenient meal.

organisms kept by marine aquarists that will eat smaller fish. Anemones, mantis shrimp and many species of crabs and cone shells are also very efficient fish eaters.

Foraging on sessile invertebrates such as live corals, sponges or tubeworms is less dramatic than the sudden ingestion of a smaller fish, but it too qualifies as predation. Butterfly fishes, angels, many large wrasses, most tangs and trigger fishes all rely to a greater or lesser degree upon such prey in nature. It is thus hardly surprising that they take an acute gustatory interest in the invertebrate fauna of a marine community! Many gastropods and echinoderms also pose a serious threat to the sessile invertebrates that can be successfully cultured in a marine aquarium. Short of keeping diners and dinners apart from one another, there is no effective way to manipulate the expression of predatory behavior to advantage in

captivity. This tendency of many coral reef fishes to graze on a tank's invertebrate fauna adds another element of challenge to successfully maintaining a mixed community tank. Predatory species and their feeding preferences are clearly indicated in the Catalog section. This facet of their behavior must always be carefully considered **before** adding them to an established community or introducing tankmates to their quarters.

**Territoriality** is the behavioral factor that operates most often to limit the compatibility of coral reef fishes in captivity. Reef fishes display two basic types of territorial defense. In the first instance, the territorial proprietor vigorously excludes other fish of the same species from a patch of reef that supports sufficient food to meet its nutritional requirements. All algae-grazing damsels, most sessile invertebrate browsers such as butterfly and angelfishes and even cleaner wrasses defend such feeding territories in nature. These territories are usually very large relative to the size of their defenders. I have seen subadult Beau Gregories, *Eupomacentrus leucostictus*, barely 7.6 cm (3″) overall length defending territories nearly 2 m (c. 6′) on a side! A pair of butterfly fish may hold an area ten times larger still. The aquaristic corollary of this behavior is quite simple: **No more than a single individual (or more rarely, a single pair) of any species that displays this mode of territoriality should be kept in a given tank!** Public aquaria can often make an exception to this rule, but few private persons can accomadate tanks large enough to house several individuals of any territorial species without undesirable consequences.

Although they pose little danger to smaller fishes, many coral reef dwellers share the tendency of the six-banded angelfish, *Pomacanthus sexstriatus*, to treat a tank's sessile invertebrate residents as live food.

Herbivorous damselfishes that cultivate algal "gardens" are notoriously territorial. This juvenile Garibaldi, *Hypsypops rubicundus*, will defend an area several meters square against both conspecifics and other herbivorous fishes in nature.

If this were the end of the matter, selecting an assortment of compatible coral reef fishes for a marine community tank would be a simple matter indeed. However, as already noted in Chapter 1, many coral reef fishes practice **interspecific** as well as the more traditional **intraspecific** defense of a feeding territory. At one time, it was thought that such behavior represented the malfunctioning of an otherwise adaptive behavior pattern. The Austrian ethologist, Konrad Lorenz, noted that territorial coral reef fishes were more likely to attack other fishes whose color patterns closely resembled their own than tankmates whose color patterns were dramatically different. Aquarists have confirmed this observation many times over. The conclusion drawn from these observations was that interspecific territoriality was largely a function of mistaken identity. Other species were attacked because similar elements in their color patterns automatically elicited an aggressive response from a territorial proprietor.

However. field ethologists have also observed interspecific territorial defense in nature. Under these circumstances, it seems that the heterospecific intruders most likely to be attacked by a territorial resident were those with similar dietary requirements regardless of their coloration. It thus seems that interspecific territoriality is anything but maladaptive in its normal context.

Clearly captive fishes are under no pressing need to exclude possible competitors from their territory in order to assure access to an adequate food supply. Their keeper is more than ready to satisfy their needs in this respect! However, such behavior is essentially "hard-wired" into their nervous systems. As such, it is effectively resistant to any external attempts to modify its expression. Thus, in order to keep aggression in his marine community tank at a minimum, the prudent aquarist will take two additional guidelines into consideration when selecting its residents, to whit,

(a) **never attempt to house two different species with similar coloration in the same tank,** and

(b) **never attempt to house two different species with identical or very similar feeding patterns in the same tank.**

This might seem to set extremely severe conditions upon the selection of a compatible community of coral reef fishes. In reality, the selection of species available commercially is so great that it is a very simple matter to assemble a compatible, behaviorally interesting and aesthetically pleasing marine community tank.

Many other coral reef fishes defend a small core territory that contains a shelter to which they can retreat in the face of danger. This

It is much easier to satisfy the space requirements of fish like the green-bandes goby, *Gobiosoma multifasciatum*, that defend only a shelter and its immediate vicinity in nature than it is those of species that hold large feeding territories.

Like these powder blue tangs, *Acanthurus leucosternon*, many coral reef fishes are highly social in nature, yet prove very intolerant of conspecifics in the more restricted environment of the home aquarium.

The coral catfish, *Plotosus anguillaris*, is typical of those highly social marine fishes that retain their preference for the company of conspecifics in captivity.

may also be the resident's nightime resting place. Typically, these species range for considerable distances away from their shelter to feed. While these species will chase potential usurpers away from their chosen shelter, they usually ignore them when away from its vicinity. Clownfishes, grammas, dottybacks, many wrasses and virtually all gobies and blennies practice this sort of territorial defense. These species are much more easily managed in captivity, as increasing the ammount of shelter available in the tank usually goes far towards minimizing aggressive interactions.

It must also be noted that many coral reef fishes are not territorial in nature. Some species, such as the lionfishes of the genus *Pterois*, are effectively indifferent to the proximity of conspecifics. Others, like the cardinalfishes and plankton feeding damsels, are highly social animals that do best in the

A number of marine fishes are, like the Pacific seahorse, *Hippocampus kuda*, indifferent to the proximity of conspecifics both in nature and in captivity.

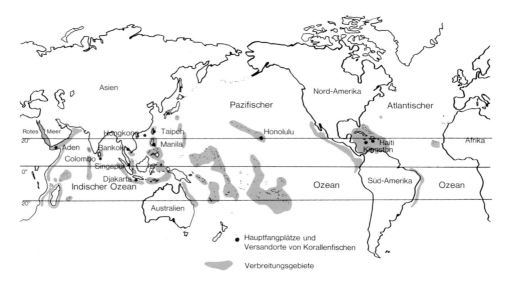

The map labels visible: Asien, Nord-Amerika, Pazifischer, Atlantischer, Rotes Meer, Hongkong, Taipeh, Honolulu, Afrika, Aden, Bankok, Manila, Haiti, Kingston, Colombo, Singapur, Djakarta, Indischer Ozean, Australien, Ozean, Süd-Amerika, Ozean

● Hauptfangplätze und
Versandorte von Korallenfischen

Verbreitungsgebiete

**The distribution of reef-building corals.**

company of their fellows. However, marked sociality in nature does not always translate to a tolerance of conspecifics in captivity. A critical number of individuals may have to be present for the fish to shift from a territorial to a social mode of behavior. Many tangs, for instance will live amiably in groups of four or more in captivity. However, efforts to house two specimens together result in open and unremitting warfare until one of the contenders is either removed from the tank or killed.

The Catalog also addresses the degree of sociality characteristic of each species covered. As with its predatory tendencies, this aspect of its behavior must be carefully considered when deciding whether or not it has a place in a given community of marine organisms.

# Choosing residents
# for the Marine Aquarium

Save for the fortunate minority who live in sufficient proximity to coral reefs to collect their own specimens, marine aquarists must rely upon commercial channels of distribution to secure specimens for their tanks. While retailers in both Europe and North America offer a remarkable selection of coral reef fish from all over the world, the aquarist familiar with freshwater fishes is apt to be somewhat taken aback by both the prices and the anticipated mortality rates of their marine counterparts. The nature of the trade in marine organisms accounts for both phenomena.

First of all, with very few exceptions, all marine organisms are collected from the wild. Tank-raised clownfish of several species as well as neon gobies are sometimes available through commercial channels, and progress continues to be made in the experimental culture of other coral reef inhabitants. All the other animals offered for sale by the retailer were at one time swiming, slithering or scuttling over a coral reef. Their price must reflect not only the cost of their collection, but the very considerable expense entailed in transporting them by air from their locality of origin to their final destination. In many instances, the cost associated with shipping a given fish exceeds the price demmanded for it by the collector!

Secondly, both the collecting and shipping processes are unavoidably stressful to their objects. Leaving for subsequent consideration the deplorable practice of using cyanide as a means of collecting coral reef fish, even trapping or netting a fish from its native waters is a traumatic experience. Marine fish are not fed for at least 24 hours prior to shipping in order to minimize the ammount of waste excreted in the shipping container. This is a necessary practice, but in consequence, the fish loose weight and may suffer from internal disturbances. Each fish is packed in a single plastic bag containing the bare minimum of water for shipping. This again is a necessary step imposed upon the shipper by the need to save weight. However, such a move seriously limits the fish's mobility while exposing it unavoidably to an elevated concentration of its own wastes for a period of 8 to 36 hours, depending upon the distance between its point of origin and its final destination. Though shipping bags are inflated with pure oxygen, marine fish inevitably suffer from respiratory stress in transit because of the buildup of dissolved carbon dioxide in their water. Finally, even carefully packed shipments of fish suffer some degree of chilling in transit.

Given the multiple stresses to which marine organisms are subject before they ever reach the retailer's tanks, it is hardly surprising that roughly 25% of all imported animals survive no more than 8 weeks after their initial collection. The retailer hopes that his suppliers have absorbed most of this anticipated mortality, but knows from experience that he will also sustain losses. This factor definately enters into the prices he must charge for these animals if he is to turn sufficient profit to remain in business. The consumer likewise prefers to operate on the assumption that the retailer has absorbed most of the losses inevitably associated with a given shipment of fish. However, the laws of probability make it equally inevitable that he too will be afflicted by a certain percentage of premature mortality among the animals he purchases. This being the case, it behooves the aquarist to select both his retailer and his purchases

wisely. The liklihood of an unpleasant experience can be greatly reduced if the prospective purchaser of marine organisms learns to recognize obvious indications of trouble and tailors his subsequent behavior accordingly.

## Choosing a Dealer

Because the care marine organisms receive immediately prior to their purchase has a considerable impact upon their prospects for long-term survival, it pays to deal with a competant retailer. Because marine organisms are not inexpensive, it also pays to deal with a retailer who will stand behind his merchandise. A reasonable guarantee policy, *i.e.*, gratis replacement of animals that die within 24 to 48 hours of purchase on presentation of the cadaver, is a pretty good indicator that the retailer in question is both competant and reputable. His prices may be somewhat higher, but the quality of his livestock and his willingness to back his claims to competance with concrete action more than compensate for any difference in cost.

A reasonable guarantee policy is only one indication that a dealer knows what he is about. Astute scrutiny of his tanks will provide many others. Check the color of their water. A pronounced yellowish tint indicates an overworked filtration system and an unseemly reluctance to make water changes. Neither bodes well for the survival prospects of animals that have had the misfortune to reside in such an environment for any length of time. Ask the dealer about his filtration system. If he has a high capacity central system, high stocking rates in his display tanks need not be a cause for alarm. If not, crowded display tanks are an excellent reason for the prospective buyer to take his business elsewhere. Inquire whether the dealer maintains a prophyllactic concentration of copper in his system. A positive answer may suggest that the absence of parasites on his fish has more to do with such suppressive treatment practices than with the animal's inherent good health.

Examine tanks for excessive acumulations of mulm or uneaten food, patches of blue-green algae on the gravel or dead fish. All are signs of poor management. Note that a single casualty in a row of tanks does not automatically indict a retailer for incompetent husbandry, but a series of tanks containing dead or dying residents is another matter altogether.

Watch the staff's interaction with other customers. Reluctance or inability to respond in a helpful manner to questions about the maintenance of a marine system or the behavior or maintenance requirements of a particular fish or invertebrate are hardly positive signs. Neither is a willingness to allow prospective buyers to make uninformed purchases of an imprudent character. One may legitimately entertain doubts about either the competance or the business ethics of a sales person who encourages a customer to purchase a panther grouper, a lionfish and a clownfish for his newly set-up 60 l aquarium!

**Captive marine fish should be captured by manuvering them into a glass or clear plastic container, never chased down with a net.**

Finally, watch how the staff catches a customer's purchases. Does the owner or salesperson manuver the fish into the net or cathing container with a minimum of commotion or does he chase the intended purchase helter-skelter about the tank until its exhaustion allows it to be captured? Does he traumatize the animal further by removing it from the water before putting it in the shipping bag or does he carefully scoop it from the net with an apprpriately sized container, then add it to the bag? Does he have a bag already filled with water to receive his capture, or does he allow it to thrash about in the net or holding container until he prepares one? Netting trauma is a frequent but completely avoidable source of stress for marine fishes. A shop whose staff is either unaware of this fact or so ignorant of the behavior of the livestock it offers for sale that it cannot capture individual animals with a minimum of trauma is unlikely to prove very knowledgable about other, equally important aspects of marine aquarium keeping.

## Choosing Healthy Fish and Invertebrates

Selecting a competent dealer assures the prospective purchaser that the animals he offers for sale have been properly cared for up to the time of purchase. However, the condition of individual fish and invertebrates offered for sale can vary considerably, often due to circumstances beyond the retailer's control. It is up to the individual purchaser to know enough about his prospective purchases to make an informed choice, either to buy or not, and should he opt for the first alternative, which individual in a group of animals is most likely to adapt successfully to life in his tank. Thus the need to be familiar with the relevant characteristics of a given species before setting out to purchase it.

The first factor the prospective buyer should consider is whether a given species has any biological characteristics that mitigate against its successful maintenance in captivity. Many beautiful butterfly fish, for instance, are obligate live coral feeders. Most specimens never accept alternative foods in captivity, while those few that do invariably waste away, victims of dietary deficincies. The strikingly marked cleaner wrasses of the genus *Labroides* represent yet another example of marine fish whose dietary needs cannot be satisfactorily met in captivity. **Removing such animals from their native habitat is tantamount to pronouncing an irrevocable death sentence on them. Purchasing them is essentially an exercise in sadomasochism and simply provides further economic motivation for their capture and exportation.** Given the tremendous selection of strikingly colored coral reef fish and invertebrates available today, there is simply no justification for the purchase of animals whose needs cannot be properly met by the amateur aquarist.

Above: Butterflyfishes that feed primarily upon live coral polyps such as *Chaetodon trifasciatus*, will not survive in captivity unless their special dietary needs are met.

Cleaner wrasses such as *Labroides dimidiatus* represent another group of specialized feeders that rarely survice long in captivity.

Adult groupers like this magnificent *Cephalopholis boenack* usually outgrow their welcome in even the largest home aquaria.

Even the many species whose nutritional and other needs can be met in captivity vary considerably among themselves is hardiness and longevity. It clearly is to the neophyte marine aquarist's advantage to initially select those species that have established a reputation for both characteristics. The Catalog addresses both points and should be consulted whenever a purchase is contemplated. It is also worth noting that the difficulty of managing a given species increases exponentially with its size. Larger specimens generate a significantly heavier waste load, a factor which complicates successful nitrogen cycle management. Their notions of what constitutes adequate living space also tend to undergo a dramatic upward revision as they grow larger. The problems arising from both factors require a considerable degree of hands-on experience to manage successfully. Thus, unless he is fortunate to enjoy access to tanks of 400 l (c. 100 US gallons) capacity or larger, the beginning marine aquarist would do well to eschew any species whose adult length exceeds 15.0 cm (c. 6") standard length unless he is prepared to part with his pet once it exceeds that size. Most

groupers, snappers and triggerfish definately can be counted upon to outgrow their quarters. So can most angelfishes of the genera *Pomacanthus* and *Holocanthus*. As it is not always easy to find a home for such "lunkers", it is a good idea to sound out the dealer's willingness to take them back in trade for smaller specimens **before** making the decision to add one of these robust species to one's marine community. In any event, it is never pleasant to part with an animal that may have become a real pet during its stay in the household. Once the marine aquarist feels fully comfortable with his system, he will have plenty of opportunities to work with these more robust coral reef residents.

The final general consideration that should influence the buyer's selection of marine animals is how they were collected. Until very recently, the overwhelming majority of marine fishes exported from the Philippines were collected by the use of sodium cyanide as a "tranquillizing" agent. Even relatively slight exposure to this extremely toxic substance causes serious liver damage to fishes which, however, may not manifest itself until well

Many coral reef fish exported from the Philippines, such as the zebra angelfish, *Centropyge multifasciatus*, have a reputation for delicacy. It now appears this is largely due to the delayed effects of exposure to sodium cyanide, which is widely used as a means of stunning fish for capture in that country.

after the initial intoxication. Fish so poisoned can appear to be perfectly healthy, showing normal behavior and coloration and even displaying a healthy appetite. However, after an interval of a few days to several weeks, they loose their appetites, develop a peculiarly intense coloration, display signs of respiratory distress and die. There is no effective treatment for cynaide poisoning, and it appears that the reputation many Indo-Pacific coral reef fishes have garnered for fragility under aquarium conditions stems from their modality of capture rather than from any inherent peculiarities of their biology.

Efforts are underway to replace cyanide fishing in the Philippines by less ecologically disruptive, non-toxic capture techniques. Regretably, until every exporter in the archipelago can be given a clean bill of particulars with regard to cyanide use, the possibility that marine fish of Philippine provenance have been exposed to cyanide during capture cannot be dismissed out of hand. The only way the consumer can protect himself is to avoid buying such specimens.

Restricting one's purchases to species native to areas where drugging is not used as a collecting method, such as the Caribbean, the coastal waters of Baja California and Hawaii is one way to avoid poisoned fish. However, this precludes the possibility of maintaining some of the most beautiful and popular coral reef fishes. Fortunately, very few Indo-Pacific species are restricted to the waters of the Philippine archipelago, so the aquarist who is willing to be choosy can usually count of alternative sources of supply for a given species.

Reputable dealers are as eager to avoid the problems associated with poisoned fish as are their customers and are usually prepared to make strenuous efforts to secure sound specimens for sale. Note that fish captured by other methods are usually more expensive than those that have been drugged. This is due as much to the fact that they are often imported from less accessible areas than the Philippines as to any difficulties inherent in netting or trapping. This can add significantly to their transport costs. However, in the long run $20.00 fish that lives for a year or longer is a better bargain than a $5.00 fish that dies within a week of purchase. So do not be shy about asking where a given animal came from and do not hesitate to go elsewhere to purchase fish if a straightfoward answer is not forthcoming.

Finally, avoid buying newly-arrived fish or invertebrates. Many common parasitic infestations of marine fish are provoked by shipping stress. This, it is only common sense to allow newly arrived animals to recuperate to a degree from the multiple traumas they have endured before stressing them with yet another change of venue. Equally to the point, it is clearly to the aquarist's advantage for any weak sisters in the shipment to quit their mortal coil in the dealer's rather than in his tank. A fish that is alive and feeding well a week after its arrival at a retailer's establishment has an excellent liklihood of being in the same condition six months later.

These general caveats aside, the signs of a health are much the same for marine as they are for freshwater fish. Choose active animals with clear eyes, crisp coloration, intact fins and an unblemished body. Avoid specimens with badly damaged fins, patches of missing scales, or any sort of light spotting or lesions on the body and fins. Individuals showing obvious respiratory distress or loss of coordinated swimming ability are clearly terminal cases and should never be considered acceptable risks. As a rule, highly reclusive specimens are highly stressed in the bargain, but the behavior of coral reef fishes is characterized by sufficient variability to inspire a certain degree of caution in interpreting such shyness. Though the observation may seem heartless, individual fish that are harrassing their tankmates are better survival prospects than those being harrassed.

**Never buy a marine fish that refuses to eat when offered food.** Do not hesitate to ask a salesperson to feed the inhabitants of the tank containing a potentially interesting fish, and do not accept excuses if the animal in question refuses to take food. **Loss of appetite is inevitably the prelude to serious and potentially lethal problems.** A reputable dealer will not hesitate to offer a prospective purchase food if asked to do so by a customer. It is not worth the risk of doing business with any retailer who refuses such a request.

It is extremely important to know something of the behavior of a given species when assessing its state of health. Individuals of the royal gramma, *Gramma loreto*, like to keep their ventral surface in contact with the substratum. This can result in an individual hanging upsidedown in a cave or under a ledge. Some hawkfishes and gobies of the genus *Gobiodon* are fond of resting, bird-like, in the branches of a coral head. Either of these behavior patterns would be highly suspect in the generality of coral reef fishes, but they are quite normal for these species. Refer to the Catalog section for information on the behavioral idiosyncracies of the major groups of coral reef fishes.

Marine invertebrates are such a diverse group that it is impossible to provide general guidelines to the prospective buyer. Refer to the appropriate sections of the Catalog for information relevant to each major group.

# Transporting marine organisms

Marine organisms, like their freshwater counterparts, are usually transported in plastic bags containing a volume of water under a bubble of oxygen. Because a shipping bag acts much the same as a newly setup aquarium, special care must be taken to minimize the possibility that a newly purchased specimen will be severely stressed in transit to its new home.

First of all, make certain that the salesperson packs the specimen in a sufficient volume of water. A good rule of thumb is for the depth of water above the animal's back to equal the depth of its body in a bag at least 5.0 cm (2") longer than its total length. If a journey of more than an hour separates the retailer's from the fish's final destination, the bag should be at least 10.0 cm (4") longer than its inhabitant's overall length.

Secondly, be sure that the bag is inflated with oxygen rather than compressed air. Remember that seawater can hold less oxygen in solution than freshwater, even when briskly aerated. The reduced rate of gas exchange at the surface of what is essentially a stagnant pocket of water obviously does nothing to improve the situation. Increasing the ammount of oxygen available at the air-water interface is the only means of compensating for this state of affairs.

The carbon dioxide produced as a byproduct of respiration will tend to push the pH of the water in the bag downwards and will eventually interfere with its resident's ability to absorb oxygen even when the latter gas is present in abundance. If time in transit is no more than a few hours, carbon dioxide accumulation is unlikely to cause problems on either account. If a longer journey is anticipated, it is prudent to add a commercial buffering agent to the bag's water. Used according to the manufacturer's directions, Trizmaà 8.3, a product of the Sigma Chemical Company of St. Louis, MO, will hold pH changes to no more than 0.2 of a pH unit over a 24 hour interval. Independant studies have shown that the pH in the same volume of unbuffered sea water would decline by a full pH unit over the same period of time.

The third point to remember is that nitrogenous wastes will accumulate in the water of a shipping bag exactly as they would in a newly set-up aquarium. The longer the bag's resident is in transit, the greater the concentration of toxic ammonia to which it is exposed, and the larger its resident, the sooner the point of acute toxicity will be reached. It is sometimes suggested that either naturally occuring zeolitic clays or synthetic resins with an affinity for ammonia be used to keep the concentrations of this dangerous substance at sublethal levels in shipping bags.

This approach works well enough in fresh water. However, chemical interference from dissolved salts makes these substances useless in sea water. Experienced marine aquarists have long been in the habit of scattering a handful of thoroughly innoculated gravel from the bed of a undergravel filter over the bottom of a shipping bag. The rationale behind such action is that the *Nitrosomonas* bacteria present will break down any ammonia as quickly as it is produced. Research has confirmed the validity of this precautionary measure.

Obviously, the more innoculated gravel used, the greater the positive effect. Conversely, the larger the specimen transported, the more innoculated filter medium necessary to keep the ammonia build-up at a tolerable level. Experienced aquarists recommend adding a quantity of this gravel sufficient to cover the entire bottom of the shipping bag with a thin layer of material. Such precautionary measures are in order if the specimens in question are to be in transit for more than a few hours regardless of their size, and should always be taken when transporting specimens 15.0 cm (6″) overall length despite the length of their journey.

**Commercial buffers should only be used as an adjunct to the shipping of marine organisms in conjunction with an addition of innoculated filter medium to the shipping bag.** Remember, the total ammount of free ammonia present in solution is affected by the pH of the water. In the absence of a buffer, the pH of the water in the shipping bag declines over time. This tends to keep the proportion of toxic ammonia present more or less constant by favoring the formation of harmless ammonium ion. In a buffered system, the pH remains high, which alows the total ammount of ammonia to increase rapidly to lethal levels. A liberal portion of innoculated gravel added to the shipping bag provides insurance against such an eventuality.

Inquire beforehand at what temperature and specific gravity the dealer maintains his tanks. This information will simplify the process of acclimating purchases to their new home. Finally, always carry bags of marine organisms in a styrofoam box or cooler. As previously noted, they are much more susceptible to temperature stress than their fresh water counterparts. Such a contingency is easily avoided if they are transported in a well insulated container.

# Introducing specimens to a Marine Aquarium

Immediately upon arrival at the fish's destination, open the bag in which it has been transported, roll back its rim several times until a recognizable "collar" has been formed, and float it in the tank. **Never float fish or in-**

**vertebrates in a sealed bag!** Polyethylene bags work well as fish transport containers because their molecular structure permits limited gas exchange between their interior volume and the outside. Immersing a sealed bag in water prevents the polyethylene from "breathing" normally. This can impose serious respiratory stress on its resident very quickly.

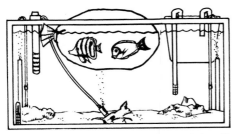

**Floating a** CLOSED **plastic bag containing live animals in an aquarium for any length of time can cause them severe respiratory distress.** ALWAYS OPEN THE BAG BEFORE FLOATING IT.

If the conditions the animals have been living under in the dealer's tanks do not differ greatly from those in their new residence, acclimating them is a fairly straightfoward matter. Remove and discard from a quarter to a third of the bag's original contents and replace it with an equivalent volume of water from the tank. Repeat this performance 10 to 15 minutes later, and alow the bag to float for an addition 10 minutes. At the end of this interval, tip the bag gently on its side and allow its resident to swim out into its new home. If a fish or invertebrate seems reluctant to leave the bag, simply leave it in position until its resident leaves of its own volition. This rarely takes more than a few moments.

If one has no information on the prior living conditions of newly received specimens, it is prudent to proceed a bit more cautiously in acclimating them to their new home. After floating the bag in the receiving tank, take the pH and specific gravity of its contents. Measuring the specific gravity will almost certainly entail removing a sample of the water to a specific gravity cylinder in order to secure an accurate reading from the hydrometer. If

the pH of the bag's contents difers by more than half a unit from that of the tank, or if the salinity reading differs by more than 2.0 ppt, it is prudent to acclimate the fish more slowly to its new home. Half a dozen 10% water replacements, seperated by 10 minute intervals, are less likely to prove stressful to the new arrival under such conditions than fewer, larger changes over a comparable interval.

Sound husbandry dictates submiting all new arrivals to a 7 to 10 day quarantine period before introducing them to an establishes community. The stresses associated with capture and transport seriously compromise any organism's inherent resistance to disease. It is thus no surprise that newly purchased fishes are often attacked by such parasites as *Oodinium* or *Crytocaryon*. Quite apart from this risk that such infestations might be transmitted to a tank established residents, the treatment of these diseases inevitably stresses even otherwise healthy fishes to a degree. This trauma can be avoided if the treatment need only be given to the affected animal.

A further advantage of such a quarantine period is that it allows a new arrival a quiet interval to rebuild its strength and regain its behavioral equilibrium. This increases the likelihood that it will be able to make a place for itself with minimum diffculty when it is finally added to an existing community of organisms. To assure that a newly purchased fish will feel at home as quickly as possible, be certain to provide the quarantine tank with a selection of shelters. The mechanics and proper use of a quarantine tank are considered in greater detail in Chapter 8.

If it is impractical to quarantine a newcomer before introducing it to an established community tank, there are a few steps that can be taken to facilitate its smooth integration into its existing network of social interactions. First of all, give the tank's existing residents a good feeding. A full stomach tends to mellow their reaction to the sudden appearance of a new tankate. It is also prudent to shake up the existing peck order a bit by either changing the position of some of the tank's infrastructure or adding a few new elements to its decor. A few large mollusc shells, a new clump of finger coral or a cluster of barnacle shells goes far towards increasing the ammount of unoccupied shelter in a marine tank. This in turn makes it more likely that a newly introduced animal will be able to secure a refuge without having to fight for it.

It is inadvisable to offer newly introduced fishes or invertebrates food until they have become familiar with their new surroundings. Usually it requires no more than a few hours before they feel secure enough to begin swimming briskly around, although it may take somewhat longer before they are comfortable in the presence of their keeper. It is preferable to offer new purchases the type of food to which they have grown accustomed for their first few meals. There will be plenty of time to wean them over to alternate diets once they have become thoroughly accustomed to their new surroundings. An excellent choice of initial food for most non-piscivorous marine fish is live adult *Artemia*. It is both taken eagerly by most marine species and will live long enough in the tank for even the most retiring newcomer to have the opportunity to feed upon it.

Once the new addition has had a chance to eat, shut the tank lights off. Reducing the ammount of available light tends to slow down behavioral interactions to a degree, making it easier for a new arrival to work himself into the existing pattern of space utilization and social interactions in a community aquarium. The tank can be returned to its normal lighting schedule the next day. Watch interactions between the newcomer and its tankmates closely for a week or so after its introduction. Brief squabbles are nothing to be alarmed about. However, if the new fish proves the persistant looser or cannot leave its refuge without being attacked, the only alternative is to remove either the bully or its victim to new quarters. Such an outcome is less likely if the least aggressive of a tank's intended residents is the first stocked. Add more belligerent species in order of their increasing aggressiveness, with the most aggressive species the last added.

Introduce relatively unaggressive fish such as the royal gramma, *Gramma loreto,* first to a community aquarium. A period of prior residence will allow them to better cope with more belligerent subsequent additions.

Extremely territorial species, such as the blue devil, *Chrysiptera cyanea,* should always be added last to a community tank. If added first, they will usually liquidate less aggressive companions as fact as they are introduced to the aquarium.

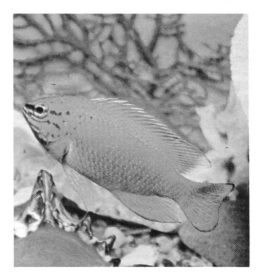

# CHAPTER 6.

# Feeding the Marine Aquarium

## Setting up a feeding programm for Marine Organisms

Doubtless because commercial mariculture is still in its infancy, much less is known about the nutritional requirements of marine fishes than of many of their freshwater counterparts. Data garnered from many years of rigorous experimentation permit feed technologists to prepare rations that maximize the growth and ensure the well-being of such diverse species as trout, channel catfishes, carp and tilapias. Much of this information is directly relevant to the nutritional requirements of other representatives of the families to which these important food fish belong. Thus the freshwater aquarist is considerably better off than his marine counterpart when it comes to putting together a feeding plan that will guarantee the health and reproductive success of his pets.

If precise information on the nutritional requirements of marine organisms is largely lacking, a considerable body of data on the feeding patterns of both coral reef fishes and invertebrates has been accumulated over the past 35 years. It is at least possible to identify those species whose dietary preferences are so specialized as to render their successful maintenance anything from extremely costly to virtually impossible for the amateur aquarist. One can also assign those marine species that are successfuly kept under home aquarium conditions to one of three broad trophic categories, to whit, **carnivores**, **omnivores** and **herbivores**. Within the carnivore category, it is both possible and useful to distinguish between piscivorores, invertebrate browsers, mollusc eaters and plankton feeders. Such information, which is included

in the Catalog, permits the aquarist to make educated judgements about what to feed his pets.

In light of the present state of knowledge or lack of it about the nutritional requirements of marine organisms, the best advice to offer the marine aquarist is to offer his pets a diet that is both **varied** and **fresh**. This can sometimes prove a challenging task. Quite apart from the observed fact that many marine organisms have species specific dietary preferences, a good deal of trophic idiosyncracy often occurs within a given species. Where one individual snaps up flake food with relish, another will totally ignore all offerings save live food. Fortunately, contemporary marine aquarists can offer their pets a remarkable selection of live, fresh, frozen and prepared foods. Thus while putting together a feeding plan that marine organisms will find both palatable and nutritious may well entail both persistance and a certain reliance on trial and error, the many options available virtually guarantee success to the diligent hobbyist.

It is impossible to overemphasize the importance of palatability when selecting a diet for marine fishes. The most nutritious food is valueless to an organism if its flavor – or lack thereof – precludes consumption by its intended beneficiary. It is particularly important to provide newly acquired specimens with food sufficiently to their liking to guarantee its prompt and repeated consumption. Live nauplii and adult brine shrimp are excellent for this purpose. Remember that newly imported animals are usually suffering from the effects of a prolonged fast by the time they arrive in a hobbyist's tank. It is absolutely essential to their well-being that they begin eating immediately. Once they have regained the weight lost following capture and during transit and are in better condition, efforts can be made to persuade them to adopt a different diet.

Because of the impact overfeeding can have upon nitrogen cycle management, it is equally essential to exercise great care when feeding marine organisms. **NEVER GIVE A MARINE AQUARIUM MORE FOOD THAN ITS INHABITANTS CAN COMPLETELY**

**CONSUME IN 5 MINUTES!!** Any food remaining on the bottom the tank after this interval should be netted or siphoned out. If the fish still seem hungry after a single feeding, wait half an hour and offer them another small meal. Quite apart from considerations of good aquarium hygiene, there is another very good reason for offering marine fishes many small meals rather than one or two large daily feedings. With the exception of piscivorous species, coral reef fish nibble at their prefered food items more or less constantly during the daylight hours. Very few have the expanded foreguts necessary to hold large ammounts of food for future processing. A regime of repeated light feedings thus corresponds far more closely to their natural pattern of food intake.

The frequency with which marine organisms should be offered food varies considerably between species. Very small specimens, up to 3.75 cm (1.5″) overall length, should be offered small quantities of food at least 5 times daily. Newly hatched brine shrimp nauplii should make up at least half of their diet. Larger specimens do not require more than three feedings daily. Herbivorous species such as tangs, are an exception to this rule. They browse constantly in nature and do very poorly in captivity unless their keeper duplicates this feeding pattern with 4 or 5 small daily feedings. Large predatory specimens, such as groupers or lionfish, should be fed no more than 2 or 3 times a week. It is prudent to impose a weekly fast day on established marine tanks. This practice, from which only very young fish should be exempted, simplifies nitrogen cycle management to a degree and assures that the tank's inhabitants will retain a hearty appetite.

A tank's more assertive residents will often monopolize access to particularly choice food items. This can result in its timider inhabitants getting less than their full share. If this appears to be a problem, offer food at both ends of the tank. It sometimes helps to drop one or two items in front of the usual refuge of a particularly retiring species. If time is available, one can also allow the more aggressive fish to eat their fill, wait five minutes, and re-sume feeding. Once their stomachs are full, even the most gluttonous individuals are usually too lethargic to seriously inhibit the efforts of their more retiring companions to secure a meal.

It is also necessary to take a marine organism's natural cycle of activity into account when offering it food. Cardinalfishes, for example, tend to feed at dusk and dawn in nature. In captivity, they are often inhibited by a tank's intense illumination and tend to get less than their share at feeding time. Many invertebrates are also crepuscular or nocturnal feeders. The aquarist who keeps such animals as pets should be certain that he offers them food at the appropriate time. The easiest way to meet this requirement is to shut the tank lights off while leaving some other source of illumination in the room where it is located, then add food to the tank. Diurnal fishes are less efficient at locating food in such dim light, thus affording their crepuscular or nocturnal tankmates the advantage they need to secure a full meal.

The healthy appetites of marine fishes makes every feeding a special pleasure for the hobbyist. The bolder of a tank's residents quickly learn to take flakes or other morsels of food from their owner's fingers. Such behavior promotes the sort of intimate contact between an aquarist and his fish that helps to sustain a lively interest in the aquarium and its residents.

# Suitable Foods for the Marine Aquarium

### Prepared and Freeze-dried Foods

For reasons of both convenience and economy, most marine aquarists prefer to make prepared foods the backbone of whatever feeding program they design for their pets. Flake foods are most usually employed to feed marine organisms. This is due principally to the fact that flakes tend to sink slowly through the water than do pellets, thus affording the fish more time to snap them up before they hit the bottom. The soft texture of moistened flakes also makes it s simple

**Once they have learned to recognize them as edible, a surprisingly large number of marine fishes will enthusiastically feed on flake foods.**

matter for the smaller arthropods and molluscs to manage such offerings. This confers another advantage upon flake foods from the invertebrate enthusiast's perspective. Pelletized foods are useful chiefly in feeding the larger marine fish, such as surgeons, triggerfish and the more robust angels. TetraTips are particularly useful for this purpose, for they can be pressed against the glass sides and front of the tank where the fish can nibble on them undisturbed by their keeper's proximity.

The flake foods of choice are products formulated specially for use in the marine aquarium, such as TetraMarin. Such foods contain a selection of ingredients that enhances their palatability while providing their consumers with most of the vitamins and trace elements they need to remain in good health. Formulations based by a high proportion of plant material, such as Tetra Conditioning Food, are relatively low in protein but high in roughage. They are thus an essential element in the diet of herbivorous species such

**Large fishes such as *Lycodontis favigeneus* tend to prefer pelletized over flake foods.**

**Prepared foods formulated specifically for use in the marine aquarium are formulated with the dietary needs of coral reef fishes in mind.**

as tangs, many damsels and butterfly fish and most large angelfish.

To minimize the ammount of uneaten food that gets swept into the filter or lodges under the tank's infrastructure, it is preferable to select a product with very large flakes. Both TetraMarin and Tetra Conditioning Food are available in large flakes, a fact that further

*Herbivorous fishes appreciate regular feedings of flake foods enriched with green vegetables.*

enhances their suitability for use in the marine aquarium. If the fish to be fed seem too small to mamage very large flakes, it is a simple operation to break them into smaller fragments before feeding them.

Bear in mind that newly imported marine fishes are likely to find prepared food of any sort rather confusing at first. They will almost certainly be very reluctant to take flakes from the surface. If they are housed with companions who have already learned to feed from the surface, it usually takes no more than one or two feedings for the newcomers to catch on and join in the feeding frenzy. If such exemplars are not present, it is best to soak the flakes in water before adding them to the tank. The fish are more apt to take them as they drift slowly to the bottom. Once they learn to recognize them as food, they are more apt to modify their usual foraging behavior and come to the surface to feed. When offering flake food, it is a good idea to reduce the flow or completely shut off the tank's filter for the duration of the feeding. This minimizes the chance of flakes being swept into corners and crevices where the fish cannot reach them.

Some individual specimens are quite obstinant in their refusal to try prepared foods for the first time. A simple way to overcome such reluctance is to soak the flakes in a small ammount of clam juice before offering them to the fish. Bottled clam juice is available at most supermarkets and sufficiently inexpensive to make such a strategy of flavor enhancement feasible. Even very picky eaters respond positively to this tactic. Once the fish have learned to recognize the flakes as edible, it is usually possible to progressively dilute the concentration of and finally completely eliminate the clam juice without affecting the palatability of the flakes.

A respectable selection of freeze-dried live foods is also available to the marine aquarist. These items are typically characterized by both high price and high palatability. Their one disadvantage is extreme buoyancy. This reduces their utility in feeding newly imported specimens dramatically. Once fish have learned to take food freely from the surface, freeze-dried foods such as krill or brine shrimp can be used with great success as a dietary supplement for most coral reef fishes.

## Frozen Foods

Fresh frozen foods represent another convenient source of suitable nourishment for marine organisms. Aquarists can choose between whole frozen food organisms such as adult brine shrimp, zooplankton, mysid shrimps and bloodworms or prepared mixtures of fresh seafood, marine algae and vegetables supplemented with vitamins in an agar or gelatin matrix. Both types are chiefly useful as a means of providing marine fishes with a palatable and nutritious dietary supplement, though food value tends to vary from one product to another. Frozen adult *Artemia*, for example, are useful chiefly as a source of roughage and trace elements, because their exoskeletons rupture when they are frozen. This causes most of their body mass to be lost when they are thawed for feeding. Euphasiid shrimps, the dominant component in frozen zooplankton, mysids, smelt and bloodworms, on the other hand, respond more favorably to freezing and thawing. They retain virtually all of their food value. Such foods are highly palatable to the great majority of coral reef fishes. They are thus preferable to prepared formulas when feeding newly imported marine specimens.

Many aquarists simply break off a chunk of frozen food and drop it into the tank for the fish to pick at. This practice is unwise for a number of reasons. First of all, there is some reason to believe that ingesting very cold food on an ongoing basis is harmful to the health of marine fishes. Secondly, allowing a chunk of food to thaw in the tank releases large ammounts of nitrogenous substances into solution. These can impose a serious short-term burden on a tank's biological filter, particularly in an aquarium that is stocked to near carrying capacity. Finally, adding the food as a single chunk allows the tank's more aggressive inhabitants to monopolize access to it, to the detriment of their less assertive tank mates.

When feeding a frozen prepared mixture, break off a piece large enough for a single feeding, place on a saucer and allow it to partially thaw. It can then be easily cut into smaller pieces, which in turn can be offered to the residents of a marine aquarium. These foods should be used with great care, as their often elevated protein content can result in serious problems if any appreciable quantity should go uneaten in the tank. The five minute rule is particularly relevant to the feeding of such formulas.

Before feeding frozen whole food organisms, thaw the piece of food out beforehand in cold tap water. Hot water should be avoided, as it may lower the nutritional value of the food in question by destroying essential vitamins. Once it is completely thawed, pour off the water and replace it with fresh water of the same temperature. Allow most of the food items to settle to the bottom of the container and pour off the supernatant water. Repeat the procedure until the the water standing over the food is perfectly clear and free of any suspended matter. Now pour off most of the water and replace it with salt water from the tank to be fed. The now thoroughly cleaned food items can be offered to the fish a few at a time with a kitchen baster.

## Fresh Foods

Virtually any type of seafood relished by people will be appreciated by marine fishes. Fish, shrimp, crab, lobster, clams, scallops and mussels are highly palatable and nutritious additions to the menu of most marine organisms. To assure that the fish receive the full nutritional benefit of such offerings, use only fresh seafood. Frozen seafood tends to loose its food value if it sits too long in a freezer. The easiest way to feed these items is to partially freeze the food, then cut it into strips about the width of a pencil. It can then be fed at once. Any surplus can be immediately frozen for future use.

Seafood intended for small fish should be finely minced and dispensed from a baster, as described for frozen food. If the object is to tempt larger specimens, such as triggerfish, snappers, groupers or lionfish, place a piece of the appropriate size on the ent of a piece of wire or a sharpened wooden stick and move it gently to and from in front of the intended consumer's mouth. Once the fish learns to recognize the strips as food, such care in presenting them becomes unnecessary.

The ideal vegetable foods for marine fishes are green macroalgae such as *Caulerpa* and sea lettuce (*Ulva*). Many coral reef fishes, among them surgeonfish, some butterflies and the moorish idol, *Zanclus cornutus*, grow better when their diets are supplemented with algae than on an exclusive regime of prepared foods. However, few aquarists live close enough to the coast to make gathering the latter feasible, while the hearty appetite such herbivorous coral reef residents as surgeonfishes for the latter precludes growing sufficient quantities to satisfy their demands. Frozen algae are available commercially, but at a cost that makes reliance upon alternative vegetable foods seem quite attractive.

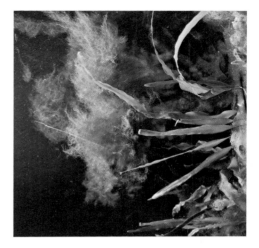

Fortunately, most leafy vegetables are quite palatable to marine fishes if properly pre-

**Filamentous green algae are greedily eaten by many coral reef fishes.**

An Achilles tang, *Acanthurus achilles* (lower right) and a yellow tang, *Zebrasoma flavescens,* enjoying a meal of fresh lettuce. Herbivorous marine fishes relish regular offerings of such vegetable food in captivity.

pared. Romaine lettuce and spinach are most commonly thought of in this context, but any leaf lettuce, Swiss chard and broad, or Italian, parsley are all excellent fish foods, rich in essential vitamin C and the pigment precursor substances marine fish require to retain their intense coloration. Thinly sliced young marrow squashes, such as zucchini and summer squash, are also quite acceptable to most herbivorous fishes.

To prepare such vegetables for the fishes' consumption, place the portion to be offered them in a collander and slowly pour several quarts of boiling water over it. Rinse the scalded greens under cold water, drain and fasten each portion to a small stone or piece of coral with an elastic band. The stone and its attached burden can then be added to the aquarium and the fish allowed to graze at leisure. As the decomposition of any uneaten vegetables can lead to nitrogen cycle management problems, it is prudent to leave such offerings of greens in the tank no more than half an hour before removing them.

Though all of these fresh foods are highly nutritious, some species of coral reef fish appear to have difficulty recognizing them as food. Most of these are browsers, accustomed to nibbling their food from the solid reef surface. An alternative approach to offering fresh foods to such picky eaters exploits their normal feeding behavior. With a food processor, reduce clams, mussels, shrimp or a combination of all three to a stiff paste. Use a high-quality flake food like TetraMarin as a thickening agent and clam juice as a thinner. Either green macroalgae or fresh vegetables can be added if the mixture is to be offered to herbivorous species.

The paste should have the same consistency as butter frosting and be easily spreadable in a thin layer over the surface of a stone or a piece of coral. Brain and mushroom coral are excellent for this purpose. Now dry the food-covered rock or coral in the oven at a temperature of 70° C. (c. 125° F.) for ten minutes. After drying, such a "feeding stone" can either be placed immediately in the aquarium or stored in a plastic bag in the freezer until needed. Most chaetodontids, conspicuous among them the long-nosed butterfly, *Forcipinger longirostris*, and the dwarf angels of the genus *Centropyge* are particularly fond of this type of food. Be certain to remove such "feeding stones" after 15 to 20 minutes of exposure in the tank.

## Live Foods

Live foods offer the ultimate in palatability to the marine aquarist. Coral reef fishes not only find their taste appealing, but respond to their movement as to an irresistable feeding stimulus. Live foods tend to be quite costly. This fact obliges most aquarists to restrict their use to the acclimation of newly acquired specimens or as a "treat" for established ones. Note that while most of the coral reef fishes available to aquarists readily adapt to a diet based on prepared and frozen foods, some species never learn to take non-living food items. Such species are indicated in the Catalog. Only the hobbyist prepared to meet the dietary requirements of such species should consider working with them.

By far the most versatile live food available to the marine aquarist is the brine shrimp, *Artemia salina*. Their durable cysts can be purchased by the hobbyist in an quantity he needs at most pet shops. Their nauplii are easily hatched and eagerly taken by all of the smaller and a surprising number of medium-sized marine fishes and invertebrates. Many different commercial systems for hatching out brine shrimp nauplii are available. The essential elements in any hatching system are water of the appropriate salinity and pH, vigorous aeration and warmth. As the salinity preferences of the cysts varies according to their locality of origin, follow the hatching instructions that come with them carefully to obtain the best results. For a prompt and complete hatch, keep the brine solution between 25° C (77° F.) and 30° C. (85° F.). It should require no longer than 36 hours to obtain a 95% hatch of the eggs added to a hatching container.

*Artemia* nauplii are strongly attracted to a bright light. Once the aeration is shut off, they will congregate in great numbers around a powerful beam of light shone into the hatch-

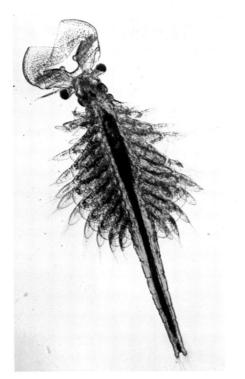

**An adult male brine shrimp, *Artemia salina*. Its ability to survive indefinately in salt water makes the brine shrimp an ideal live food for marine fishes.**

ing container. This makes it a simple matter to siphon them off into a fine meshed net. They should be rinsed under a gentle stream of luke-warm water, allowed to drain thoroughly, then placed in a small container of sea water from the tank where they are to be fed. They can then be offered to its residents with a large eye dropper or a kitchen baster.

It is not a good idea to feed unrinsed nauplii or nauplii suspended in the hatching solution directly to marine organisms. The hatching solution is typically saltier than the sea water in a marine aquarium. Constant addition of saltier brine will drive the salinity of the tank upwards to a dangerous degree. Note also that most of the nutritional value of *Artemia*

nauplii lies in their large yolk sac, which is consumed over the passage of time. To get the most out of brine shrimp nauplii, feed them within 12 hours of hatching. When feeding *Artemia*, both nauplii and adults, remember to shut the filter off until the fish have eaten their fill. Unless this precaution is taken the brine shrimp, weak swimmers at best, will all end up in the filter bed rather than inside the fish!

One can raise *Artemia* nauplii to adulthood, but the process is messy, time consuming and not particularly productive. Adult brine shrimp are available from retail dealers in most parts of the country for most of the year. They are collected from San Francisco Bay and various salt lakes in the western United States and shipped by air to their various destinations. Their availability is thus subject to the vagaries of both the weather and airline schedules. Sporadic availability and cost both make it impractical for most marine aquarists to rely heavily upon live adult brine shrimp as a fish food.

This is perhaps for the best, as *Artemia* are deficent in a number of vitamins and amino acids vital to the long-term well being of marine fishes. However, because they will live indefinately in sea water, they have an uncontested advantage over the majority of live foods available to the marine aquarist. When added to the aquarium, they constitute a "living larder" available to its inhabitants over a long period of time. Furthermore, the jerking motion of both nauplii and adult *Artemia* entice the fish to snap at them and thus encourage timely feeding. As noted, this is particularly important when dealing with newly imported specimens.

Small fish are the other live food source of importance to marine aquarists. Piscivorous species such as groupers, snappers and scorpionfishes often refuse to take any other nourishment, and even those specimens that learn to take pieces of fresh fish or shellfish do best when offered live fish once or twice weekly. Many small to medium sized coral reef fishes with omnivorous feeding patterns in nature also relish a meal of live fish of the appropriate size. Guppies and mollies make

**Although they can be easily taught to take alternative foods, large groupers relish the occasional "treat" of live fish.**

excellent live food for marine fishes because they adapt rapidly and will live for extended periods in sea water. Other poeciliids are somewhat less salt-tolerant, but can be counted to live long enough in a marine aquarium to serve their intended purpose. The brackish water killifishes of the genus *Fundulus* that are widely used as bait by sport fishermen along the Atlantic and Gulf coasts of North America will also live indefinately in sea water. Their size makes them practical only as a food for large predators, while their use does pose a certain risk of introducing parasites into the aquarium.

Feeder goldfish, which are most commonly offered to large fishes as food, have virtually no salt tolerance and die within moments of being placed in sea water. This is not usually a serious problem, as the larger piscivorous reef fishes typically snap up such offerings as soon as they hit the water. Feed them only one or two at a time and take care to remove any immobile specimens immediately. Other-

wise, they are as likely to provoke a filter overload as any other dead fish that goes unremoved from the system.

Other live foods such as white worms, earthworms and *Daphnia* all suffer from the same disadvantage of dying rapidly after immersion in sea water. They should only be offered in small quantities and great care must be taken to remove any uneaten portions before they foul the tank. *Tubifex* worms should never be used to feed marine fish. Quite apart from the fact that they carry significant numbers of potentially harmful bacteria, they will burrow under the gravel of a marine aquarium and die there. This behavior does nothing to simplify nitrogen cycle management. The marine aquarist who lives on the seashore will often be able to collect considerable numbers of small crustaceans, such as mysids, as well as live snails, mussels and other shellfish. These are perfectly acceptable sources of live food and should be exploited whenever possible.

Sessile marine invertebrates are less tolerant of elevated nitrite and nitrate levels than the generality of marine fishes. Hence very rogen cycle management is essential to their successful culture.

# CHAPTER 7.

# Maintaining the Marine Aquarium

## Managing the Nitrogen Cycle

The secret of a succesful marine aquarium is maintenance of high standards of water quality. This means successfully managing the nitrogen cycle in the tank. This fact is complicated by the fact that aquarists typically deal only with one sequence of the catabolic phase of the nitrogen cycle, in which proteins and other complex molecules containing nitrogen are broken down in a stepwise fashion to nitrate. Unless he has opted to experiment with a dentrifying unit in his filter system, the aquarist is faced with an unavoidable build-up of nitrate in his tank.

There is no direct evidence that even elevated nitrate levels ($> 10.0$ ppm) are toxic to marine fishes, although they clearly are not relished by hard corals and a number of other sessile invertebrates. However, the exercise of a bit of common sense will suggest that animals that never encounter significant concentrations of a particular substance in nature are unlikely to benefit from being marinated therein in captivity, however physiologically innocuous the compound in question appears to be. Furthermore, nitrate build-up appears to occur in lockstep with the accumulation of other substances that are likely to prove harmful to marine organisms. The aquarist is thus faced with the necessity of periodically reducing the concentrations of Hese substances to acceptable levels. This requires a program of regular partial water changes.

Of equal importance to proper nitrogen cycle management is the care of a marine tank's biological filters. Both undergrvel and canister filters eventually suffer a loss of flow-through capacity because of mechanical fouling of their media by large waste particles. By reducing the flow of oxygen-laded water through the filter bed, such blockage can seriously compromise the functioning of a biological filter, with predictably disagreable results. Regular purging of the filter bed is thus absolutely essential to the continued well-being of a marine aquarium.

## Water Changes in the Marine Aquarium

It is a simple matter to change water in a freshwater aquarium. In the overwhelming majority of cases, tap water, suitably treated to remove chlorine or chloramine, is perfectly acceptable to the tank's residents. The only precaution the aquarist must take is to match the temperature of the fresh water with that of the tank. Because fresh sea water must be mixed beforehand, water changes in a marine aquarium are a good deal more time consuming, and unless carefully thought out in advance, can often prove considerably more laborious in the bargain. This explains why marine aquarists are so concerned to keep water changes at a minimum.

There are no hard and fast rules to be offered on how much or how frequently water should be changed in a marine aquarium. Both the frequency and volume of such changes depends upon the kinds of organisms kept, the stocking rate of the tank and the type of filtration employed. A 200 l (c. 50 gallon) aquarium with a properly set up Dutch mini-reef containing mainly sessile invertebrates with symbiotic algae and one or two small fish may need no more than a 10% water change every 6 to 8 weeks. A tank the same size housing a large grouper or two adult lionfish may require replacement of a comparable volume of water weekly or a more substantial water change every 2 to 3 weeks. Incorporating a protein skimmer into the filtration system also tends to stretch out the interval between water changes because it removes considerable quantities of nitrogenous wastes entirely from the system. The use of activated carbon in the filter system also significant prolongs good water quality in a closed system.

Until the novice marine aquarist has learned enough about his system to base an informed judgement upon other data, he ought to check the nitrate level in his tank weekly. If the nitrate concentration is > 10.0 ppm, 25% to 30% water change is in order. If he takes the trouble to record the dates of such water changes in his notebook, he will shortly be able to calculate the average interval between them and schedule a regular program of water replacement accordingly. Bear in mind that this rule of thumb only refers to water changes that constitute routine maintenance for a marine aquarium. Other factors than can dictate an immediate and more more substantial water change will be considered in the next chapter.

The first step in carrying out a water change is to calculate the precise volume of water to be replaced. Remember to calculate this as a percentage of the **actual volume of water in the tank**, not its rated capacity. The displacement of the tank's infrastructure guarantees that these two figures will be quite different. This is a relatively simple calculation to carry out if the aquarist has prudently written down the actual volume of water in his system in his notebook. In any event, it is recommended to siphon the water into buckets of known volume the first time a water change is done and keep track of the ammount removed whilst actually conducting the operation. The water level in the tank can be recorded in the aquarist's notebook for future reference. This eliminates the need for such careful monitoring of the volume of water siphoned off in the future.

The next step is to mix 25% again the volume of water to be removed from the tank. It is always a good idea to mix extra sea water before doing a water change. It sometimes happens that more water than originally anticipated has to be removed from the tank. Alternatively, it may prove necessary to wash decorative materials or filter media, an operation that also requires clean sea water. The aquarist who has kept a careful record of the ammounts of salt mix used to generate his original volume of sea water will have little difficulty determining how much he will need to prepare the quantity required for a water change. It is preferable to prepare the new sea water a day ahead of time using cold tap water, then raise it to the temperature of the tank with an immersion heater.

If this is not practical, allow the hot water to run 3 to 5 minutes before using it to bring the temperature of tap water to the desired level prior to adding the salt mix. This should reduce the risk of metal contamination to acceptable levels, but to be absolutely certain that none of these substances are present, add Tetra AquaSafe to the final volume of water at the dosage recommended on the bottle. This product will form an organic complex with any heavy metal ions present, tieing them up in a form that is harmless to marine organisms. If necessary, now is the time to add the appropriate volume of dechlorinating or dechloraminating agent to the water.

The next step is to add the appropriate volume of salt mix to the water. Stir and aerate briskly until **ALL** of the salt has gone into solution. Undissolved salt accretions should never be added to the aquarium. Fish can mistake them for food, often with grave consequences. This is a further advantage to mixing fresh sea water well ahead of its moment of use. With practice, the hobbyist will become quite proficient at mixing sea water of the required salinity in one pass. Until he reaches this point, prudence dictates checking the specific gravity before adding freshly mixed sea water to an established tank. Follow the procedures outlined in Chapter 2 to adjust the salinity upwards or downwards as necessity dictates.

By this time, it should be clear why the novice marine aquarist was advised in Chapter 2 to invest in a number of plastic carboys or similar vessels of large volume. Considerable holding space is necessary both to mix fresh sea water and receive old water from the tank. Much sloshing and splashing of seawater will be eliminated if the aquarist has taken the precaution of setting the container

of fresh sea water on a wheeled dolly that allows it to be brought right up the the tank rim. Alternatively, one can simply purchase a length of clear plastic tubing long enough to reach from the location where the sea water is prepared to the tank. The newly mixed water can then be pumped into the tank with a minimum of fuss and bother. As a certain ammount of splashing is inevitable in the most efficiently conducted water change, prudence dictates spreading a plastic dropsheet around the base of the tank before commencing operations.

Disconnect the tank's heater as well as any filters whose pump mechanisms rely upon continous water flow for cooling. If the water level falls to the point where such pumps are no longer drawing water, their motors are otherwise likely to burn out. It is also a good idea to periodically remove one or two of the larger pieces of decorative infrastructure before starting to drain water from the tank. This affords an opportunity to siphon out any detritus that may have accumulated beneath their bases. This is also the moment to remove any coral that is due for bleaching and clean the inside surfaces of the tanks front and sides of algae with a magnetized scraper or a soft abrasive pad.

To simultaneously purge the tank substratum of accumulated waste, aerate the bed of an undergravel filter and remove old water, use the Tetra HydroClean when making water changes. This versatile and useful piece of equipment enormously simplifies the task of tank maintenance in both fresh and salt water aquaria by making it unnecessary to stir the filter bed before doing a water change. Unless the tank is very heavily stocked, it is not usually necessary to purge the entire substratum at each water change. Most aquarists do from a third to half the bottom at a setting. It is a prudent measure to work the intake bell of the instrument around the base of particularly large pieces of coral or rockwork each time the tank is cleaned. These are precisely the spots where detritus is likely to collect and anaerobic conditions develop.

Once the predetermined volume of water has been removed, replace any pieces of decora-

**The substratum of any aquarium should always be purged of accumulated detritus during the course of a water change.**

tive material that were taken out at the onset of the operation. Take care to place their bases solidly on the filter plate or tank bottom! Now top the tank up with fresh sea water. Once the aquarium has been refilled, plug the heater back in, start up the filter siphons, if necessary, and reconnect their pumps. Discard the old water. It is a good idea to run the cold water tap at full force and pour only small volumes of the dirty sea water down the drain at any one time if the house relies upon a septic tank to process household waste. A sudden influx of sea water otherwise runs the risk of upsetting its operation.

All that remains for the aquarist to do now is to clean up in the vicinity of the tank, put away his equipment and wipe up any water that may have dripped onto the outside surface of the tank. Counting the preparation of fresh sea water and clean-up afterwards, it is usually possible to carry out a 25% to 30% water change in a 220 l (55 U.S. gallon) tank in just under two hours. Assuming the need

for a water change every two weeks, the hobbyist can anticipate a monthly investment of four hours in this essential aspect of tank maintenance. This is really a very small price to pay to enjoy the beauty of a marine aquarium. Anyone who balks at devoting this much time to its care is better off adopting some other hobby, as he is most unlikely to succeed as a marine aquarist!

**Filter Maintenance**

An undergravel filter can be purged of accumulated particulate waste during routine water changes. Other filter types require special attention to insure their continued efficient functioning. Protein skimmers should have their cups emptied daily. The output of bubbles from their airstones should also be carefully monitored. If it seems to have fallen off, replace the affected stone with a clean one and take remedial action to clear the blockage responsible for the problem.

Sintered glass and pumice airstones will

initially respond to an overnight soak in white vinegar, followed by a few hour's operation in fresh water. Eventually they will become so heavily encrusted with minerals that such treatment does not clear them away sufficiently to restore satisfactory performance. Once this point has been reached, discard and replace the afflicted airstone. Wooden air releasers can often be salvaged by soaking them for a few hours in chlorine bleach and leaving them overnight in a gas oven. The heat generated by the pilot light is sufficient to drive off any moisture, but not so great that the wood block is likely to warp or split.

Outside power filters should be checked daily for waste accumulation and their media replaced or purged as needed. This can mean a daily filter change in heavily stocked tanks or those housing messy feeders. In such instances, it makes sense to pay the somewhat higher initial price and purchase an efficient, reusable mechanical filter medium such as Eheim's EhfiFix. It is difficult to determine the point at which activated carbon loses its capacity to adsorb wastes. As it will begin to release such substances back into solution once this point has been reached, prudence dictates replacing it frequently. Most marine aquarists find it convenient to replace at least a portion of the carbon in their system whenever they make a water change. There is certainly no harm in making partial carbon changes more frequently.

Sponge filters should be cleaned weekly. It is much easier to prevent severe blockage or algal overgrowth than to correct either problem after it has manifested itself. Remove the sponge to a vessel of clean sea water of the same temperature and salinity as that in the tank or origin. If the outer surface of the sponge is blocked in any manner, scrub it vigorously with a soft plastic brush. Then immerse it in the vessel of clean sea water, shake it vigorously several times, remove it from the bowl and squeeze it dry. Repeat the proceedure until the surface of the sponge is unobstructed and the water that runs from it when squeezed is free of particulate matter. Discard the first bowl of sea water. Slowly pour clean sea water over the sponge and squeeze it dry over the empty bowl. Repeat until the runoff from the sponge is clear or nearly so, then return it to the tank. **Never rinse a sponge under freshwater!** To do so will seriously compromise its function because of the toxicity of fresh water to its salt-adapted bacterial population.

Canister and trickle filters stand in need of attention whenever their return flow seems reduced from its original level. Disconnect and disassemble the filter unit, taking care to have a bucket at hand to receive any dirty water trapped within or, in the case of a trickle filter, remove its trays from their place in the system. Replace the prefilter or clean it under a stream of lukewarm fresh water as circumstances dictate and discard any spent carbon.

Transfer the dirty ceramic or plastic medium to a container with a tight-fitting cover. Fill it half full with clean sea water, stir its contents virouously with a wooden spoon or a length of CPVC pipe, then pour off the now dirty water. Repeat this proceedure until the water is mostly free of large particles of detritus. Now fill the container two-thirds full, cover it tightly, and shake it vigorously for two or three minutes. Pour off the water and repeat until the decanted liquid is almost totally free of particulate matter of any sort. Once again, take care not to disrupt extant bacterial populations by traumatizing them with a shower of tap water.

The canister proper or the trays should be scrubbed clean under a stream of lukewarm fresh water and toweled dry. It may also be a good idea to run a pipe cleaning brush up the plastic tubing that connects the filter unit to the tank. Significant deposits of organic matter can build up along their interior surface. This reduces their effective diameter and can markedly reduce water flow through the filter.

The purged medium can now be returned to the filter unit. Remember to add fresh carbon to the system and to replace the dacron "cap" in a canister unit with a fresh pad. Reconnect the units's plumbing, restart any necessary siphons, and turn the filter back on again. A greatly enhanced return flow should at once be evident.

The coral reef is characterized by great stability with regard to such significant environmental factors as temperature, salinity, dissolved oxygen level and pH.

# Maintaining other Aspects of Water Quality

## pH

The pH of sea water in tropical reef habitats ranges from 8.1 to 8.3. There is little information on the effects of longterm exposure to lower values on the well being of their inhabitants. However, common sense alone suggests the desirability of keeping the pH in a marine aquarium within the range of naturally occurring values simply to avoid introducing another source of stress into an already quite alien environment. As the pH drops towards 7.0, the ammount of carbon dioxide sea water can hold in solution increases. This in turn interferes with the respiratory efficiency of fish, which in and of itself can seriously stress an animal.

It is widely believed that calcareous substrata such as coral gravel, dolomite chips or crushed oyster shell will provide sufficient natural buffering capacity to keep the pH in a marine aquarium within acceptable levels. This is not true. None of these materials is soluble at pH values greater than 8.0. Thus, while these substances will keep the water on the alkaline side of neutrality, the best any of them can do is to buffer the water at 7.6–7.8, a level 50 to 60 times more acidic than encountered over coral reefs. These substances will afford protection against abrupt drops in pH, but over the course of time, the accumulation of acidic waste products of animal metabolism will drive the pH in a marine aquarium inexorably down from its initial optimal value.

Both foam fractionation, the operating principle behind a protein skimmer, and filtration with activated carbon will slow the progressive acidification of sea water by removing acidic waste products from the tank before they can react with its natural buffering system. Indeed, the chief functional benefit of carbon filtration seems to be the adsorbtion of weakly acidic organic compounds from sea water. However, while the use of a protein skimmer and activated carbon will delay the decline in pH of a marine aquarium they cannot arrest it indefinately. At some point, the aquarist will have to intervene to restore the pH to an acceptable value.

Assuming a tank to be lightly stocked or furnished with a liberal growth of green algae, nothing more may be required to keep pH values within the acceptable range than regular partial water changes and periodic replenishment of the filter's activated carbon. Heavily stocked tanks may require a more direct form of intervention to accomplish the same end. In any event, the pH of a marine aquarium should be monitored on a weekly schedule and corrective action taken if it falls to 8.0 or lower.

The method of choice to employ in raising the pH in a marine aquarium is the addition of measured quantities of **sodium bicarbonate** to the tank. Commercial products with **sodium carbonate** as their active ingredient are not recommended for this purpose. Unless used with great care, they can boost the pH upward too abruptly. Sudden large changes in pH are extremely stressful to marine organisms and should be avoided at all cost. **A good rule of thumb is to change the pH by no more than 0.1 pH unit daily.** Five grams (a level teaspoonful) of sodium bicarbonate per 76 l (20 US gallons) of water will raise the pH to just that extent.

To adjust the pH upwards, measure out the precise quantity of dry sodium bicarbonate necessary. This again requires knowing the actual volume of water present in the aquarium. Remove 3.5 to 4.0 l (about 1 US gallon) of water and dissolve the premeasured baking soda therein. Now add the resulting solution slowly to the tank. Dry baking soda should **never** be added directly to an inhabited aquarium.

The pH of the tank will **drop** immediately after the addition of the bicarbonate solution to the water. This is perfectly normal and is no cause for alarm. The pH will slowly increase to a higher value than that initially measured. The more vigorously the tank is aerated, the more rapid the rise. After 12 hours, test the pH of the tank water again. If it is still below 8.1, repeat this proceedure daily until the desired value is reached. If the pH is sligthy higher than the optimal value, there is no need to take further action. Slightly elevated pH values are harmless to marine organisms and will in any event slowly drop back to the prefered range without human intervention.

## Trace Elements

The role of dissolved trace elements in maintaining the health of marine fishes is unclear. At least some of these elements, *e.g.*, iron and manganese, should be available to animals in their food. There is no disagreement on the importance of dissolved trace elements in the successful culture of marine macroalgae and most sessile invertebrates with symbiotic zooxanthellae. Many trace elements tend to be removed from sea water as organic complexes. Such removal is an unavoidable by-product of biological filtration. Both foam fractionation and the use of activated carbon also remove trace elements from solution.

It is thus important to replenish a tank's supply of dissolved trace elements on a regular basis. A synthetic salt mix of high quality will contain most of these substances, so partial water changes partially address this problem. However, it usually proves necessary to make use of trace element solutions in order to keep concentrations of these substances at biologically significant levels. Several brands of trace element solutions are comercially available. If used according to the manufacturer's instructions, they will serve this purpose admirably.

# CHAPTER 8.

# Troubleshooting in the Marine Aquarium

At some point in his efforts at maintaining a marine aquarium, even the most diligent novice hobbyist is apt to encounter management problems of major proportions. Despite the most stringent adherence to the guidelines presented to date, circumstances beyond his control can lead to situations that require prompt corrective measures if a major disaster is to be avoided. Thje object of this chapter is to train the aquarist to recognize incipient problems and to suggest effective means to combat them **before** they grow to crisis proportions.

## Learning to be a careful observer

Major crises in both fresh and salt water aquarium management are invariably preceded by slight but accurate warning signs. The ability to recognize these warnings for what they are requires both well developed observational skills and a baseline against which such observations can be compared. Reference works such as this and the experiences of other aquarists can supply a basis for comparison, but the aquarist himself must cultivate the habit of closely observing what goes on in his aquarium. This skill can be learned by anyone with sufficient motivation. The best way to start is draw up a checklist and systematically cover all the points enumerated therein every day. Within a very short time, this observational routine will become so deeply ingrained that the hobbyist will automatically run through it every time he finds himself in front of an aquarium! At least once a day, the hobbyist check his aquarium against the following list:

(1) Is all the equipment in the tank functioning properly? (Check filters and pumps for normal operation. Check the outside filter to see if it needs cleaning. Check the return flow of canister or trickle filters to see if it has dropped off from its initial discharge of clean water. Check all airstones to see if their discharge of bubbles is in any way impaired. Check the thermometer to see if the heater is working properly.)

(2) Has there been any change in the condition of the tank since it was last examined? (Check the water level for evidence of evaporation. Is the water cloudy or discolored? Does it have a sour or rotten smell? Are there any discolored patches on the gravel surface or substantial deposits of detritus on the tank bottom? Have either macroalgae or sessile invertebrates undergone a sudden change in appearance? Has their been a sudden "bloom" of either suspended or attached algae?)

(3) Are all the tank's residents present and accounted for? If a pinch of food doesn't elicit a response from everyone, why not? (Check behind the infrastructure, in rear the corners and at the surface for bullied or injured specimens, bodies or exoskeletal husks. Check the cover glass for possible escape routes and the floor for any trace of the missing. If the missing animal is one of the tank's smaller residents, check the larger of them for signs of a recent heavy meal, such as a bulging stomach and reduced appetite.)

(4) Do the tank's residents look different in any way? (Look for changes in coloration, the appearance of spots or blemishes on the body or fins, missing scales, torn fins, distended gill covers or sudden bloating of the abdominal region.)

(5) Are the tank's residents behaving differently than usual? If so, are all of them or only a few individuals acting strangely? (Note differences in swimming ability and patterns of movement, respiration rate and response to food. Note a sudden incidence of scratching against the bottom

or other hard surfaces or any tendency for fish to hang either in the stream of bubbles from an airstone or just beneath the water surface. Monitor behavioral interactions closely. Note any sudden increases or decreases in levels of aggressive behavior as well as any changes in the targets of such behavior.)

Finally, on a weekly basis it is prudent to check the specific gravity of the tank's water and run pH and nitrate tests.

This might seem like a tall order to carry out on a daily basis. In practice, it will take most people about ten minutes to work their way through this checklist initially. With practice, it is possible to cut the time to less than five minutes. Anyone unwilling to take that much time daily to assure the well being of his aquarium should take up another hobby. He clearly has no future as an aquarist!

A number of the itemized problems suggest their own solutions. Evaporative losses must be made good with dechlorinated or dechloraminated tap water. Non-functioning equipment must be restarted, repaired or replaced. Potential exit points must be identified and sealed off. Persistant bullies or their victims need to be relocated to new quarters. Alternatively, the ammount of cover in the community tank needs to be increased so that more shelter is available to its residents. Deviations from optimal salinity and pH values must be corrected in the manner previously described. The remainder of the chapter will address those problems whose solutions are not necessarily self evident.


## Coping with power failures

There is nothing quite like a local blackout to strike panic into the heart of a marine aquarist. His first thought in a summer power loss is a tankful of asphyxiated fish, in a winter outage, a collection of frozen corpses! In practice, few interruptions in the electrical supply last long enough for either bleak outcome to eventuate if the hobbyist has taken a few elementary precautions to mitigate their effects upon his aquaria.

The first step to take in the event of a blackout is to shut off all tank appliances. Electrical equipment in general does not respond well to the sudden surge of current that follows the reestablishment of service. Apart from this, it may not be desirable for filters to suddenly come on line again after a prolonged period of inactivity. Shutting their pumps off allows the aquarist to implement appropriate precautionary measures before returning them to service.

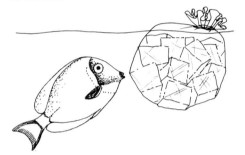

**Floating a plastic bag filled with ice cubes in a marine aquarium will provide some short-term relief from the effects of extremely high ambient temperatures.**

Summer or winter, the greatest danger a blackout poses to marine fish is asphyxiation. It is therefore essential to restore a normal flow of air to the tank as quickly as possible. Inexpensive battery-powered air pumps are widely sold in sporting goods stores. Sport fishermen use them to keep their bait buckets aerated. These units run for several hours on one or two C batteries. They put out about the same volume of air as an inexpensive diaphragm air pump. The prudent marine aquarist will keep a couple of these pumps and sufficient batteries to power them for 8 to 12 hours on hand. In the event of a power failure, they can be immediately pressed into service in place of the tank's normal air supply. If it comes to a choice between running an air stone or keeping an air-driven undergravel filter in operation, absolute priority should be given to the filter. The reason for this will shortly become apparent.

If a house enjoys an alternative source of heat, a winter power failure is not likely to result in dangerous chilling of a marine aquarium. In a situation where the heating system is entirely dependant upon electricity, the situation is somewhat grimmer. The outcome of the episode will depend upon the outside temperature, how well insulated the house is, and how long the interruption of service lasts. The most the aquarist can do is buy himself as much time as possible be reducing the rate of heat loss to the tank's surroundings. This is best accomplished by taping styrofoam panels cut to fit its front. back and sides to the tank and covering the ensemble with a thermally reflective survival blanket. Sheet styrofoam is readily available at hardware stores and home building centers. Survival blankets can be purchased at any sporting goods store that specializes in camping or hiking equipment.

If the tank relies upon a sponge, undergravel or trickle filter, no special precautions need be taken before reconnecting the tank's filters unless the power outage has lasted longer than 12 hours. The dissolved oxygen concentration will remain high enough under these circumstances to preclude serious damage to their nitrifying bacteria and consequent reduction of nitrate to nitrite, and ultimately, ammonia. If the outage lasts longer than 12 hours, the operation of these filters will be compromised.

Under such circumstances, it is advisable to either add an outside power filter charged with a pad of PolyFilter to the tank or add PolyFilter to the unit already in service before reconnecting the biological filter. Test the tank water for ammonia and nitrate immediately after the filter has been restarted and monitor concentrations of both of these substances carefully for several hours thereafter. As a rule, the use of PolyFilter in the system will prevent either ammonia or nitrite from reaching toxic levels while the filter bed is reestablishing a normal level of activity. However, if concentrations of either metabolite rise above trace levels despite such measures, a major water change is in order.

In the case of a canister unit, anoxic conditions arise much more rapidly following the interruption of water flow through the filter media. A power cutoff of no more than three hours can result in the production of dangerous ammounts of nitrite and ammonia within the filter bed. Before restarting a canister filter that has been off line for several hours, direct the return flow tube's discharge into an empty bucket. Turn the filter back on. The resulting flow of water will be heavily laden with particulate matter and have a foul odor. The filter should be allowed to discharge its flow into the bucket until it runs clear and odor free. Depending upon how long it has been inactive, several bucketfuls of water may have to pass through the canister to purge its media thoroughly. Throw the polluted water out.

Once the filter bed has been purged, take a sample of the return flow and test for ammonia and nitrite. The unit can be restarted without any further attention if neither can be detected in its outflow. If the test results give readings above the trace level, break down the filter, rinse the media as recommended for ordinary maintenance, and add a pad of PolyFilterà to the system when reassembling the unit. The filter can now be safely returned to service. An alternative to adding the chemically active medium to the canister would be to run an identically charged outside filter concurrently with the newly purged canister filter for a few days. Remember to replace the water that was lost during the initial purge of the filter with clean sea water.

## Pollution induced trauma

This is a comprehensive term for a wide range of symptoms caused by the contamination of an aquarium by toxic substances. Because such pollution causes an overall deterioration of environmental quality, **ALL** the residents of an affected tank will be affected to some degree. Fish display the following characteristic symptoms:

(1) labored breathing, often in conjunction with lethargic movement and a tendency to hang at the water' surface;

(2) extreme sensitivity to such external stimuli as sudden movement, vibrations or bright light, manifested by frantic dashes from one end of the tank to the other, and

(3) marked intensification in coloration, often accompanied by a dullness or cloudiness of the eyes.

In the most extreme case, affected fish will gasp at the surface of the water and display a loss of equilibrium. Eventually they simply lie on the bottom, often in a contorted posture, barely breathing and totally unresponsive to outside stimuli. Once this point has been reached, death follows shortly.

**PROMPT** implementation of corrective measures is essential when responding to pollution induced trauma (PIT). The sooner the source of stress is removed from the aquarium, the greater the liklihood that intoxicated fish will make a successful recovery. Hence the importance of correctly identifying the toxic agent responsible for the problem.

## Ammonia Poisoning

A sudden build-up of ammonia, provoked by inadvertant nitrogen cycle mismanagement, is the usual source of PIT in the marine aquarium. In extreme cases of ammonia intoxication, the tank's water will manifest a milky or greyish turbidity and a foul smell. However, it is quite possible for a tank to be crystal clear and still support toxic concentrations of ammonia. Hence the necessity of testing for ammonia as soon as anything appears amiss in a marine aquarium. **Readings > 0.10 ppm indicate the presence of dangerous concentrations of ammonia that require immediate corrective action.**

The following corrective measures are dictated when confronted by ammonia poisoning:

(1) **Immediately** add a chemically active medium such as PolyFilterà to the filtration system. Either add a pad to an already operating outside filter or else set such a filter up for this purpose.

(2) Remove any obvious sources of nitrogenous waste, such as cadavers or a large accumulation of uneaten food, from the tank.

(3) Make a major water change. Replacement of at least 50% and as much as 80% of a tank's volume is in order, accompanied by a concurrent and thorough purging of its substratum.

(4) Thoroughly clean the media of canister or trickle filters, as outlined in the previous chapter and return them to service.

(5) If possible, add a fully matured sponge filter to the affected tank to supplement the operation of its newly cleaned units.

It is important to bring chemically active media on line before making a water change. A significant increase in pH may follow such action. This in turn can result in a short-term but still dangerous **increase** in the ammonia concentration. Hence the necessity of already having on hand sufficient capacity to absorb ammonia as rapidly as it forms.

Ammonia poisoning is most likely to occur when the hobbyist fails to thoroughly run his biological filter in before adding organisms to the system, when he adds new animals to the system too rapidly, or when he exceeds the recommended stocking rate for his tank. Overfeeding is another frequent source of problems. Two often unsuspected causes of a sudden upsurge of ammonia in an otherwise healthy tank are the use of a household cleanser containing ammonia as an ingredient in the vicinity of a marine aquarium or the close proximity of a cat litter box. Never use any product containing ammonia in the same room as a marine aquarium unless PolyFilterà has been added to the filter as a prophyllactic measure. Litter box contamination is most easily prevented by moving it elsewhere in the house. If this is not possible, make a practice of changing its contents frequently and mixing an ammonia absorbing product with the litter.

As is the case with all types of PIT, it is much easier to prevent the occurence of ammonia poisoning by adhering to sound management practices, than to correct the problem after the fact. Regretably, most neophyte marine aquarists seem to require at least one brush with ammonia poisoning before they fully grasp the implications of this fact.

## Nitrite Poisoning

Acute nitrite intoxication is a relatively infrequent problem in the marine aquarium, simply because few if any organisms would likely survive the upsurge in ammonia concentration that would ordinarily precede it! Virtually the only circumstances that could lead to a sudden increase in dissolved nitrite without an anticipatory ammonia surge would follow the sudden resumption of water flow through a filter following a prolonged power outage. In the absence of oxygen, nitrate is reduced to nitrite in the filter bed. When such a filter comes back on line before precautionary measures are taken, there is the liklihood that dissolved nitrite could exceed the 0.50 ppm threshold usually accepted as productive of acute toxic effects. Elevated nitrite levels require the same sort of response as mandated for ammonia poisoning.

Chronic nitrite poisoning can occur if marine organisms are exposed to concentrations between 0.20 ppm and 0.05 ppm for extended periods of time. Any of the symptoms listed above that manifest themselves in a tank whose water shows a distinct yellowish tint should prompt an immediate nitrite test. If the results fall within the critical range, a partial water change is in order to alleviate the immediate symptoms. Over the long run, reducing the tank's population and purging the filter media more frequently are the only measures that will prevent a recurrence of the problem.

## Poisoning by Insecticides or Other Outside Agencies

Symptoms of PIT present in a tank that tests negative for either ammonia or nitrite are the

**A yellowish tint is often indicative of deteriorating water quality. If a white chine plate appears yellow when lowered into a marine aquarium, it is tume for a water change.**

result of poisoning by some outside agency. The most lethal and commonly encountered of these are insecticides. Even minute concentrations of the products commonly sold for household use can be lethal to marine organisms. An immediate water change, complete replacement of the activated carbon present in the filter system and its supplementation with PolyFilter may save some of the tank's inhabitants. Regretably, it often happens that by the time the aquarist notices that anything is amiss, the situation is past saving.

**NEVER USE INSECTICIDES IN THE VICINITY OF A MARINE AQUARIUM OR ITS AIR SUPPLY!**

This prohibition applies as strongly to slow release products such as insecticidal strips or pesticide treated shelving paper as it does to aerosol sprays. If this rule must be broken, as might be the case if an apartment is to be sprayed for roaches, take appropriate measures to protect the tank's inhabitants. Wrap the pump and cover the tank tightly with barely damp towels. If the tank is serviced by a trickle filter, wrap the base of the tank in plastic sheeting and tape it securely shut. Leave these protective wrapings in place until the last traces of odor from the spraying are gone and keep PolyFilter in the filtration system for a week after the spraying.

Also take care to keep activated carbon well away from insecticides. The carbon readily adsorbs these substances from its surroundings. When added to a filtration system, such contaminated carbon will release these poisons slowly into the water, eventually resulting in a major crisis in the aquarium. Activated carbon will also pick up other toxic aerosols if afforded the opportunity to do so. The surest means of preventing such accidents is always to store activated carbon in a tightly sealed container.

While insecticides clearly surpass other outside agencies in toxicity, there are other products that have the potential of causing problems in the marine aquarium. Mention has already been made of household cleansers containing ammonia. Hair sprays, aerosol deodorants, furniture care products and tobacco smoke are all toxic to marine organisms to a greater or lesser degree. Prudence thus dictates keeping them as far away from the marine aquarium as possible, or failing that, to make certain that its surroundings are thoroughly ventilated if their use therein cannot be avoided.

Assuming he has followed the recommendations made in Chapters 2 and 3 with regard to equipment and tank furnishings, the aquarist should not have to worry about most types of metal poisoning in his tank. As a rule, misuse of copper-based medications is the only way toxic metals can get into a marine aquarium. If fish display the symptoms of PIT shortly after a copper-based medication has been used in their tank, test the copper concentration immediately. If it proves higher than the manufacturer's recommended dosage, immediately add Tetra AquaSafe to the tank at the rate of 1 ml/l (4 ml/US gallon) of water and add PolyFilter to the filtration system. Check the copper level in the tank at hourly intervals. It should drop quickly into the safe range following treatment.

The safe use of copper as a theraputic agent will be discussed in greater detail in the next chapter. Suffice it for now to state that copper-based medications must **ALWAYS** be used according to the manufacturer's instructions and should **NEVER** be used unless the aquarist has a reliable copper test kit at hand to measure the concentration of copper actually present in the tank.

# Algae Blooms

Explosive proliferation of algae in the marine aquarium can take two forms. The usual manifestation of this problem is the sudden appearance of a dark velvety growth that spreads alarmingly over virtually every solid surface in the tank. This condition is the result of the rapid colonization of the aquarium by "black" – actually blue-green – algae. Less frequently, the offending alga is dark red or reddish brown. Blooms of suspended algae, which turn the tank water yellowish green,

are relatively unusual in marine aquaria. This condition, which is analogous to "green water" in the freshwater aquarium, seem to occur most frequently during episodes of warm weather.

Algae blooms arise when a tank contains a superabundance of plant food – nitrate – and receives either too much light or the wrong sort of light. There are several ways of treating these unsightly conditions, but unless the aquarist makes fundamental changes are made in his management practices, the problem will certainly recur.

Elevated nitrate levels are a symptom of overstocking. Water changes will knock them back for a short time, and a vigorous growth of macroalgae will slow their buildup to some degree. However, the only practical means of lowering the concentration of dissolved nitrate on a long-term basis is to reduce the number of animals present in the tank. An algal bloom should thus be regarded as a relatively benign warning of a situation that may well prove dangerous if allowed to go uncorrected.

Blooms of brown algae are caused by diatoms. They are usually the result of insufficient light. Leaving the lights on a few hours

An infestation of blue-green algae is an unsightly indicator of poor water quality in a marine aquarium.

**Blooms of red algae are due to inappropriate lighting. They can be eliminated at changing a tank's illumination to full spectrum flourescent tubes or by supplementing it with warm white flourescent bulbs or an indandescent light source.**

longer each day will usually suffice to eliminate the problem. Blooms of "black" and dark red algae are due to too much of the wrong kind of lighting. They can be eliminated by either replacing the tank's existing flourescent tubes with full spectrum bulbs or by supplementing their output with light from warm white flourescent tubes or incandescent bulbs. As the undesired attached algae die off, they will usually be replaced by flourishing growths of filamentous green algae, a state of affairs that will be greatly relished by the tank's herbivorous inhabitants.

Managing blooms of suspended algae is a bit trickier, as their sudden die-off can result in oxygen depletion and nitrogen cycle management problems. The safest approach is to filter the tank for several hours with a diatom filter, then leave its lights off for 2 or 3 days. Such a treatment removes most of the algae from the system and discourages the proliferation of any that might have escaped the clutches of the filter.

It is not a good idea to use copper sulfate as an algicide, notwithstanding its efficacity in that regard. The algae take up the copper ion from solution, then die. As they decompose, they release copper back into solution in an unpredictable manner. If the copper in itself does not prove toxic to the tank's inhabitants, there is the risk it may interact with other medications, such as Tetra's General Tonic to cause mortalities. If copper proves the only means of eliminating an algal bloom, make an effort to remove as much of the dead algae from the aquarium as soon as possible after it has been killed and add PolyFilter to the filtration system for a week to 10 days to scavenge any residual copper from solution.

## First aid in the Marine Aquarium

If a community tank's residents are carefully selected with an eye towards behavioral compatibility, the liklihood of damaging fights between its residents is small. However, as fish grow in size, their spatial requirements often increase exponentially. Thus a damsel that proved a model citizen in a 120 l (c. 30 US gallon) aquarium at 2.5 cm (1") overall length stands a good chance of turing into the terror of the tank at 7.5 cm (3") total length. Quite apart from such ontogenic changes in behavior, most fish display sufficient individual variability with regard to their behavior to make blanket statements about how they will act in captivity of questionable value to the aquarist. A description of a given species behavior is essentially a probability statement about how most individuals act under most circumstances. Every aquarist has met his share of fish that have never read reference books and consequently behave exactly as they please rather than the way they are supposed to!

There is thus an excellent chance that the marine aquarist will find himself faced with the need to treat a battered fish at some point in his career. There is an equally good chance that he will also confront the necessity of treating himself. Quite a few marine fish possess sharp spines capable of inflicting a nasty puncture wound. If this were not enough, a fair number of very popular coral reef residents are more or less venomous in the bargain. Finally, large wrasses like the harlequin tuskfish, many puffers and all trigerfish and morays can deliver serious bites if mishandled. The remainder of this chapter will outline simple first aid proceedures for both injured fish and their traumatized keepers.

## Physical Injuries to Fish and their Treatment

Fish that have suffered moderate fin damage or are missing only a few scales do not usually require heroic treatment to recover from their injuries. They should be isolated from their persecutor(s) in a dimly lit tank containing several hiding places. Add 1 ml/2l (2ml/US gallon) of AquaSafe to the water and let nature take its course. If the fish will take Tetra Medicated Food, offer the fish a regular diet of the antibacterial formulation for several days. If not, offer the fish its favorite foods during the interval of isolation. Tissue regeneration should occur fairly rapidly.

If the injured specimen has suffered extensive scale loss or had its fins bitten back to their bases, it is almost inevitable that they will contract secondary bacterial infections that must be treated before normal regeneration will occur. The medications of choice for this purpose are the furan-ring based antibiotics. These compounds are extremely effective against pathogenic bacteria but have minimal impact upon the operation of a biological filter. An excellent selection of propietary products formulated for use in the marine environment are available commercially. Used according to the manufacturer's instructions, they will give very satisfactory results.

So will such antibiotics as tetracycline hydrochloride, but at the cost of the tank's nitrifying bacteria. If the aquarist must employ one of these unselective antibiotics, he should remove the hospital tank's sponge filters and run them in a bucket of untreated sea water until treatment is completed. As a rule, a 24 hour bath suffices to treat most superficial infections. At the conclusion of treatment, replace the hospital tank's water completely with fresh sea water of the same temperature and reintroduce the sponge filters.

**Marine fish suffering from minimal damage, such as this common clownfish, *Amphiprion ocellaris,* require nothing more than a period of respite from their tankmates' attentions to recover fully.**

Regardless of the medication chosen, the course of treatment will be considerably accelerated if the injured fish can be persuaded to take medicated flakes concurrently with its antibiotic bath. Oral dosage is really a far more efficient method of delivering antibiotics to where they are needed than marinating the injured fish in medication. However, as loss of appetite is often a prominent symptom of bacterial infections, there is often no alternative to the cruder technique of the antibiotic bath.

The presence of cotton-like tufts along the margins of a wound indicate a secondary infection by fungi. Such infections are easily treated in their initial stages but grow less responsive to treatment with the passage of time. Tetra's GeneralTonic added to the tank water at the rate of 1 ml/2l (2 ml/US gallon) in conjunction with the recommendad dose of AquaSafe. As with the treatment of bacterial infections, eradication of fungal infestations is accelerated if the afflicted fish will take medicated food. Tetra's antifungal/antiparasitical formulation should thus be offered to any specimens that will take it over the course of treatment.

Remember that these measures simply

**Palatable medicated flake foods represent the most efficient means of delivering antibiotics to a diseased fish.**

address the grosser manifestations of what is essentially a behavioral problem. There is little point in successfully treating an injured fish only to return it to an environment where history can be expected to repeat itself. Providing more hiding places in the victim's tank of origin may alleviate the situation some-what, but in the last analysis, the only way to prevent serious fighting between a tank's inhabitants is to give them more living space or find another home for one or the other of the two combattants.

## First Aid for Fish Keepers

Simple puncture wounds are the most common injuries suffered by marine aquarists. As already noted, most coral reef fishes have strong spines in their fins. Angelfish supplement this armament with pungent opercular spines, surgeonfishes with one or two pairs of "switchblades" on their caudal peduncles. All of these weapons can deliver a very nasty wound if their bearers are not carefully handled. This is as good a reason as any for using only large, deep nets when moving those marine fishes too large to be manipulated into rigid containers for this purpose.

Deep puncture wounds should be immediately washed with soap under warm water. If possible, try to induce bleeding to flush as much alien matter from the wound as possible. If there is serious local swelling or

**The retractable caudal spine (lower left) of such surgeon-fish as *Zebrasoma xanthurum* can inflict painful, slow-healing wounds on careless aquarists.**

The preopercular spine of angelfishes, clearly visible on this *Centropyge eibli* can inflict a nasty puncture unless their bearers are carefully handled.

the victim feels either progressive numbness spreading from the vicinity of the wound or acute pain, there is the possibility that the slime and skin injected into the wound are proviking an allergic reaction. In the face of such symptoms, get the injured party to the nearest hospital emergency room **IMMEDIATELY**. A visit to the doctor is strongly recommended as soon as possible after receiving such an injury, for regardless of what instrument delivers them, puncture wounds carry with them a risk of tetanus.

Simple prudence dictates a tetanus booster shot under the circumstances.

Moray and wrasse bites should be treated in the same manner as puncture wounds. Moray eels are sometimes said to have a venomous bite. This is not true, but moray teeth are particularly filthy. The wounds they inflict thus stand an excellent chance of becoming severely infected. They should therefore receive expert medical treatment as quickly as possible. Triggerfish and puffer bites usually result in the removal of a size-

A bite from a black trigger, *Odonus niger,* or any large triggerfish can require stitches to close. Droll appearance and often friendly manner notwithstanding, these fish deserve their keeper's full respect.

Moray eels are not venomous, but their bites are very apt to become seriously infected. Anyone unfortunare enough to be bitten should promptly seek a doctor's care.

able piece of flesh, with concommitant profuse bleeding. Though adults of some of the larger triggerfish can do sufficient damage to require stitching of the resultant wounds, the specimens kept by private aquarists are much more limited in their offensive abilities. Their bites, while acutely painful, are seldom serious enough to require more than the routine first aid required by any serious abrasion.

The spines of quite a few marine fishes are associated with venom glands. Cone shells are also venemous, but use modified teeth as the delivery system for their potent neurotoxin. While the bites of all the larger cone shells should be regarded as life-threatening, there are no reports of fatalities among aquarists who have been "stung" by any of the venomous fishes generally available through commercial channels. Nevertheless, fish

Their smaller adult size notwithstanding, dwarf lionfishes such as *Dendrochirus zebra* (left) and *D. brachypterus* (right) are just as venomous as their larger and more flambouyant relatives of the genus *Pterois*.

"stings" are excruciatingly painful and pose a serious risk of extreme allergic reactions, up to and including anaphylactic shock.

Holding the wound under the hottest stream of water that the victim can bear followed by wrapping in a hot compress will alleviate the intense pain of an envenomed wound to a degree, as heat tends to break down the active ingredients of the toxins. However, as anyone unfortunate enough to have experienced the effects of envenomation will attest, the only appropriate response to such an incident is an **IMMEDIATE** trip to the nearest hospital emergency room! When checking the victim into the emergency room, make certain that the attending physician is fully informed of the circumstances of the injury. This includes the **scientific name** and the **family** of the offending organism. Most doctors have no prior experience in treating such injuries and will need this information to retreive relevant data on how to treat the problem from a poison control center.

It should be noted that with the exception of cone shells, which use their venom to overcome their prey, the delivery systems of all the venomous marine fishes commonly kept in aquaria are geared to defense rather then offense. Even cone shells "bite" only when provoked in some manner by their keeper. With the exercise of a modicum of common sense in handling these animals, the aquarist can enjoy the pleasure of their often spectacular presence in his tank with minimal risk to his well-being. Venomous animals are clearly indicated in the Catalog section, so if he wishes, the ultracautious hobbyist can easily avoid them altogether. As they are a decided minority among commercially available marine species, it is quite possible to have beautiful display without including any potentially dangerous organisms among its residents.

**A lovely pair of** Anampses rubicaudata, *the red-tailed wrasse, representatives of the overwhelming majority of coral reef fishes that pose no threat whatsoever to their keepers!*

# CHAPTER 9.

# Common diseases of Marine Fish and their Treatment

Novice marine aquarists have a tendency to regard outbreaks of disease as isolated disasters that afflict their fish in an unpredictable manner. Their usual response is to initiate a course of action intended to eliminate the obvious symptoms of the condition with the expectation that once they are gone, so is the problem. Quite apart from its inherent difficulties, this reactive approach to fish disease often fails because the neophyte often does not recognize their initial symptoms and thus misses his best chance to treat them effectively. The aim of this chapter is to outline an approach to disease that will greatly reduce the liklihood of serious outbreaks in the marine aquarium and to familiarize the aquarist with the symptoms and appropriate treatments of the most commonly encountered diseases of marine fishes.

## Stress and disease

The pathogenic organisms that cause outbreaks of disease are an integral part of the natural environment of coral reef fishes. Yet recognizable bacterial infections or parasite infestations are virtually never reported in nature. This is due to the fact that under normal environmental conditions, the fishes' immune systems either prevent pathogens from gaining a foothold or else surpress the ability of any that do manage to enter a potential host from reproducing successfully. Furthermore, the density at which even highly social fish live in nature poses serious obstacles to the infective stages of most pathogenic organisms. A betting man would not wager a great deal on the liklihood of any given *Oodinium* dinospore or *Cryptocaryon* tomont making it to a suitable host on the reef!

Disease outbreaks occur in nature only when the environment deteriorates sufficiently to seriously stress its inhabitants. The resulting stress effectively disables their immune systems, thus allowing the uncontrolled multiplication of pathogens human observers refer to as disease. The obvious corollary to this observation is that captive fish should be kept in a stress-free environment in order to avoid outbreaks of disease. Unfortunately, this is easier said than done. An aquarium is an extremely artificial environment. Water quality, temperature and diet often differ to a greater or lesser degree from what coral reef fish regard as normative. Furthermore, space limitations mean that fish must necessarily live in closer to proximity to one another in the aquarium than they do in nature. This can greatly speed up the tempo of behavioral interactions between a tank's residents. Aquarists often think of stress entirely in terms of gross environmental factors such as water chemistry and temperature. However, behaviorally induced stress is at least as important a determinant of the health of captive fishes.

Withal, it is remarkable that marine fish manage as well as they do in captivity. If he avoids gross errors in nitrogen cycle management, furnishes the aquarium with the behavioral needs of its residents in mind, errs on the conservative side in stocking his tank(s), and feeds his fish a varied diet based on his knowledge of their natural feeding patterns, the marine aquarist usually has few complaints about the health of his fish. There are, however, sources of stress that are not entirely under his control. It is the operation of these factors that often produce an outbreak of disease in well-managed aquaria.

Chief among these is the prior history of his aquarium's inhabitants. Fish can be stressed prior to purchase and not develop obvious health problems until some time after being brought home. In fact, given the unavoidable stresses involved in their capture and shipping, all newly purchased fish should be regarded as biological time bombs requiring only the appropriate environmental trigger to go off in an established community tank, usually with devastating results. Infestations, particularly those of a parasitic nature, can spread very rapidly to all of a tank's inhabitants because the limited volume of an aquarium enormously increases the liklihood that their infective stages will find a suitable host. It can happen that so many parasites manage to colonize the tank's established residents that by sheer numbers, they overwhelm the fishes' natural defenses, with predictably serious consequences. The result is what most observers would describe as an outbreak of disease.

## Prophyllaxis as a means of cambatting disease

As with all the other problems the marine aquarist is likely to encounter, diseases are more easily prevented than cured. However, there is considerable confusion over what constitute effective prophyllactic measures. It might at first seem that the obvious way to prevent outbreaks of disease would be to exclude all pathogens from the marine aquarium. Both ultraviolet sterilization of the tank's water and prophyllactic administration of ozone are often advocated as effective means of accomplishing this objective. Regretably, neither approach is capable of accomplishing this end.

Ultraviolet (UV) sterilization depends on passing the tank's water sufficiently close to an energetic source of ultraviolet light for any suspended pathogens to be killed by its output of lethal radiation. Unfortunately, UV penetrates only a short distance in water. Thus pathogens must pass very close to the UV source if they are to be killed by its output. If this were not complication enough, the germicidal effectiveness of UV is reduced by the presence of dissolved organics and suspended matter in the stream of water to be treated.

These factors, taken with the limitations imposed by filter design on how much water can flow through a sterilizing unit during a given interval seriously limit the effectiveness of UV sterilizers. Furthermore UV bulbs have short effective lives and are expensive in the bargain. Under **ideal** conditions, these units can destroy 90% to 95% of the pathogens present in an aquarium. Given the rate at which these microorganisms multiply, this level of efficiency offers no real protection against such parasitic diseases as velvet and saltwater ick.

Prophyllactic dosage with ozone is a theoretically more effective approach to sterilizing a marine aquarium. However, it too has serious shortcomings. First of all, ozone is an extremely toxic substance. Unless the dosage is carefully regulated, it can kill fish and invertebrates in a tank outright. Secondly, pathogens vary in their sensitivity to ozone. Concentrations that kill one species have minimal effect upon another. Of even greater import to a marine aquarium's inhabitants is the susceptibility of nitrifying bacteria to ozone poisoning. A dose that will kill the infective stages of all common pathogens will also blitz a biological filter in the bargain. Swapping the probability of contracting velvet or *Cryptocaryon* for the certainty of ammonia poisoning cannot, by the remotest stretch of the imagination, be viewed as a very favorable trade-off!

Finally, both UV and ozone sterilization only work against the **free-swimming** stages of pathogens. Many disease-causing bacteria and some established *Oodinium* individuals can persist for considerable periods of time **inside** a host without provoking obvious disease symptoms. A fish may thus appear to be superficially "clean", yet be carrying the potential for another flare-up of symptoms. With exposure to stressful conditions, these cryptic pathogens can resume their uncontrolled multiplication, provoking a recurrence of the original outbreak. Thus even assuming 100% success against free-swimming pathogens, neither UV nor ozone sterilization can guarantee the total eradication of all disease producing organisms from a tank containing fish without killing them in the bargain.

The most effective prophyllaxis the marine aquarist can implement in his tanks is to maintain his fish in as stress-free an environment as possible in conjunction with the prudent quarantine of new arrivals. If systematically implemented, the techniques of marine aquarium management presented thus far will go a long way towards eliminating major sources of stress. If he exercises common sense in selecting residents for his aquarium, the aquarist will have effectively eliminated yet another source of problems from his system. It thus remains only to discuss the role and mechanics of quarantining newly purchased specimens.

# The role of quarantine in disease management

Quarantine is the practice of isolating individuals exposed to an infectious disease long enough for the infection, if present, to manifest its characteristic symptoms. It is based upon the observed fact that the major communicable diseases oh humans and terrestrial animals characteristically have a specific incubation period. Individuals who do not develop symptoms within this interval can thus be assumed free of infection. The object of quarantine is primarily to prevent the spread of disease to unexposed populations of potential victims and secondarily to facilitate the treatment of the quarantined individual should circumstances render this necessary.

As practiced by some marine aquarists, quarantine is taken to mean prophyllactic treatment of newly purchased specimens with a selection of anti-parasitical agents during their period of isolation. The assumption is that by the end of the quarantine period, the animal in question will have been purged of any parasites it might be carrying and can thus be introduced to its ultimate destination without risk to itself or its tankmates.

This is, for a number of reasons, a highly questionable assumption. Chemical baths, like UV and ozone sterilization, only work against the motile or free-living stages of pathogenic organisms. They are not effective against pathogens already present within a host. Secondly, the anti-parasitical agents in

most common use, copper sulfate and formalin, are themselves quite toxic and prolonged exposure to them can severely stress any fish. This in turn can depress the animal's immune system sufficiently to permit the unchecked proliferation of those organisms that have already established a toehold. This objection does not extend to the antibiotics commonly used to combat bacterial infections. However, the unrestrained prophyllactic use of these medications can inadvertedly lead to the emergence of antibiotic-resistant strains of the very pathogens their use is intended to eliminate.

**Fish should never be medicated unless their condition clearly warrants treatment.** The aquarist is much better off if he designs the quarantine period as an interval of isolation in a stress-free environment that allows a fish to recover naturally from the traumas to which it has previously been exposed. If he takes care to select specimens that have already made a partial adjustment to captivity in the dealer's tanks and are free of any obvious disease symptoms, 10 to 14 days of good feeding in an environment devoid of aggressive interactions should be all the treatment necessary to prepare them for life in a new community setting.

# Setting up and managing a quarantine tank

While he may reasonably hope that a newly purchased fish will spend an uneventful two weeks regaining an acceptable level of resistance to disease, the prudent aquarist will plan for the possibility that the newcomer will develop symptoms that require treatment when setting up his quarantine facility. As it can serve equally well as a hospital tank for established residents in need of treatment, a quarantine tank should be a permanant part of the hobbyist's set-up. A 60 l to 80 l (15–20 US gallon) tank serves this purpose admirably. Larger quarters are uneceesary, as no more than a single specimen should be treated at a time. It should be equipped with one or more biologically active sponge filters, a thin layer of quartz gravel and several non-calcareous hiding places. Plastic plants, small clay flower pots or pieces of CPVC pipe serve this purpose admirably. Coralline or dolomite gravel, crushed oyster shell, pieces of whole coral and large shells should be avoided at all cost. These calcareous materials absorb copper from solution. This makes it extremely difficult to maintain theraputic copper concentrations in their presence.

It is a good idea to keep a small outside power filter on hand for eventual use on a quarantine tank. Because many medications depress or inhibit totally the activity of a biological filter, it is best to remove such units from the tank and run them in a bucket of clean sea water until the treatment has been completed. An outside filter will suffice to filter the tank in their absence. It will also prove useful as a receptacle for PolyFilterà and activated carbon when the time comes to remove a given medication from solution. A supplementary airstone should always be used in conjunction with a power filter.

The quarantine tank should have its own heater and a tight-fitting lid. It need not be brightly lit. In fact, a few days of subdued lighting often does wonders to restore the self-confidence of very shy specimens and bring them out into the open, where they can be more easily watched for signs of disease. Because some symptoms, such as the golden sheen of velvet, are more evident when the affected fish is illuminated from the side, it is a good idea to keep a flashlight next to the quarantine tank as well.

In the event that a quarantined fish does come down with a treatable disease, one or more complete water changes are likely to prove necessary before it can be pronounced cured. It is a good idea to anticipate this fact and have sufficient fresh sea water to make at least one such change mixed up beforehand. This is yet another reason for investing in a number of plastic carboys when setting up a marine aquarium.

Newly arrived specimens cannot be expected to recover from shipping trauma and other sources of stress unless they eat. Hence the importance of getting them to feed as soon as possible after arriving. Live *Artemia*, either nauplii or adults depending upon the size of the fish, are an excellent first food for most coral reef fishes. A small piece of "living rock" will often serve to start most invertebrate browsers feeding, while a piece of *Caulerpa* or other macroalgae serves the same purpose for herbivorous fishes. After a few days of such luxury fare, they can be gradually introduced to frozen and prepared foods. The injunction to feed sparingly but frequently applies with particular force to fish in quarantine.

Because bacterial pathogens are effectively ubiquitous in the environment and several parasites seem capable of persisting for extended periods in an aquarium as spores, the notion that a fish that manages to stay free of symptoms for a given interval need no longer be considered at risk for the diseases in question is erroneous. It is more accurate to say that a fish that has stayed "clean" during the quarantine period has probably recovered sufficient natural resistance to infection that it runs minimal risk from exposure to any pathogens present in its environment. Thus there are no hard and fast rules governing the length of quarantine. Prudence would suggest a stay of at least ten days in isolation for fish that seem free of obvious problems. On the other hand, it would probably be wise to allow newly imported specimens or those that have come from questionable circumstances as long as a month in isolation before adding them to an established community tank.

# Commonly encountered diseases of Marine Fishes

### Knot Disease or Lymphocystosis
**Causative agent.** Knot disease results from the activities of the virus *Lymphocystis*. The condition is not highly contaigous, nor does it usually appear to seriously inconvenience its victims.

**Diagnosis.** A *Lymphocystis* infection firsts manifests itself as a series of white, knot-like thickenings along the margin of the gill

The small white nodules characteristic of a light *Lymphocystis* infection are clearly visible on the pectoral fin of this queen angelfish.

The larger nodules of a more severe case of lymphocystosis aare clearly evident along the margins of this scat's vertical fins.

covers, on the margins of the fins and around the mouth. It may later spread to other parts of the body.

**Treatment.** As with all viral diseases, there is no known cure for lymphocystosis. Improving the fish's living conditions, adding supplemental vitamins to the diet and raising the temperature a few degrees in the hope of triggering the fish's own immune system will sometimes produce short-term remission of symptoms. Affected portions of the fins can be trimmed with a sterile razor blade and painted with an antiseptic solution. However, there are no guarantees that the regenerated portion of the fin will not be reinfected, while this treatment is undoubtedly far more traumatic to the patient than the original infection. Interestingly, knot disease is one of the few conditions to which marine fish are prey in captivity that profitably engages the attentions of cleaner fishes and shrimps. Their attentions are likely to prove as effective in slowing the progress of the disease as crude surgical intervention and are certainly much less stressful for the patient!

## Fin Rot

**Causative agent.** This condition is ccaused by the activites of the pathogenic bacteria *Aeromonas*, *Pseudomonas* and *Vibrio*. These organisms are always present in marine aquaria, but are incapable of attack-ing unstressed fish. Fin rot is invariably associated with a major deterioration of water quality, *e.g.*, elevated nitrite levels, low pH or inapprpriate salinity.

**Symptoms.** The fins, particularly the unpaired fins, take on a ragged appearance and trail whitish filaments from their distal margins. If the disease is unchecked, erosion can progress all the way to the base of the fins.

**Treatment.** Immediately take whatever steps are necessary to restore water quality in the affected tank. Remove the infected specimen to a hospital tank and treat with 3.8 mg of nifurpirinol (Furanace)/40 l (10 US gallons) of water. Continue the treatment for 5 days, then make a 50% water change and add PolyFilter to the filtration system to remove the final traces of the antibiotic. Nifurpirinol is not toxic to nitrifying bacteria, so if necessary, an entire community tank can be treated with

A blue chromis suffering from acute fin rot. Once the infection has reached the caudal peduncle, as in this instance, treatment is pointless and the infected fish should be humanely destroyed.

A scat heavily infected with skin fungus. Fortunately, even such serious cases respond favorably to a wide range of proprietary medications.

no risk to its filter bed. The course of treatment will be accelerated if the fish can be induced to eat the antibacterial formula of Tetra's Medicated Flakes.

### Ulcer Disease, or Vibriosis
**Causative agent.** This disease is caused by the pathogenic bacteria *Vibrio anguillarum*. Like fin rot, it is an infallible indicator of poor environmental environmental quality. Unstressed fish have little difficulty resisting infection.

**Symptoms.** Loss of color and appetite and erosion of the fins are the initial symptoms, followed rapidly by the appearance of open, bloody ulcers on the flanks and a red appearance to the fin bases and in the vicinity of the vent. The progress of the untreated infection is rapid and inevitably results in death.

**Treatment.** As for fin rot. Like all bacterial infections, vibriosis is much more easily prevented than cured. Ulcer disease responds to the same regime indicated for treatment of fin rot. Because it spreads far more rapidly than fin rot, early diagnosis and treatment are essential if the victim is to be saved.

### Skin Fungus
**Causative agent.** Several species of saprophytic fungi will invade damaged tissue of marine fishes on an opportunistic basis. Skin fungus usually appears as a secondary infection on wounds or lesions caused by bacteria or other pathogens. It can also develop if a fish's skin has been damaged by prolonged exposure to substandard living conditions. Hence it is prudent to immediately check the pH and nitrite levels in a tank where fungus suddenly appears. As a rule, such outbreaks indicate that a water change is in order. Clownfish seem particularly susceptible to skin fungus.

**Diagnosis.** Discrete cottony tufts, usually along the fin margins or around the edges of open wounds, are characteristic of skin fungus. Greyish patches may also appear on the flanks where the skin has been damaged by the attacks of parasites.

**Treatment.** The first step in the treatment of skin fungus is to improve living conditions in the affected tank. A water change is the obvious first step. The filter bed should be thoroughly purged and fresh carbon added to the system. It may also be necessary to lower the stocking rate of the tank to effect significant long-term improvements in the situation. Affected fish should be moved into the quarantine/hospital tank and treated with 1.0 ml of Tetra's GeneralTonic 2 l (10.0 ml/5 US gallons) of water. If large areas of the body are effected, addition of 1 ml of AquaSafe 2 l (2.0 ml/US gallon) of tank water will make it easier for the fish to osmoregulate until it has regenerated its damaged skin. Treatment should persist until all traces of the fungus are gone, a period of 5 to 7 days.

Ichthyosporidiosis, or *Ichthyophonus* Disease
**Causative agent.** This condition arises from an infection of the internal organs by a parasitic fungus of the genus *Ichthyophonus*. The life cycle is complex and the mode of transmission uncertain. It is believed the parasite may be carried by marine copepods. Be that as it may, the condition does not appear to be highly contaigous under aquarium conditions. Most infections arise when fish already hosting the parasite are stressed by poor water conditions, which depress their resistance to disease and permit the unchecked proliferation of the parasite.
**Diagnosis.** Initially the skin develops a roughened appearance, reminiscent of sandpaper. Sometimes abcesses form on the skin and burst open, while the fins erode for no apparent reason. Infected fish become pale and loose weight regardless of the ammount of food they eat. Later the fish will tend to turn on its own axis with a rocking motion and swim with its mouth constantly open. While the roughened skin and locomotor dysfunction might seem to permit a positive diagnosis, a postmorten examination of liver or kidney tissue for cysts is the only way to confirm the presence of the pathogen. In the trade, ichthyosporidiosis has been made the scapegoat for the delayed symptoms of cyanide poisoning.
**Treatment.** There is no known cure for ichthyosporidiosis. Addition of supplemental vitamins to the diet sometimes causes a

spontaneous remission of symptoms. The course of the disease might also be slowed by regular feedings with the antiparasitical formulation of Tetra Medicated Food. Severely affected fish should be humanely disposed of.

**Marine Velvet**
**Causative agent.** Often refered to simply by the name of its causative agent, *Oodinium*, marine velvet is probably the most frequently encountered parasitic infestation of marine fishes. Clownfish seem particularly susceptible to this complaint. It is caused by the dinoflagellate *Oodinium ocellatum*, a protozoan whose complex life cycle is represented in the accompanying diagram. Like its freshwater counterpart, marine velvet is usually brought on by a deterioration of water quality, so scrupulous attention to nitrogen cycle management is the best preventative an aquarist can implement against this frequently lethal disease.

Life cycle of Oodinium

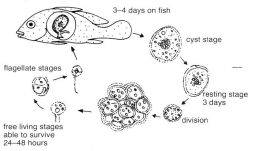

**Sympotoms.** The first signs of velvet are accelerated respiration, a tendency for the fish to hold its fins clamped shut, and repeated attempts by infested specimens to rub against solid objects. These behavioral manifestations are characteristic of other parasitic complaints, so it is necessary to check for the actual presence of the parasites to make a positive diagnosis. Individual *Oodinium* **trophonts**, the actively feeding cells whose activities cause the symptoms of marine velvet, can attack the body and fins, the gills and the intestine. Infestations of the gills and intestine are obviously not superficially apparent. Those of the skin are.

Look for white, greyish or yellow pinpoint dots on the body and fins. Barely visible to the naked eye, they are most likely to be visible on the transparent portions of the fins or against the more darkly pigmented areas of the body. It is advantageous when searching for *Oodinium* to examine the fish **head on**. These minute dots are also more easily seen if the fish is illuminated from the side. Once the parasite has established a firm foothold and begun to multiply unchecked, the entire fish will appear covered with a golden sheen, hence the origin of the name velvet disease for *Oodinium* infestations.

*Amphiprion clarkii* **with an obvious** *Oodinium* **infestation.**

**Treatment.** Regretably, novice aquarists are usually unaware that a problem exists until the infestation has become acute. Once the infestation has progressed to this stage, successful treatment becomes extremely difficult and the victim's prognosis is not favorable. Hence the importance of spotting the initial symptoms and initiating treatment immediately thereafter.

*Oodinium* infestations are difficult to treat because neither the trophonts nor the resting cysts formed when the parasite drops off of its host can be easily attacked. The parasites are vulnerable to medication only for the relatively brief period – between 24 and 48 hours – the they exist as free-living **dinospores**. There is some evidence that even the dinospores are not killed by theraputic agents, but rather, their ability to grow and multiply is somehow inhibited by the presence of drugs. It is suggested that this accounts for reports of the sudden reappearance of marine velvet once medication is removed from the system. It should now be appreciated why an outbreak of marine velvet in a community tank causes such concern, for the only certain way to eliminated the parasite is to remove all its residents to another aquarium for at least ten days. This is sufficient time for any resting cycts present to release their complement of dinospores. In the absence of suitable hosts, these will die off, leaving the tank free of *Oodinium*.

The first stage in treating marine velvet en-

tails freeing the infested fish of trophonts. This treatment is best carried out in the quarantine/hospital tank. It is accomplished by treating the infested fish with quinine hydrochloride, which causes the trophonts to drop from their hosts. The recommended dose is 10.0 mg/l (40 mg/US gallon). Dissolve the medication in a small volume of sea water from the affected tank, then add the resulting solution to the aquarium. The fish should be completely free of parasites within 24 hours of the onset of treatment.

Quinine hydrochloride was formerly widely used to treat freshwater ich outbreaks, but it has been largely displaced from the aquaristic pharmacopeia by other medications. It will thus probably be necessary to secure this drug through the good offices of a doctor or veterinarian. Quinine hydrochloride is harmless to both invertebrates and nitrifying bacteria, so this phase of therapy can be carried out in the community tank if necessary. Regardless of where treatment was initiated, 50% to 75% of the tank's water must be replaced within 24 hours of its onset. Make a point of taking water from the bottom of the tank and poke the siphon into all accessible caves and crevices to remove as many cysts from the system as possible.

The next stage of treatment entails a copper bath to attack any dinospores produced by resting cysts that were not removed when the tank water was changed. Regretably, not even moving affected fish into an entirely new tank can guarantee that further dinospores will not be produced. Resting cysts can adhere to the mucus coating of the gills and release their dinospores without ever leaving their host. Concentrations of 0.8–1.0 ppm of dissolved copper are effective against *Oodinium* without acutely stressing the fish under treatment. A wide selection of commercial products containing copper sulfate as their active ingredient will give satisfactory results if used according to the manufacturer's instructions. However, these formulations vary considerably in their potential toxicity to fish and the ease with which theraputic levels of copper can be maintained in solution. Amine-complexed copper sulfate has to date proven the most effective formulation for use in the treatment of marine velvet. This product is distributed by SeaChem Laboratories under the brand name CupriPlex.

Treatment should persist for two weeks. Take extreme care not to overfeed during this interval. The fish's appetite will be depressed to begin with, while the presence of copper in the water tends to reduce the efficiency of biological filters. Dissolved copper is extremely toxic to *Artemia*, so take particularly care when feeding brine shrimp to fish under treatment not to offer more than they will immediately consume. At the conclusion of treatment, make a 50% water change and add PolyFilter to the filtration system. As it absorbs dissolved copper, PolyFilter turns blue-green, then dark brown. Once this point has been reached, replace it with a fresh piece. Continue to keep PolyFilter in the system until the water tests entirely free of dissolved copper.

If the treated fish remains free of symptoms for an additional week, it can safely be introduced or reintroduced to an established community tank. As already noted, complete eradication of *Oodinium* from an infected fish is virtually impossible. The treatment outlined above will keep the parasites from destroying their host, and may buy it time to rebuild its natural defenses against attack. A sudden reappearance of marine velvet after an apparently successful course of treatment often indicates a persistantly depressed immune system. Some fish seem never able to reconstitute their natural defenses against *Oodinium*. The most humane course of action in such cases may be to destroy the specimen in question, as it is otherwise condemned to spend the remainder of its usually brief life in a dilute copper solution as the price of survival.

A brief consideration of the behavior of copper in marine aquaria is in order at this point. Copper ion tends to leave solution quite rapidly under aquarium conditions. In marine aquaria, it is adsorbed by the magnesium carbonate present in calcareous materials to form an insoluble precipitate. Unless the copper ion is protected in some manner against this process, it is necessary to monitor the level of dissolved copper in the water with a reliable copper test kit at least twice daily. If the concentration has dropped below the recommended theraputic level, additional medication must be added to the tank to restore it to the recommended level. This is why it is preferable to use a product like amine-complexed copper when treating marine fish as well as why calcareous substrata and hiding places should not be used in a quarantine or hospital tank.

The copper that has thus been precipitated from solution has not left the system. It accumulates in the substratum and infrastructure of a marine aquarium in a form whose solubility is influenced by the pH of the water. If the pH in the tank drops, some or all of this complexed copper can return to solution. Because copper is extremely toxic to marine organisms, this can have a negative impact on an aquarium's residents. Even sublethal doses are stressful to fishes and there is evidence that copper also depresses the activity of a biological filter. This can result in an abrupt increase in dissolved ammonia, a further source of stress.

Quite apart from its acute toxicity to higher invertebrates, this is as good a reason as any for never using copper-based medications in a community tank. It also underlines the main shortcoming to using copper as a prohyllactic measure against marine velvet or any other parasitic disease. Any substance that increases the stress level in the marine aquarium has no place in a rational management plan no matter how effective it purports to be against parasitic infestation.

An alternative treatment for velvet that can be used safely in a community tank entails using a combination of chloroquine, a widely available anti-malarial drug, and a combination of non-metallic compounds that will kill the dinospores without harming the fish. Such a formulation is marketed by Tetra under the trade name Marine-OMed. Used according to instructions, this product will eliminate *Oodinium* infestations within 3 to 5 days. It is harmless to higher invertebrates at low concentrations, has no effect on the normal functioning of a biological filter and is easily removed from solution by the use of Poly Filter. **Do not use any form of copper-based medication in conjunction with Marine-OMed therapy!** The interaction of these compounds can prove fatal to the fish.

### Marine "Ich"

**Causative agent.** Like velvet, marine "ich" is caused by a parasitic protozoan, in this case a ciliate, *Cryptocaryon irritans*, whose complex life cycle is illustrated in the accompanying diagram. Like its freshwater counterpart, marine "ich" appears to be brought on after fish have been subjected to severe stress. This is probably the reason this disease occurs so frequently in newly imported specimens.

**Diagnosis.** Marine "ich' is much easier to diagnose than is velvet. The initial behavioral symptoms are essentially identical to those of an *Oodinium* infestation. However, *Cryptocaryon* manifests itself in whitish pimples about the size of a pinhead on the fins and body. These cysts are considerably larger than those of *Oodinium* and are thus much easier to spot. If the progress of the infestation is not checked, the victim's eyes become clouded and bloody lesions will appear on the fins. These can then become the foci of secondary bacterial infections, which can prove a more serious threat to the fish's survival than the original parasitic infestation.

**Treatment.** *Cryptocaryon* infestations are more easily treated than is marine velvet, for unlike *Oodinium*, this parasite does not produce a medication-resistant resting cyst, while its **tomites**, or infective stages, are vulnerable to a wide selection of drugs. Several effective treatments are available, listed in order of their increasing stressfulness to the patient. In all cases, treatment should persist for two days after the disappearance of the last white spots from the fish's body.

(1) Metronidazole, manufactured by Searle Laboratories and marketed under the trade name Flagyl will kill the infective stages of *Cryprocaryon* as a dose of 250.0 mg/38 l (10 US gallons) of water. Treatment can be carried out in either a quarantine/hospital tank or in an established community, though it is usually more economical to dose a smaller volume of water.

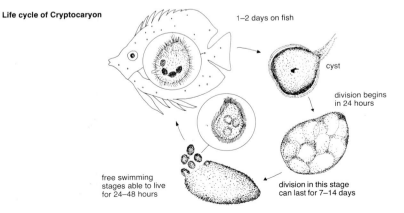

**Life cycle of Cryptocaryon**

1–2 days on fish

cyst

division begins in 24 hours

free swimming stages able to live for 24–48 hours

division in this stage can last for 7–14 days

**Cryptocaryon on the head and fins of a butterfly fish (Forciper longirostris)**

(2) Quinacrine hydrochloride, an anti-malarial drug sold under the trade names Atebrine, Chinacrine and Mepacrine is extremely effective against salt water ich at a cumulative dosage of 12 mg/ 4 l (1 US gallon) of water. The medication should be added as two 6.0 mg/gallon doses two days apart. Antimalarial drugs tend to vary significantly in potency. Hence the importance of securing a formulation that has been bioassayed to ascertain its theraputic strength. Bioassayed quinacrine hydrochloride packaged for aquarium use is distributed by Global Marine, P.O. Box 6611, St. Petersburg, FL 33736.

Quinacrine hydrochloride is light sensitive and must be stored in a dark place if it is to retain its potency. This fact also dictates that a tank undergoing such treatment should be kept darkened. This drug is toxic to neither higher invertebrates nor to nitrifying bacteria. It can thus be used safely in an established community tank. It will turn the water yellow, but this color will disppaear with the addition of PolyFilter to the filtration system.

(3) A formalin bath made by adding 1.0 cc of absolute formalin to 20 l (5 US gallons) of water is lethal to the infective stages of marine "ich". This treatment should only be carried out in a quarantine/hospital tank. Make certain that the tank is briskly aerated during treatment. The use of formalin is contraindicated if the fish to be treated has open wounds of any sort.

(4) Both encysted parasites and their mobile tomites are susceptible to a pure fresh water bath. The pH of the water in the bath should must be identical to that in the fish's tank of origin to avoid killing the patient outright from pH shock. It is a relatively simple matter to buffer fresh water in this manner with commercially available sodium bicarbonate. Immerse the infested fish in the bath for at least 5 but no more than 15 minutes. The difference in salinity between the bath and the protoplasm of the encysted parasites results in a massive inflow of water that leads to cell membrane rupture and death. Repeat the treatment every 5 days until the the fish is free of white spots.

While effective against *Cryptocaryon*, fresh water baths are stressful to marine fish. They are probably best used on larger fishes, whose smaller surface/volume ration affords them greater protection from osmotic shock, and those species with a known tolerance of a wide range of salinities, *e.g.*, scats, stripeys, damselfish and gobies.

The mobile tomites of *C. irritans* are large enough to be vulnerable to filtration through diatomaceous earth. An alternative response to a light outbreak of marine "ich" in an established community would be to run a supplementary diatom filter thereupon for three days. This approach would require that the tank's entire volume move through the filter mass several times an hour in order to trap the tomites before they find a potential host. It is thus probably more applicable to tanks of < 400 l (c. 100 US gallons) capacity than to larger aquaria.

**Brooklynellosis**
**Causative agent.** This affliction of the gills and skin is the result of infestation by the parasitic ciliate protozoan *Brooklynella hostilis*. The parasite does not appear to pose any serious threat to healthy fish. However, it will multiply explosively in animals whose immune systems have been depressed by capture and shipping trauma or by prolonged exposure to substandard water conditions. Seahorses and clownfish seem particularly

susceptible to infestation by *Brooklynella*.

**Diagnosis.** The initial symptoms are respiratory distress, loss of appetite and excessive production of body mucus, often in sufficient quantities to give the fish's color a whitish or greyish cast. Small, white lesions subsequently appear scattered over the fishes body. As these increase in number, the fishes skin actually begins to slough off of its body. Death follows rapidly thereafter.

The initial symptoms of brooklynellosis are reminiscent of those of marine velvet, "ich", and gill flukes. However, the scratching behavior associated with all three of these conditions is not characteristic of fishes attacked by *Brooklynella*. The white lesions produced by this parasite are larger than the cysts of *Oodinium*, smaller and initially less numerous than those of *Cryptocaryon*. The sloughing off of skin tissue is a reliable diagnostic feature. Regretably, the chances of saving a fish this far gone are slight.

**Treatment.** *Brooklynella* is susceptible to several treatments, listed below in order of their increasing stressfulness to the affected fish.

(1) Malachite green, at a dose of 0.13–0.15 ppm is effective against *Brooklynella*. It is best to prepare a special stock solution from **reagent grade** malachite green for use in treating marine fishes rather than rely upon commercially available formulations sold for use in fresh water tanks. These are often made from the less expensive technical grade dye, which can contain trace ammounts of heavy metals that can prove troublesome to marine animals. To mix the stock solution, add 100.0 mg of reagant grade malachite green to 100.0 cc of deionized water. To attain a theraputic level of 0.13 ppm, ad 0.5 ml of this stock solution/3.8 l (1 US gallon) of water.

Malachite green tends to be inactivated by contact with organic detritus. It is thus much easier to maintain theraputic levels of this medication if treatment is carried out in a hospital/quarantine tank rather than an established community aquarium. However, established tanks can be safely treated with this drug, as it will harm neither higher in-vertebrates nor nitrifying bacteria.

(2) Freshwater baths have been used successfully to combat this parasite. The affected fish should be dipped for 2 minutes in buffered fresh water, as described in the section dealing with marine "ich". Repeat the baths until all symptoms have disappeared.

(3) A 50 to 60 minute bath in a solution of 1.0 ml of absolute formalin/3.8 l (1 US gallon) of water controls *Brooklynella* most effectively. Remember to aerate constantly during treatment. Usually a single bath suffices to eradicate the infestation. Formalin is contraindicated in cases where erosion of the skin has resulted in the appearance of open wounds.

Regardlesss of the treatment chosen, it is important to treat the fish for secondary bacterial infections at its conclusion. The patient should be transfered to a quarantine/hospital tank and medicated in the manner recommended for treating such bacterial infections as fin rot and ulcer disease. If extensive lesions are present on the flanks, addition of 1 ml of AquaSafe 2 l (2.0 ml/US gallon) of tank water will make it easier for the fish to osmoregulate until it has regenerated its damaged skin.

## Gill Flukes

**Causative agent.** Several genera of mongenetic trematodes, of which *Neobenedenia* is the most frequently encountered, will commonly attack the gills of marine fish in captivity. Because the life cycle of these microscopic worms does not entail passage through one or more intermediate hosts, they are capable of extremely rapid multiplication and pose a serious threat to the health of afflicted fishes. Angelfish, butterflyfish and surgeonfish seem most susceptible to gill flukes.

**Diagnosis.** A dramatic increase in the rate of gill movements accompanied by loss of appetite are the most obvious symptoms of gill flukes. Check the tank for other possible causes of respiratory distress (elevated temperature, non-functioning airstones or filters, low pH or elevated nitrite levels) and the fish for the other symptoms of velvet or marine "ich". If none of these factors appear to

**Gently open the gill covers to inspect the gills –
they should be a clean, dark red**

account for the rapid breathing, remove the affected fish from the water, and while holding it gently but firmly in the net, lift a gill cover and examine the gills. If they are pinkish or greyish white rather than dark red, flukes are the likely cause of the problem. Adult *Neobenedenia* are c. 4.0 mm long and are readily apparent to the naked eye. However, many smaller trematodes are also known to attack the gills of fishes, so the absence of visible parasites hardly constitutes a clean bill of health.

**Treatment.** There are three recommended treatments for gill flukes. They are presented herein in order of their increasing danger to the patient.

(1) Freshwater bath. Place the fish in a well aerated 10% solution of of sea water (1 part sea water:9 parts fresh water) at a temperature of 26° C. (79° F.) until the fish shows obvious signs of distress. Depending upon the species under treatment, this interval can range from 15 minutes to 6 hours. If the patient is obviously in poor condition, or is very expensive, such a freshwater dip should only be carried out if the fish can be observed throughout the course of the treatment. Return the fish to the hospital tank for a 12 hour recuperation period and examine it for

symptoms. If they persist, repeat this procedure until the fish is breathing normally again. Do not be afraid to attempt this seemingly radical cure. It costs nothing and can be used repeatedly until the affected fish are healthy again. The most delicate fish species have been treated successfully with this method. Even specimens that had refused food for days beforehand and had become extremely emaciated have made a complete recovery when treated with a freshwater bath.

(2) Formalin bath. Dip the affected fish in a solution of 1.0 ml of absolute formalin/1 l (1 quart) of water for 10 minutes or until it shows obvious signs of distress. Be sure to aerate the medicinal bath throughout the treatment. Return the patient to the hospital or quarantine tank and repeat the bath in 24 hours if the symptoms persist. If the second bath proves ineffective, wait at least 5 days before repeating the treatment.

(3) DTHP bath. This should be considered the treatment of last resort for flukes. DTHP (dimethyl (2,2,2 trichloro-1 hydroxymethy) phosphonate) is an extremely powerful organophosphate insecticide sold under the generic name trichlorfon and the trade names Dylox, Masoten, Neguvon, Chlorophos and Dipterex. It is widely used to treat fish under pond culture for external parasites. DTHP is an effective antiparasitical agent but has a number of drawbacks when used in the marine aquarium. Even a slight overdose is instantly fatal to fish and some species have no tolerance for this product whatever. Furthermore, even brief skin contact or exposure to its fumes can make a human very sick. DTHP must therefore be handled with great care. **Always wear plastic gloves when handling DTHP and take care to work with it only in well ventilated surroundings!** The theraputic dosage is 0.5 g of an 80% DTHP solution/1000 l (260 US gallons) of water, which yields a concentration of 0.5 ppm of active ingredient. The fish should remain in the medicated bath until the symptoms disappear, a period that should not exceed 8 days.

If the fish has been very heavily parasitized, it is advisable to remove it to a separate quarantine/hospital tank and treat it for possible secondary bacterial infections. The treatment recommended for fin rot will give satisfactory results.

## Skin Flukes
**Causative agent.** As in freshwater fishes, skin flukes represent an infestation of monogenetic trematodes of the genera *Gyrodactylus* and *Dactylogyrus*. These parasites can multiply very rapidly under aquarium conditions. The damage they do their host is usually compounded by secondary bacterial and fungal infections.

**Diagnosis.** A greyish, slimy appearance to the fish's body, accompanied by repeated scratching behavior are the superficial symptoms of skin flukes. They are sometimes confused with those of marine velvet, but fish afflicted with flukes never display the discrete, pinpoint dots characteristic of *Oodinium* trophonts. The diagnosis of flukes can be readily confirmed by examining a scraping of mucus under a low-power microscope. The individual worms, which measure c. 1.5 mm in length, are clearly visible in the sample.

**Treatment.** Skin, like gill flukes, respond to freshwater and formalin baths. The treatment should be repeated until the symptoms of skin flukes have disappeared. After each treatment, the fish should be returned to a hospital tank containing a solution of 1.0 ml of Tetra GeneralTonic 2 l (10.0 ml/5 US gallons) in order to combat the secondary fungal infections that usually accompany an outbreak of skin flukes.

## Gill Maggots
**Causative agent.** Parasitic copepod crustaceans of the genus *Ergasilus* can infest the gills and feed upon their filaments in much the same manner as gill flukes.

**Diagnosis.** The superficial symptoms of a gill maggot infestation are identical to those of flukes. However, when the gills are examined, the individual copepods are readily visible to the naked eye as small white organisms c. 2.0 mm in length moving about the surface of the gill filaments. The greyish-

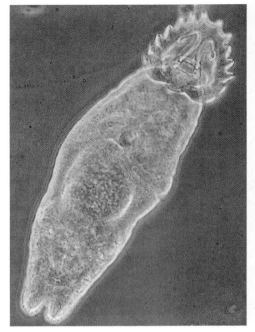

Enlarged view of a skin fluke. Note the hook-like mouth parts.

brown egg cases of the parasite can also be readily seen interspersed between individual filaments. Only after an infestation has attained acute proportions will the gills display the pinkish appearance so characteristic of the presence of gill flukes.

**Treatment.** It is fortunate that *Ergasilus* infestations are more rarely encountered than gill flukes, as these parasitic copepods are more resistant to treatment. Two approaches will give satisfactory results. Both should be implemented very cautiously, as they are quite stressful to the patient.

(1) Formalin bath. The same regimen recommended for gill flukes will also work on gill maggots. Remember to aerate the medicated bath vigorously during the course of treatment.

(2) DTHP bath. A fifteen minute bath in a 10.0 ppm solution of Dylox, Masoten or any other product containing 80% DTHP as an activer ingredient (1.0 g/100 l (26 US gallons)) will eradicate *Ergasilus*.

In the case of severe attacks, post-treatment supportive therapy as recommended for the victims of heavy gill fluke infestations is in order.

## Marine Fish Lice

**Causative agent.** The crustacean genus *Argulus*, which comprises many species parasitic on freshwater fishes, includes a number of representatives that attack their marine counterparts. Adult fish lice can move from one host to another, but it is not known whether their larval stages can survive long enough in captivity to successfully colonize a host. For whatever reason, serious outbreaks of *Argulus* in captivity are rare.

**Diagnosis.** The flat, rounded parasites measure 2.0–5.0 mm a diameter and have large, dark eyes. They are easily visible to the naked eye, particularly when they lodge at the bases of the vertical fins.

**An adult** Argulus sp. *Fish lice are large enough to be readily seen with the unaided eye.*

**Treatment.** *Argulus* are not easily killed. If the louse has parasitized a large fish, the easiest course of action may simply be to pull it off with forceps. A freshwater bath, as recommended to treat gill flukes, will cause some species to drop off of their hosts and swim freely about the treatment container. A 15 minute DTHT bath, at the dosage recommended to eradicate gill maggots, will also kill *Argulus*.

Once all the parasites have left the affected fish, it can be returned to the hospital or quarantine tank and given the same care recommended for victims of severe gill fluke infestations. There is always the possibility that the puncture wounds left behind by the parasites will develop secondary bacterial infections unless appropriate preventative measures are taken.

## Degenerative Blindness

**Causative Agent.** Degenerative blindness in marine fishes is frequently caused by a combination of excessive illumination of the aquarium in conjunction with a diet deficient in Vitamin A. Fish maintained under 24 hour illumination are incapable of regenerating the retinal pigments necessary for normal vision. Fish whose diets lack sufficient carotenes cannot synthesize the vitamin A necessary for the production of visual pigments.

Blindness can also be one of the symptoms of piscine, tuberculosis, caused by the pathogenic mycobacterium.

**Diagnosis.** Though their eyes are clear and show no sign of physical injury, afflicted fish have a hard time moving about the tank and locating food. They further fail to respond to obvious visual stimuli such as a concentrated beam of light shone in their eyes. With the passage of time, fish afflicted with tuberculosis become emaciated, develop ragged fin edges and open pits in the nuchal region somewhat reminiscent of the "hole in the head" syndrome of fresh water fishes, and swim around with wide open mouths, though no other signs of respiratory distress are evident.

**Treatment.** Degenerative blindness is more easily prevented than treated. Afford the fish 6 to 8 hours of darkness daily and see to it that they have regular access to foods rich in the precursons or vitamin A. Herbivorous species like angelfish and tangs, which seem particularly susceptible to degenerative blindness, should be offered fresh vegetable foods or flake foods soaked in a vitamin supplement several times weekly. Fresh grated frozen liver is an excellent source of vitamin A for carnivorous fishes. If they are reluctant to accept fresh liver, soak strips of their prefered food items in a vitamin supplement before presenting them to their intended consumers. As long as they can be induced to take food, specimens already afflicted in this manner have an excellent chance of making a full recovery.

Pregretably, there is no antibioctherapy presently effective against piscine tuberculosis. Fish that do not a chieve a spontaneous remision of its symptoms should be humanely destroyed.

## Humane disposal of terminally ill fish

Notwithstanding his best efforts, the aquarist is sometimes confronted with problems beyond his abilities to alleviate or resolve. In such a situation, the only humane course is to euthanise the afflicted fish. A swift slam against a solid surface is the simplest means of efficient euthanasia available in such cases. Aquarists too squeamish to implement this direct approach will be pleased to note that a tenfold increase in the recommended dosage of commercially available tranquilizing agents kills terminally ill or incurably damaged fish just as quickly. Alternatively, add a quarter of a cup of dry baking soda to 1 l (c. 1 quart) of water taken from the aquarium. Stir the soda until it is entirely dissolved. Capture the sick fish and place it in the bicarbonate solution. The excess carbon dioxide released will render the fish uncounscious, while oxygen deprivation will quickly dispatch it. The fish can be presumed dead when gill motion has completely ceased.

**Coral reef fishes rarely suffer from disease in the wild. Most of the problems that afflict them in captivity arise from environmental stresses caused by inadequate nitrogen cycle management.**

# CHAPTER 10.

# Plants and sessile invertebrates in the Marine Aquarium

## Algae

Freshwater aquarists have long enjoyed the option of aquascaping their tanks with live plants. Marine aquarists are less fortunate in this regard. While quite a number of plants are found in the sea, only a small number bear any resemblance to the vascular plants of freshwater biotopes. However, algae do play a useful role in the management of a marine aquarium and a the macroalgae of the genus *Caulerpa* are both easily grown and sufficiently pleasing to the eye to warrant a place in any decorative scheme.

Shortly after a new marine aquarium has been set up, brown algae (diatoms) will usually appear on such solid surfaces as the sides of the tank and its infrastructure and bottom. Such infestations are unsightly but normal. Once the filter is properly run in, growing conditions will favor the proliferation

**Filamentous green algae usually appear "spontaneously" in well-lit tanks with efficient biological filtration.**

of green algae. Assuming the availability of proper lighting (See pp. 00), tufts of green algae will slowly replace the previous bloom of brown algae. This process can be accelerated successfully by the use of starter cultures of green algae. These are available from most retailers specializing in marine fish under a variety of brand names.

A rich growth of green algae in a marine tank indicates good water quality. Only under these conditions can fish and other marine organisms be expected to prosper. Green algae should thus be allowed to grow freely in a marine aquarium, for they serve a useful biological purpose. If a protein skimmer is used as an adjunct to the filtration system, it may prove necessary to add additional trace lements to the tank every few weeks. These substances tend to be removed to assure their normal growth. Any of the commercial trace element preparations on the market will serve this purpose admirably.

Green algae do not relish long-term exposure to dissolved nitrate concentrations > 20.0 ppm. This contrasts with brown algae, which can withstand values as high as 300.0 ppm and bluegreen algae, which can prosper in water containing up to 150.0 ppm. This is why the presence of brown and blue-green algae is an infallible sign of poor water quality. Notwithstanding its tendency to remove trace elements from solution, an efficient protein skimmer is a useful adjunct to green algae culture, for it removes much nitrogenous waste from the system before it can undergo decay. As a rule, to promote a good growth of green algae, make a partial water change whenever the tank water begins to develop a slight yellowish tint.

Failure of green algae to colonize an aquarium, the persistence of brown algae or the proliferation of dark red and "black" (actually blue-green) algae can also indicate insufficient illumination of the proper spectral characteristics as well as poor water quality . As indicated in Chapter 8, both problems can be successfully adressed by a regime of partial water changes and either the replacement of existing lights with full spectrum flourescent tubes or mercury vapor spot lights or the supplementation of cool white or GroLux lights with warm white flourescent tubes or incandescent bulbs.

Even desirable green algae may sometimes get out of hand in a community tank. Avoid the temptation to use chemicals to eliminate excessive algal growth. Apart from their possibile short-term toxicity to its other inhabitants, the copper they contain accumulates in the dead algae and is unpredictably released into the tank as they decay. This means **ALL** the dead algae must be removed from the tank, a tedious proposition that entails removing all of its infrastructure for a thorough scrubbing. The easiest way to curb algal growth is to introduce a small surgeonfish to the tank and allow nature to take its course. The regal tang, *Paracanthurus hepatus*, is ideal for this purpose, as it rarely exceeds 15.0 cm (6″) overall length and is inoffensive towards fish of other families.

Tangs like these *Ctenochaetus strigosus* will keep a marine tank from becoming overgrown by filamentous green algae. Unfortunately, they graze on more ornamental macroalgae with equal enthusiasm!

There are c. 60 macroalgae of the genus *Caulerpa* known to marine botanists, although space requirements preclude considering more than a handful herein. This genus of "higher" algae has been well known to marine hobbyists over the past decade and

The leaf-like ASSIMILATORS, the RHIZOME and and the root-like HOLDFASTS are clearly visible in this photo of *Caulerpa prolifera*.

is becoming as frequently used in salt water aquaria as many vascular plants are in freshwater set-ups. A "typical" *Caulerpa* consists of a **rhizome** equipped with structures resembling leaves, the **assimilators**, and roots, the **holdfasts**. Unlike vascular plants, whose roots, stems and leaves are made up of specialized cells grouped into discrete tissues, the assimilators and holdfasts of a *Caulerpa* are not even made up of differentiated cells. These macroalgae are actually a highly specialized colonial organism known as a **syncoetium**, whose protoplasm supports many nuclei within a single cell membrane. If placed in the appropriate environment, any part of a *Caulerpa* is capable of generating any of the specialized structures characteristic of the colony.

Most *Caulerpa* require **absolutely clear water** and an environment with good water movement to prosper. They are troubled by turbidity because the surfaces of their assimilators must remain free of any sediment to assure the unimpaired exchange of gases required for photosynthesis. As a rule, these macroalgae can be successfully added to a marine aquarium within a week of the appearance of the first growth of filamentous green algae. Most *Caulerpa* species like to colonize coarse-grained substrata or limestone rocks. A few species, like *C. racemosa* var. *uvifera*, are very adaptable and do not seem to be limited to a particular substratum. Their runers spread out over rocks and other items of decorative infrastructure in the aquarium.

Good growth of *Caulerpa* requires **intense** lighting. Either multiple flourescent tubes or

*Caulerpa* **can be expected to prosper in a well-lit tank that does not house herbivorous fishes.**

**The fern-like assimilators of** *Caulerpa sertularoides* **contrast pleasantly with the grape-like clusters of** *C. racemosa* **var.** *uvifery.*

116

incandescent spotlights (mercury vapor or metal halide) will yield satisfactory results in the marine aquarium. The shoots of *Caulerpa* always grow towards the strongest light source. They will branch laterally if the tank receives bright light from the side, as would be the case if the tank were situated in a window. Otherwise, they will grow quickly upwards. Some *Caulerpa* species, such as *C. prolifica*, grow so rapidly that they may actually smother small sessile invertebrates, such as anthozoans, and less prolific speciesof algae. In this event, they must be thinned periodically.

In nature, *Caulerpa* are relished as food by herbivorous fishes, sea turtles and even some humans. Hence there are a number of coral reef fishes that cannot be kept in the same tank as these macroalgae. Surgeonfishes in particular will graze a tank bare of *Caulerpa*, but the larger angelfish and many damsels can prove almost as destructive. Certain marine worms and snails as well as sea urchins will also employ these algae as food. Refer to the Catalog to determine which marine organisms cannot be safely housed in a tank with *Caulerpa*.

Because *Caulerpa* are so greedily eaten by herbivorous fishes, many marine aquarists choose to employ these algae as a dietary supplement. Indeed, an argument can be made for setting up a separate aquarium simply to grow *Caulerpa* as food! Virtually all green algae are relished by plant-eating fishes. While it is true that luxuriant growths of filamentous green algae on a tank's infrastructure are not the most eye-catching sight imaginable, their presence could someday prove the salvation of a newly acquired fish that initially refuses to eat any other type of food.

Indeed, it is possible to lay down a supply of algae against any future need if a deep freeze is available. Simply remove any surplus algae from the tank, rinse in quickly under running fresh water – this is best done in a net in the case of filamentous algae – and freeze them immediately. Such deep-frozen fare never fails to find favor with algae-eating newcomers.

*Caulerpa prolifica* is undoubtedly the most durable and easily grown macroalga. Provided it is not molested by herbivorous organisms, it will spread widely over the bottom of the aquarium. Thanks to the continual improvements in the quality of commercial salt mixes and the ready availability of supplemental trace element solutions, it is now possible to grow a much wider selection of *Caulerpa* species. *Caulerpa mexicana* and *C. sertularoides* are almost as easily grown as *C. prolifica* and their fern-like assimilator blades make a pleasing contrast to the simple oval structures of that species. The assimilators of the previously mentioned *C. racemosa* var. *uvifera* resemble minute clusters of green grapes, while those of *C. peltata* resemble stalked disks.

Initially, prudence dicatates attempting to culture *Caulerpa* in a fish-free tank, perhaps in the company of a selection of sessile invertebrates. Once the hobbyist has suceeded in maintaining and propagating several species, he can count himself sufficiently experienced to consider adding a few small, mobile invertebrates and non-herbivorous fishes to their tank.

# Invertebrates in the Marine Aquarium

The first editions of **The Marine Aquarist's Manual** dealt exclusively with the husbandry of coral reef fishes. Contemporary conditions suggest that a wider coverage of potential residents for the marine aquarium is called for this expanded treatment, for salt water hobbyists are presently taking a much greater interest in the culture of invertebrates than ever before.

Such a turn of events is less surprising than it might seem. This assemblage of animals has evolved into an immense variety of species in the coral reef biotope. In fact, a reef without a full complement of associated invertebrates is virtually dead. "Artificial reefs" have been constructed of scuttled hulks and old automobile tires in many parts of the world. While they initially provide a degree of refuge for

A marine aquarium stocked with a carefully chosen selection of marine invertebrates is as pleasing to the eye as a community of coral reef fishes.

fish and their young, only after they have been extensively colonized by invertebrates can they be accurately described as reefs.

Until a few years ago, it was the gaudy, poster-colored reef fishes that were prefered over everything else as aquarium residents. No species could be too colorful or expensive! Today, marine aquarists are tending to return to the original roots of their hobby. It is worth remembering that marine aquaristics had its first successes when anemones from the English coast were maintained in captivity.

A few thoughts on possible reasons for this return to the roots of the marine aquarium hobby are in order at this point. First of all, living coral reefs, with their associated gorgonians, anemones, sponges, molluscs, crustaceans, starfish and algae, are restricted to the tropics. While many hobbyists dream of visitng a coral reef, such localities as support them are chiefly located in parts of the world

that are off the beaten track for most aquarists. It thus should come as no surprise that there are a considerable number of enthusiasts are prepared to try recreating their own reef in miniature in an aquarium.

Initially the reef's brlliantly colored and lively fishes were the objects of aquaristic enthusiasm. But too often these fish were doomed to an early death from the moment of their capture in the wild. Many specimens were stunned with cyanide to make them easier to catch. They thus reached dealers – and ultimately hobbyists – with severe and irreversible liver damage. Expensive specimens from the Philippines and Singapore were apt to die within weeks of their importation. However, invertebrates, unlike fish, never had to be poisoned to make them catchable. Even the most active crustaceans are much less mobile than fish, and for an anemone to take flight is out of the question! Thus one important reason for the current ascendency of invertebrates in the marine aquarium thus seems largely due to the simple fact that because they are not caught with poison, these animals have an excellent chance of surviving and even breeding in the aquarium.

Finally, until quite recently, invertebrates – particularly sessile species such as corals – were shunned by aquarists as too difficult to keep. Given recent advances in aquaristic technology, this is no longer true. The ability to produce synthetic salts that recreate almost natural sea water, has removed a major obstacle ot the successful husbandry of even the most delicate invertebrates. Recent advances in filtration technology have greatly simplfied the task of maintaining adequate water quality for their culture, while the availability of high-intensity lighting systems has removed the last obstacle to successfully maintaining sessile invertebrates that live in symbiosis with intracellular algae. At least as important as these technological breakthroughs, is the simple fact that retailers who specialize in marine organisms have de-

veloped much greater expertise in their management. The hobbyists thus now enjoys the advantage of a varied selection of healthy invertebrates for his tank and access to advice on how to care for them properly.

The aim of this chapter and the following is to present the reader with an overview of the basic rules of successful invertebrate culture and to introduce him to a representative selection of colorful and generally available species. Because their maintenance requirements differ considerably, it seems prudent to treat sessile, filter-feeding organisms such as sponges, corals and marine worms apart from mobile invertibrates such as molluscs, crustaceans and echinoderms.

## Suggestions for Successful Invertebrate Culture

Scrupulous attention to water quality is an absolute prerequisite to successful husbandry of marine invertebrates. Elevated nitrate levels are not well tolerated by many sessile invertebrates. Coral polyps, disk and colonial anemones, for example, cease feeding at

Maintenance of water quality is essential to successful invertebrate husbandry. The polyps of many colonial anthozoans, such as this *Mopsella ellisi* stop feeding if dissolved nitrate levels axceed 15.0 ppm.

nitrate levels as low as 15.0–20.0 ppm, values that are quite acceptable to most coral reef fishes. Even some mobile invertebrates are uncomfortable if dissolved nitrate concentrations exceed 10.0 ppm. High nitrate levels, for example, seem to complicate molting in a number of popular and highly decorative shrimp species. Not surprisingly, invertebrates are most easily cultured in tanks equipped with protein skimmers and trickle filters. Regardless of the system chosen, it is pointless to attempt introducing sessile invertebrates to an aquarium until its filter has been thoroughly run in.

For this reason, it is much easier to establish a successful invertebrate community in the absence of fish than to attempt the introduction of most of the sessile species into an established fish community. Once established, an assemblage of invertebrates that contains a fair proportion of species with sym-

biotic algae in their tissues as well as vigorously growing *Caulerpa* is usually capable of handling the nitrate output of a few small fish.

It also does not pay to skimp when purchasing synthetic salts if one wishes to be successful in keeping invertebrates. The wisest course of action for the aquarist to pursue is to determine which brand his local dealer uses and follow his lead. It also pays to ascertain the specific gravity of his water before setting up a home tank. Invertebrates as a group seem more sensitive to changes in salinity than are fish. The more similar the density of the water in their old and new homes, the more easily they can be acclimatised to a new set of living conditions.

It is impossible to successfully maintain invertebrates that enjoy a symbiotic relationship with zooxanthellae in any save brightly lit tanks. These animals apparently cannot

Light levels that will supoort a vigorous growth of *Caulerpa* will also meet the needs of sessile invertebrates like this *Actinodiscus* species that rely largely upon symbiotic zooxanthellae to meet their nutritional needs.

sustain themselves solely on the food that they capture and consume. They require nutritional input from their algal symbionts, and these cannot flourish in dim light. Lighting that suits *Caulerpa* will also meet the needs of these invertebrates. Suitable lighting fixtures are not inexpensive – an outlay in excess of $100.00 to properly illuminate a sessile invertebrate tank is not unusual. However, the entire venture will quickly be called into question in the absence of such a committment.

Not all invertebrates require such intense illumination, of course. Most mobile species are indifferent to light intensity. Even among sessile species, there are soft corals that are best kept in dimly lit tanks or situated in the shadow of a tank's infrastructure lest they be overgown with filamentous algae. The accompanying Catalog of suitable species clearly indicates individual light preferences along with other information relevant to their husbandry.

**A scanning electron micrograph of *Brachionus*, a marine rotifer useful in the culture of many filter-feeding invertebrates and marine fish larvae.**

The feeding patterns and nutritional requirements of invertebrates vary tremendously. The species covered herein have been largely selected because of the ease with which they can be fed. However, a few particularly interesting species with unusual dietary requirements have also been included. As a rule, invertebrates will prosper on a diet of live *Artemia*, TetraTips and TabiMin (crushed

to a powder and fed in suspension if necessary), freeze-dried and frozen foods. Several brands of frozen invertebrate foods are readily available from retailers who stock a comprehensive selection of marine organisms. A few species of sessile invertebrates require regular feedings of very tiny planctonic organisms, such as the green alga *Chlorella* and the marine rotifer *Brachionus*. These organisms are not difficult to culture. The names and addresses of firms that can supply starter kits and culture instructions are given in the last chapter. Once the aquarist succeeds in sustaining cultures of these organisms, he will also be in a position to attempt rearing the larvae of marine fishes.

Established invertebrate tanks should be fed sparingly. Because invertebrates are so sensitive to elevated nitrate levels, the consequences of overfeeding are, if anything, even graver for them than they would be in a tank of marine fishes. Many successful invertebrate keepers insist on a single light feeding every other day. If the aquarium contains fish, a single daily feeding is in order. Remember to adhere rigorously to the 5 minute rule! Such a regime is less rigorous than it might seem. Sessile invertebrates with symbiotic algae derive much of their nutritional needs from the metabolic by-products of their zooxanthellae, while the rockwork of an established invertebrate tank offers many foraging opportunities to its mobile residents.

Just as the hobbyist who wishes to enjoy the prolific growth of *Caulerpa* must protect these algae from the depredations of herbivorous fishes, so must the successful invertebrate enthusiast avoid the introduction of certain fishes to his aquarium. Butterflyfish and angelfish will graze a wide variety of sessile invertebrates back to bare rock. Many herbivorous damselfish will systematically eradicate the polyps from one or more branches of stony coral in order to envourage the growth of an algal garden on the newly cleared surface. Most wrasses, sharp-nosed puffers and all triggerfish are sure death to most crustaceans and marine molluscs. Catalog entries indicate clearly which fish species can safely be housed with invertebrates. Consult

Labrids like these Mediterranean rainbow wrasses, *Coris julis,* are enthusiastic invertebrate feeders. Even large crustaceans are not safe from the attentions of wrasses immediately after molting.

*Chaetodon collare,* one of many butterflyfish species that feeds extensively on coral polyps in nature. Captive specimens will even browse on the tentacles of sea anemones in captivity!

this chapter before adding any new fish to an established invertebrate aquarium.

It must also be pointed out that even an all-invertebrate aquarium may not always prove to be the underwater version of the peacable kingdom. Sea anemones, mantis shrimps, large crabs and many species of cone shells will prey upon fish if they are afforded a suitable opportunity to do so. The last three have also been implicated in depredations upon smaller crustaceans and molluscs. For their part, many molluscs, among them most of the spectacularly colored nudibranchs, graze upon a variety of anthozoans. Take care to consult the relevant entries in this chapter before selecting the residents of an invertebrate community tank.

The novice invertebrate keeper should restrict his initial purchases to the hardiest subjects and work his way slowly up to those that require more specialized care. His initial efforts are more likely to succeed if he dedicates a separate aquarium to his collection of invertebrates. While mixed culture of fishes and invertebrates is possible, the task is best approached with due deliberation.

A final word of caution: aquarists who do have the opportunity to vacation in the subtropics or tropics are often tempted to collect

**Like all octopi,** Octopus vulgaris *is a redoubtable predator that will make short shrift of any fish or mobile invertebrates unfortunate enough to share its quarters in captivity.*

*Many colorful nudibranchs like this* Nembrotha eliora *feed upon sponges or anthozoans in nature ans will graze a "minireef" quite bare of their prefered food organisms in captivity.*

and bring back invertebrates as a living souvenir of their experience. This is not a good idea. First of all, many jurisdictions regulate the collection of marine organisms quite strictly. The hobbyist who attempts to capture specimens for his tanks in ignorance of the aposite local laws can wind up in serious difficulties with the authorities. Secondly, holding marine organisms in good condition prior to and packing them properly for shipment require considerable experience. The novice aquarist lacks such skills and even experienced aquarists seldom have the opportunity to acquire them in the normal enjoyment of their hobby. Even if they survive transport, marine animals require careful acclimation if they are to survive their change of venue. Newly arrived specimens cannot simply be dumped into an established tank and expected to prosper. Unless he has planned his activities carefully beforehand and made suitable provision for housing the specimens he collects, the aquarist should limit his contact to coral reefs to snorkelling and SCUBA diving. If he must take back a tangible memento of his visit, an underwater photograph is both more humane and likely to last longer than any animals he might collect himself.

## A Selection of Sessile Invertebrates for the Marine Aquarium

**Sessile Invertebrates**. From a purely practical standpoint, it is useful to divide the invertebrates commonly maintained by marine aquarists into two broad categories based upon their degree of mobility. Sessile invertebrates are either completely immobile as adults (sponges, corals, tubeworms) or else move so slowly or so infrequently (many anemones) that for all practical intents and purposes, they can be considered immobile by aquarists. Nobile invertebrates are those species which do move about actively as adults. As a rule, these divisions correspond fairly closely to formal taxonomic groupings as well, although there are some exceptions. Most molluscs would be considered to fall into the mobile category, but some bivalves like the giant clam, *Tridacna*, are effectively sessile as adults.

From the hobbyist's perspective, sessile invertebrates play much the same role in aquascaping a marine aquarium as plants do a fresh water display tank. However, even the gaudiest plastic plants cannot rival the spectrum of colors that such sessile invertebrates as soft corals and tube worms offer the marine aquarist. It is hardly surprising that these fascinating animals continue to engage the attentions of a growing number of enthusiasts.

Sessile invertebrates differ widely among themselves in their ease of culture. However, all are extremely sensitive to nitrogen cycle mismanagement and demand the strictest attention to the maintenance of water quality. All require good water circulation in their quarters, and those corals native to the outer reef wall will not prosper unless a strong current of water plays constantly over their polyps. Of all invertebrates, these are most adversely effected by the absence or depletion of trace elements in their water. It is therefore prudent to add supplementary trace elements to their tanks on a regular basis of a protein skimmer is in use and after every water change.

**Tube anemones like this lovely *Cerianthus* sp. will use their potent nematocysts to sting to death any anthozoan within reach of their long tentacles.**

Although they are effectively immobile, many sessile anthozoans have specialized stinging cells that they use to keep the area im-

mediately surrounding their colony free of intruders. This should be taken into account when placing these organisms in a marine aquarium. Never place colonies of these animals so close together that they are in

Anthozoans that lack symbiotic zooxanthellae, like this magnificent colony of an *Acropora* sp., feed upon zooplankton in nature. Captive specimens must be offered a comparable diet to prosper.

physical contact. Indeed, it is prudent to leave a buffer zone at least 15.0 cm (6″) wide between colonies.

Most sessile invertebrates are plankton feeders in nature. Many of the species maintained by aquarists must be offered live planktonic organisms such as *Brachionus* or *Artemia* nauplii or a prepared plankton substitute on a regular basis of they are to prosper in captivity. A number of frozen plankton substitutes are also readily available and quite suitable for this purpose when used as directed. An acceptable plankton substitute can be prepared by running a level tablespoon of Tetra-Marin and a level tablespoon of regular Tetra-Min flakes through a food processor with a cup of water until a slurry of fine particles is obtained. The resulting suspension can then be transfered to a plastic cup and offered to the invertebrates in question with a kitchen baster.

It is advantageous to release small ammounts of either live or synthetic plankton in the immediate vicinity of the animal or animals to be fed rather than attempt to saturate the entire tank with food particles. This objective sometimes requires a longer reach than an unmodified baster allows. The simplest way to overcome this problem is to secure a length of rigid plastic tubing of a diameter that fits easily over the end of the baster and cut a length sufficient to reach into all portions of the tank. Once this extension has been mated to the baster, the resulting "feeding tube" will permit the accurate placement of precise quantities of food where they will do the most good.

This discussion of sessile invertebrates will initially address the the proper handling of "living rock" and its use in the creation of a viable invertebrate aquarium. Attention will then be given to representatives of the three major groups of these organisms of interest to marine aquarists, the Porifera (sponges), the Coelenterata (corals and anemones) and the Annelida (marine worms).

"Living rock" is the term applied to stones, usually of a calcareous nature, that have become overgrown with a rich carpet of macroalgae and sessile invertebrates. This

extremely diverse community also provides a home for a myriad of more active forms, such as crustaceans, molluscs, small echinoderms and even some fish species. The generous use of "living rock" in the aquarium not only provides a colorful backdrop for specimen invertebrates but can also contribute significantly to nitrogen cycle management and provide an important source of food for many of the tank's inhabitants. Liberal use of "living rock" in the tank infrastructure is an essential feature of the so-called Dutch mini-reef school of marine aquarium keeping.

"Living rock" is available in two different forms that differ considerably on how they must be handled. **Unseasoned** "living rock" is freshly collected from the wild and sold with its full complement of associated organisms in place and at varying states of debility. Within a very short time after being placed in an aquarium, the adult stages of most of these encrusting organisms will begin to die off. Their death generates a major waste load with predictable results upon the ammonia and nitrite levels of an aquarium. Once the short-term ammonia and nitrite build-up have been disposed of by the tank's biological filter, the hardy resting stages of the rock's faunal carpet will slowly begin the process of recolonization. At this point, the material is refered to as **seasoned** "living rock".

Not all of the species originally present therein will reappear, but a sufficient proportion of its residents will reestablish themselves in time to produce a diverse and extremely attractive assemblage of organisms. Encrusting sponges, byrozoans and small anthozoans will predominate among the animal community. If the aquarist is fortunate, he will find that a number of colorful red algae, such as *Botryocladia* or *Callophylis* will reestablish themselves along with a selection of green *Caulerpa* species.

The two types of "living rock" obviously require very different initial handling. **Unseasoned "living rock" must NEVER be added to an established marine aquarium!!!** To do so is to precipitate a major crisis in nitrogen cycle management that will inevitably result in the die-off of the tank's prior

**A chunk of raw, or unseasoned "living rock".**

**A chunk of seasoned "living rock".**

residents from ammonia poisoning. Not even a highly efficient biological filter can degrade all of the ammonia produced by the die-off of the rock's associated fauna to prevent a lethal build-up.

Unseasoned "living rock" should be placed in a **bare** tank with a functioning biological filter and allowed to travel its predestined path. Ammonia and nitrite levels should be monitored regularly. When both have dropped to trace levels – the process takes from two to four weeks – the chunks of "living rock" can safely be introduced to established aquaria. Alternatively, the aquarist can begin to introduce other organisms into their presence.

Seasoned living rock can be safely added to an established aquarium with minimal risk if due account is taken of the fact that the metabolism of its associated fauna will initially contribute to the tank's waste load. In order not to overstrain the biological filter's capacity, it is prudent to add pieces of seasoned "living rock" to an established tank one at a time and to monitor the tank's ammonia and nitrite levels for several days thereafter.

A growing number of retailers are willing to devote the necessary tank space to season-

ing freshly collected "living rock". Both the space and time required for this process mean that such seasoned material is likely to prove expensive. Unseasoned "living rock" on the other hand, is usually much less costly. It is for the individual hobbyist to decide whether his circumstances make it more attractive to pay the additional price for seasoned material or to carry out the seasoning process in his own tank.

### Phylum: Porifera

Class: Desmospongiae Sponges

Over 9000 species of sponges live throughout the world's seas. This group of sessile filter feeders is particularly well represented in subtropical and tropical regions, where many species can be found even in shallow, inshore waters. Sponges can range in size from a few centimeters (c. 1") to over 50.0 cm (c. 1.5') in diameter. Sponges are colonial animals, each entity comprised of an aggregation of cells specialized to perform a particular function. Only a handful of species from the Caribbean and Indo-Pacific are of interest to aquarists.

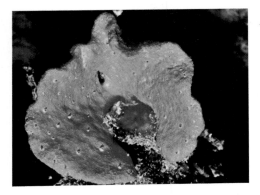

A encrusting sponge of the genus *Phakellia.*

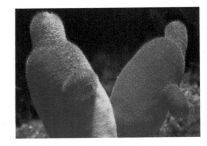

Superficial resemplance notwithstanding, these colorful sea squirts are more closely relates to vertebrates than to sponges. small colonial ascidians such as this are common colonists of "living rock".

Large sponges support a rich fauna of associated organisms, many so specialized that they cannot survive in any other habitat. The nooks and crannies their pattern of growth inadvertedly creates host a variety of small isopod and amphiopod crustaceans as well as a number of diminutive shrimp species, many belonging to the Family Alpheidae. Their exteriors are often encrusted with colonial anemones, while diminutive brittle stars crawl freely over and about their surfaces.

As aquarium residents, sponges are a mixed bag. The species that recolonize "living rock" are very hardy. The larger species imported specifically for the aquarium trade, are often fragile. They are very sensitive to a decline in water quality, are often difficult to feed and are very susceptible to being overgrown by algae. As this fate must be avoided at all cost, sponges are best kept in dimly lit tanks or placed in the shadow of other features of a tank's infrastructure. Never purchase sponges that have a greyish cast or that emit a strong putrescent odor when removed from the water. These animals are dead or dying and will simply pollute an established aquarium if added to its complement of residents.

Sponges seem to do best over a temperature range of 20°–26° C. (70°–78° F.). At higher temperatures they have a tendency to disintegrate. They should be fed frozen plankton substitutes and fine live planctonic organisms, such as *Brachionus.* When moving

sponges, take extreme care always to keep them covered with water. They should never be allowed to come into contact with air.

The larger sponges are best kept in a tank containing other filter feeders, such as sessile coelenterates, tubeworms and bivalves. The smaller crustaceans and non-grazing fish also make suitable companions. Both angelfish and butterfly fish will eat sponges greedily. In fact. sponges comprise over 90% of the diet of *Holocanthus tricolor*, the rock beauty, and *Pygoplites diacanthus*, the regal angelfish. A number of cowries and several genera of sea urchins will also graze on sponges.

Notwithstanding their striking appearance, large sponges are best attempted only by the experienced invertebrate enthusiast. The

The rock beauty, *Holocanthus tricolor,* feeds almost entirely on encrusting sponges in nature ans requires such a diet to prosper in captivity.

An interesting collection of sponges: *Haliclona permollis* (foreground lower left), *Dasychalina* sp. (center lower left) and *Pseudsuberites* sp. (midground right). The starfish is *Fromia milleporella*.

smaller encrusting species associated with "living rock", on the other hand, are an indispensable element of the fauna of any invertebrate aquarium and should be welcomed as reliable indicators of favorable environmental conditions.

## Phyllum: Coelenterata

Class: Anthozoa

Two major subdivisions of the Coelenterata furnish highly prized residents of the marine aquarium. The subclass Alcynoaria (= Octocorallia) offers the marine aquarist four orders of interest, the organ-pipe corals (Stolonifera), the soft corals (Alcynoacea), the sea fans or gorgonians (Gorgonacea) and the sea pens or sea whips (Pennatulacea). The subclass Zoantharia (= Hexacorallia) also includes five aquaristically interesting orders, the sea anemones (Actinaria), the colonial anemones (Zoanthinaria), the tube anemones (Ceriantharia), the coral anemones (Corallimorpharia) and the true or

stony corals (Scleratina). All rely upon specialized stinging cells, or **nematocysts**, to capture their prey and representatives of a number of orders support colonies of symbiotic algae in their cells whose metabolic products contribute significantly to the nutrition of their hosts. This assemblage of animals comprises several thousand described species and even the relatively small subset of aquaristic interest is too large to make a comprehensive treatment possible herein. Instead, representatives of each major group have been chosen to illustrate its salient features as aquarium residents.

Because they are sessile, inexperienced aquarists sometimes have difficulty determining the condition of a prospective purchase. In the case of colonial anthozoans such as soft corals and gorgonians, greyish patches on the surface of the colony or any other indications of damage ot its outer surface are grounds for rejecting a specimen out of hand. So are cuts or other obvious wounds on the body or basal disk of solitary forms such as

Feeding anemones like this *Actina equina* commonly contract their tentacles until their meal is fully digested.

true and tube anemones. Specimens of either of these two groups that are floating limply at the surface are clearly terminal. No anthozoan with limp, drooping tentacles is a good candidate for life insurance and specimens that have a rotten smell when removed from the water are so much carrion. On the other hand, an anthozoan that has withdrawn its tentacles is not necessarily diseased or stressed. Many species are crepuscular and their polyps only emerge under dim lighting conditions. It is also perfectly normal for the larger species to withdraw their tentacles after feeding.

Order: Stolonifera  Organ pipe corals

The green organ pipe coral, *Clavularia viridis*, forms large colonies on dead coral branches and the rocky basement of reefs. It occurs from just below the surface to depths of 8.0 m (c. 26°) in large colonies up to 20.0 cm (c. 8″) across. This species is closely related to the

A thriving colony of *Clacularia viridis*, the green organ pipe coral.

organ pipe coral, *Tubipora musica*, whose dark red skeletons make a much appreciated contribution to a marine aquarium's infrastructure. Widely distributed throughout the Indo-Pacific region, this species is exported from the Philippines, Indonesia, Singapore and Sri Lanka.

If due attention is paid to their requirements, organ pipe corals are not difficult to culture in captivity. This species relies upon its symbiotic zooxanthellae for a significant ammount of its nutrition. It therefore must receive intense light to prosper. At least three full spectrum flourescent tubes or else a battery of halogen-metal vapor icandescant spotlights are required to provide conditions for satisfactory growth. By way of compensation, *C. viridis* requires nothing in the way of special feeding. Take care to carefully monitor and regulate the number of hours of light its tank receives, as green organ pipe coral is susceptible to being overgrown by filamentous green algae. A temperature range of 20°–26° C. (70°–78° F.) is acceptable to this species. Temperatures 30° C. (86° F.) or higher are lethal. Moderately strong water movement is appreciated.

Organ pipe corals share with sponges their preference in tank companions. Apart from organisms that would feed on its polyps, large, active crustaceans, like crabs and reef lobsters, can damage colonies severely by knocking them from their perches. Anemones, particularly the highly aggressive and venomous tube anemones, tend to encroach upon organ pipe colonies, usually with unhappy consequences for their victims. They are thus best housed separately.

Order Alcyonacea  Soft corals

*Sarcophyton trocheliophorum* Leather coral

This soft coral is widely distributed over the coral reefs of the Indo-Pacific region, where it can be found to a depth of 15.0 m (c. 50'). Its growth habit varies widely. Colonies up to 1.0 m (c. 3') can be found growing on bare rock in nature. Captive specimens range from 5.0–15.0 cm (2″–6″) in diameter. Together with other species of the genera *Sarcophyton*

A fine specimen of leather coral, *Sarcophyton trocheliophorum*.

and *Sinularia*, leather coral is exported from the Philippines, Indonesia, Signapore, Sri Lanka and East Africa.

Leather coral, like green organ pipe coral, relies heavily upon the metabolic products of its zooxanthellae for nutrition. Hence its culture requirements in captivity are identical to those of the preceeding species. Supplementary feedings of live zooplankton or of plankton substitutes prepared from animal matter are relished. It is best to position the stems of this animal so thay they are completely surrounded by water and do not rest directly on the tank's substratum. Otherwise, they are subject to rotting.

It is possible to propagate *S. trocheliophorum* in aquaria with good lighting and water quality. Simply detach sections from the main colony and fasten them to a piace of clean coral limestone with nylon fishing yarn. Be sure to place these "cuttings" well away from the parental colony.

Leather coral shares most of the enemies of green organ pipe coral. Among their most important natural predators are the egg snails of the Family Ovulidae. While these are in many respects interestng aquarium residents, they should never be introduced to a tank containing *Sarcophyton*. Many species of coral shrimps are troublesome to leather corals during feeding. Their greater mobility allows them to literally snatch food from the tentacles of the feeding polyps.

### Dendronephyta klunzigeri

This colorful soft coral is representative of a number of closely related species found on the outer reef face throughout the Indo-Pacific region and into the Red Sea. Colonies can range in size from a few centimeters (c. 1″) to over a meter (3°) in length. This alcyonacean lacks the zooxanthellae of the preceding species and depends entirely upon planktonic organisms it traps with its stinging tentacles for food. Consequently, Dendronephyta is found in dimly lit locations characterized by strong to very strong water movement.

**Dendronephyta kluzingeri is one of the most spectacularly colored soft corals.**

All Dendronephyta species require considerable care to prosper in captivity. They are thus not recommended for the inexperienced invertebrate enthusiast. Take care to purchase only specimens whose outer "skin" is intact and to avoid placing even uninjured specimens directly on the tank bottom. These soft corals are very susceptible to rotting. As they demand strong water movement, they are best fastened to a coral branch or reef rock that receives the full force of the filter's return flow. As noted, these alcyonaceans lack symbiotic algae. They thus do not require intense illumination. Indeed, as they can be quickly overgown by filamentous algae, they are best kept in dimply lit aquaria or else in the shade of some prominant element of a well lit tank's decorative infra-structure.

As they cannot rely upon photosynthetic by-products for nourishment, Dendronephyta must be offered small ammounts of live zooplankton or prepared plankton substitutes at least once a day. In some manner, the polyps of a colony seem capable of sensing the approach of a feeding tube and opening fully to take advantage of the sudden appearance of food. These soft corals prefer a temperature range of 20°–24° C. (70°–76° F.) and stop feeding if the water in their tank becomes any warmer.

These alcyonaceans are best kept in a community made up exclusively of other sessile, plankton-feeding inveretbrates. If fish must be kept with them, select only small, relatively inactive species such as pipefish, sea horses, small gobies and mandarin fishes. With the exception of the commensal shrimps of the genus Periclemenes with which they occurs in nature, crustaceans do not make good companions for these soft corals. Neither do large snails or predatory echinoderms, although the smaller brittle and feather stars are acceptable tankmates. The most important predators of Dendronephyta snails of the Family Ovulidae, most of which are colored so much like their host as to be indistinguishable when foraging upon them.

Order: Gorgonaria  Sea fans or horny corals

### Anthoplexaura spp.

Gorgonians are found in all marine habitats, but are most abundant in subtropical and tropical waters. Anthoplexaura species such as this are native to the Indo-Pacific. A number of other genera are sometimes exported from the Caribbean as well. Sea fans tend to have the same habitat preferences in nature as alcyonarieans. Though specimens up to 3.0 m (c.10′) high can be encountered on the reef, aquarium specimens usually measure from 10.0–20.0 cm (4′–8′) in length.

A fine specimen of the aptly named *Dendro-nephyta aurea* (left).

Both *Dendro-nephyta divaricata* (right) and *D. aurea* require the same care as *D. kluzingeri.*

133

An aggregation of sea fans photographed in the Mediterranean. Most gorgonians live in fairly deep water in nature and are intolerant of bright light in captivity.

Like the *Dendronephyta* species whose culture requirements they share, sea fans are best attempted only by the experienced invertebrate keeper. They are dedicedly lovers of crepuscular conditions. Only the Caribbean species can tolerate any ammount of light. Illumination must be managed carefully even for light-tolerant species, as any colonization by filamentous algae can quickly prove fatal to gorgonians.

Sea fans are best kept in a sessile invertebrate community. In nature, they often live in association with tiny commensal brittle stars.

A flourishing colony of the gorgonian *Anthoplexaura dimorpha*.

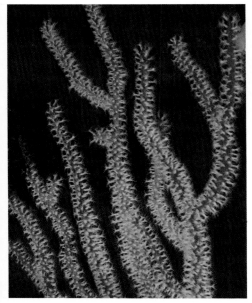

The feeding polyps of this *Anthoplexaura* sp. are clearly evident.

They are preyed upon by a number of ovulid snails and are sometimes encrusted with barnacles.

Order Pennatulacea  Sea pens

*Cavernularia obesa*

This hardy sea pen is widely distributed throughout the Indo-Pacific and is often exported from the Philippines, Singapore and Indonesia. Like all pennatulaceans, it is an inhabitant of sandy or muddy substrates. It is thus usually found on the obttom of bays and harbors rather than on the coral reef proper. Aquarium specimens rarely exceed 15.0 cm (6″) in overall length, but individuals up to 40.0 cm (c. 16″) long have been found in the wild

Possibly because of the types of habitats they come from are easily duplicated in captivity, uninjured sea pens are quite hardy under aquarium conditions. They do require at least 10.0 cm (4″) of fine sand to secure a suitable foothold. As such a substratum is inappropriate for use with an undergravel fil-

A colour of *Cavernularia obesa,* an easily maintained sea pen. The individual polyps are clearly visible in this photo.

ter, sea pens can only be kept successfully in tanks that employ an alternative approach to filtration. Moderate water movement and a temperature range of 20°–24° C. (70°–76° F.) suit them well. Temperatures in excess of 28° C. (82° F.) are lethal.

Sea pens lack zooxanthellae. They thus have no special lighting needs but require small daily feedings of live zooplankton or an appropriate synthetic substitute. They are normally crepuscular or nocturnal feeders in nature. However, in captivity they will open during the day when offered food.

Sea pens should not be kept with either true sea anemones or tube anemones. Large fish or crustaceans, most snails and predatory starfish are also unsuitable tankmates. A few

*Carotalvyon sagamianum,* another attractive sea pen.

specimens of such small, relatively "quiet" fish as gobies and mandarin fish can be kept with pennatulaceans, but all in all, they seem to do better in the sole company of other sessile, filter-feeding invertebrates. Some sea pens display a degree of bioluminesence when exposed to long-wave uiltraviolet light.

Order Actinaria  Sea anemones
Sea anemones are probably the most anatomically generalized of the coelenterates kept in marine aquaria. They are solitary, though some species occur in large aggregations made up of the asexually budded progeny of a single individual, and do not form a calcarieous or horny skeleton, in the manner of the previously discussed alcynoarians and the true or stony corals. They hold fast to their chosen substratum with a well developed pedal disk, which also affords them a degree of mobility. Their ability to attach themselves securely to the botton may account for their success in colonizing the intertidal zone as well as deeper waters in areas of strong current.

Anemones range in size from tiny species barely a centimeter across to the huge carpet anemones of the tropical Indo-Pacific, whose disks can exceed 30.0 cm (1') in diameter. While all anemones feed to a substantial extent upon zooplankton, they have the ability to sting to death and consume much larger

The symbiotic relationship between Indo-Pacific carpet anemones and clownfishes such as these *Amphiprion clarkii* has long fascinated scientists and aquarists alike.

prey items. Most fish therefore take pains to avoid them. A number of organisms, among them the clownfishes of the genera *Amphiprion* and *Premnas*, the anemone shrimps of the genus *Periclemenes* and the anemone crabs of the genus *Neopetrolisthes* have learned how to neutralize the stinging response of the larger anemones and thus enjoy a privileged sanctuary from predation among their deadly tentacles.

Many intertidal or shallow water anemones are brilliantly colored. Their characteristic red, orange and violet pigments protect their bearers against the harmful effects of the sun's ultraviolet radiation. In the absence of the appropriate precursor substances and the stimulus of intense illumination, these colors tend to fade in captivity. Many sea anemones enjoy a symbiotic relationship with intercellular algal colonies. Like other coelenterates that bear such zooxanthellae, these anemones derive a significant ammount of nourishment from their algal symbionts. Captive specimens only prosper in brightly lit aquaria.

The ease with which sea anemones can be maintained in captivity varies considerably between species. Beginning aquarists should limit their efforts to subtropical species, such as the Florida anemone, *Condylactis gigantea*. Once they have mastered the husbandry of these species, they can undertake more ambitious efforts, such as the maintenance of the tropical carpet anemones of the genus *Radianthus*. Regardless of the species chosen, purchase only undamaged specimens. Tropical anemones in particular seem very vulnerable to bacterial infection of wounds inflicted on their bodies or pedal disks. Hence great care must be taken when moving a specimen not to tear this structure when removing it from the aquarium. If at all possible, remove both attachment site and anemone from a tank in preference to trying to detach the animal from its perch.

All anemones appreciate good water movement in the aquarium. It is not unusual for specimens to relocate themselves immediately under the return flow from a tank's filter. Individuals of zooxanthellae-bearing

genera, such as *Condylactis* and *Radianthus* will also position themselves in the most brightly lit areas of a tank. In fact, often the only way to keep a particular specimen in an aesthetically pleasing location is to shine a beam of light onto that portion of the tank! A temperature range of 20°–24° C. (70°–76° F.) suffices for subtropical and tropical species. Mediterranean and other warm temperate zone anemones do not tolerate temperatures in excess of 20° C.

Anemones require regular, though not always frequent feeding. Weekly offerings of food suffice for species that lack zooxanthellae. Those that possess algal symbionts can go much longer between meals. Pea to lima bean sized morsels of fish, shrimp, crab or other shellfish are relished. Either fresh or frozen seafood can be utilized, but take care to allow frozen offerings to thaw before offering them to the anemone(s). Most species will take TetraTips without demur, and all appreciate an occassional treat of live *Artemia* nauplii. Aquarists faced with loss of color in their anemones will find it helpful to make a stiff paste of TetraRuby and stuff it into the empty thoracic cavity of a shrimp exoskeleton. Anemones will accept such offerings readily. Regular feedings of such color-enhancing foods will go far towards restoring their coloration to its original intensity.

Take care when feeding anemones to offer them only small morsels. Large pieces of food may be ingested, but are invariably regurgitated a short time later, surrounded by an "envelope" of mucus. Unless removed immediately, these rejected meals can quickly pollute a tank. If an anemone rejects food in this manner, give it a 24 hour rest and offer it a smaller portion of the same item.

When contented with their surroundings, anemones grow quite rapidly. Many species simply divide to form two separate individuals once they attain a certain diameter. Others will bud off new individuals from the base of their bodies. It is not unusual for anemones to shed eggs and sperm in an attempt to reproduce sexually. Under appropriate circumstances, such as those encountered in a Dutch mini-reef style aquarium, at least a few of the resulting planula larvae may successfully metamorphose and settle out of the plankton to produce new individuals. Their usual fate is to be sucked into the filter bed and perish therein.

Anemones should not be kept with other anthozoans, for they tend to aggressively encroach upon their colonies and sting them to death with their tentacles. It is equally advisable to avoid housing small, slow-moving fish such as pipefish, sea horses, mandarin fish and most gobies and blennies with anemones, as they have a tendency to end up as unscheduled offerings of live food! At the other extreme, butterfly and angelfish, some wrasses and trigger fish will nibble the tentacles of most anemones right back to their bases. The chief predators of sea anemones in nature are nudibranchs. These exquisitely colored molluscs will devour an anemone right down to its pedal disk. The consequences to the anemone of this fondness for what must be highly spiced fare hardly require elaboration! Large crustaceans can also damage anemones as they clamber about the tank, so they too are best kept elsewhere. Anemones do well in the company of sponges, tubeworms, bivalves and small to medium-sized crustaceans.

It is tempting to try and keep carpet anemones and their clownfish symbionts together. This requires a fair ammount of expertise in invertebrate culture and is best postponed until the aquarist has mastered keeping the anemones alone alive and healthy. Clownfish will adopt a wide selection of alternate "exotic" anemone hosts, so it may be preferable to work with a hardier species. such as *Condylactis*, in preferable to the rather delicate *Radianthus*.

Order Zoanthinaria  Colonial anemones

*Zoanthus sociatus* green colonial anemone

Colonial anemones are encountered in all seas, although like the true anemoness of the order Actinaria, they are best represented in warm waters. *Zoanthus sociatus* is a commonly imported Caribbean species. Their morphology is reminiscent of the true anemones, but as their name implies, they differ in a colonial life style. Individual polyps are quite small, often less than 1.0 cm (0.5″) in diameter, but individual colonies can be very large, up to 30.0 cm (1′) in diameter. Different species will colonize living sponges and sea fans, dead branches of coral and bare rock. Zoantharians are typically found in shallow, brightly lit habitats.

All tropical colonial anemones are liberally supplied with zooxanthellae. Indeed, many species of the genera *Zoanthus* and *Palythoa* forgo the uptake of animal food and obtain all

**The green colonial anemone, *Zoanthus sociatus* (above).**

***Parazoanthus axinellae* (below), another attractive colonial anemone.**

of their nutrition from the metabolic products of their algal symbionts. Intense illumination is thus a prerequisite to their successful culture in captivity. The aquarist who takes care to meet this need will find zoantharians to be easily cultured, notwithstanding the need to protect them from being overgrown by filamentous algae. Their other culture requirements are identical to those of disc anemones, as is the roster of suitable tankmates.

A commonly encountered predator of colonial anemones is small, unidentified black and white banded snail about 1.0 cm across. These snails apparently are inadvertedly imported with the zoantharians and are thus introduced into the aquarium. They feed by piercing the epidermis of the colonial anemones and sucking out their body fluids with their proboscis. These snails are quite cryptic and are capable of doing much damage before they are detected. It is therefore prudent to inspect established colonies periodically with a magnifying glass for signs of damage and remove any snails that are noticed..

Order Corallimorpharia  Coral or disk anemones

*Actinodiscus* spp.

These attractive anthozoans are intermediate in appearance between true anemones and true corals. They form colonies of large, rather short-tentacled polyps through a process of serial division. Disk anemones are restricted to tropical seas and are especially common in the Indo-Pacific, the Red Sea and the Caribbean. They typically colonize dead coral in areas of moderate water movement. Individual polyps range from 3.0–10.0 cm (1.25″–4″) in diameter. Colonies can attain a diameter of 40.0 cm (c. 15″) in nature as well as under favorable conditions in captivity. When satisfied with their living conditions, they often reproduce by budding from the pedal disk.

Disk anemones are an ideal beginner's subject as long as he takes care to provide their tank intense illumination. All known species possess zooxanthellae and rely very heavily

An interesting *Actinodiscus* sp. (above).

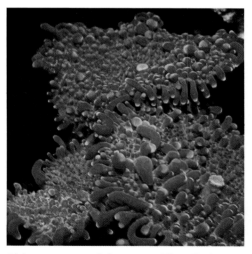

Disk anemones of the genus *Ricordia* (below) require the same intense illumination to prosper in captivity as do *Actinodiscus* spp.

upon the activities of their algal symbionts for nourishment. They can be expected to thrive under the same conditions that satisfy organ-pipe corals. If maintained under sufficiently intense illumination, disk anemones do not require frequent feeding. Only the smallest live or synthetic zooplankton should be offered as food. They appreciate good water circulation but are not as partial to strong currents as the true anemones. Unlike them, disk anemones are sedentary. Though they have a well-developed pedal disk, they will detach themselves from the substratum only if water conditions in the tank have undergone serious deterioration. They prosper over a temperature range of 20°–26° C. (70°–78° F.). Temperatures greater than 30° C. (86°F.) are lethal.

Disk anemones can be kept with other anthozoans provided they are positioned a safe distance at least 10.0 cm (4″) – from their colonies. They will live happily in the company of other filter-feeding sessile invertebrates, small shrimps and hermit crabs, herbivorous sea urchins, brittle stars and small, non-predatory starfish. Small, non-browsing fishes make acceptable companions. The larger coral reef species, with the exception of surgeonfishes, do not. Predatory snails and starfish, large crabs and shrimps of the genus *Rhynchocinetes* also make inappropriate tankmates.

In nature, disk anemomes are preyed upon chiefly by ovulid snails and nudibranchs. Imported specimens are sometimes inhabited by commensal turbellarian flatworms. These are harmless to both the disk anemones and any other organisms present in the tank. Some disk anemones flouresce when illuminated with longwave ultraviolet light.

Order Ceriantharia Tube anemones

*Pachyceriathus maua*

Tube anemones also enjoy a cosmopolitan distribution in the world's seas. Tropical and subtropical species are particularly colorful. Ceriantharians are not inhabitants of the coral reef. They are characteristic inhabitants of sandy or muddy bottoms in areas of moderate current. Unlike true sea anemones, tube anemones have two distinct types of tentacles. The long, peripheral tentacles capture and immobilize prey, while the shorter

The graceful but deadly tentacles of this beautiful *Cerianthus* apecies are reminiscent of the petals of a spider chrysanthemum.

140

*Pacycerianthus maua,* a tube anemone often available through commercial channels.

*Cerianthus filiformis* (above).

The strikingly colored *Cerianthus membranaceous* (below).

internal ones carry food to the mouth. They further lack the pedal disk of true anemones, instead constructing a tube in the substratum to accomadate their long-stalked bodies. Tube anemones can sport bodies up to 20.0 cm (8°) long and a crown of tentacles of almost the same diameter.

Ceriantharians are among the most durable of invertabrates. Specimens have lived for over 30 years in aquaria. Contented specimens will shed gametes regularly and it is not unusual for a few of the resulting planula larvae to metamorphose and settle down successfully. This makes them excellent subjects for the beginner. However, their distinctive mode of living makes several demands the aquarist must take pains to address if his efforts to maintain these lovely animals are to succeed. These animals prefer to construct a tube at least twice the maximum length of their bodies. As this would require a substratum nearly a meter deep to happily accomadate a 40.0 cm long individual, it is clear that an alternative approach to satisfying this requirement is a prerequisite to their successful culture.

The easiest way to house tube anemones is to cut a piece of CPVC tubing or pipe twice the maximum body length of the specimen to be housed. The pipe should have a diameter slightly greater than that of the body of the animal in question. These "artificial tubes" should be inserted in crevices in the rockwork and the anemones placed therein. Ceriantharians find these housing arrangements quite satisfactory and they offer the further advantage of allowing the aquarist to place his specimens were they will have the greatest visual impact.

Ceriantharians prefer a moderate water flow. A very strong current will cause them to leave their tubes. So will the accumulation of detritus in their immediate vicinity. Hence the importance of regularly purging the substratum in their tank. Direct aeration of their aquarium is not recommended. Air bubles tend to become trapped in their gastric cavities, giving rise to dangerous gas embolisms. Tube anemones do not possess zooxanthellae. Hence they have no special lighting requirements. Tropical species prefer a temperature tange of 20°–24° C. (70°–76° F.). Subtropical species should not be kept warmer than 20° C.

Tube anemones must be fed on a regular basis. Finely chopped fresh or frozen seafood and deep frozen or freeze dried zooplankton are relished. So are periodic feedings of *Artemia* nauplii. Whatever the food selected, take care to chop it finely. Ceriantharians will ingest and successfully digest substantial chunks of food. However, during the entire interval devoted to assimilating such offerings, their magnificent tentacles will be contracted. This greatly reduces their visual impact in the aquarium.

It is inadvisable to house tropical and subtropical ceriantharians together. They do not tolerate each other's company and will attempt to sting each other to death. Tube and true anemones can be housed together provided the former are in the minority and the latter are represented by species that are not inclined to move about the tank. Ceriantharians most emphatically should not be housed with sessile anthozoans. Their colonies will be aggressively encroached upon and stung to death by the tube anemones.

It is also not a good idea to house these coelenterates with fish. Tube anemones are extraordinarily venomous. Their numerous stinging cells can even provoke a noticeable response where the tentacles come into contact with human skin. Small fish will inevitably be stung and eaten. Furthermore, there is some evidence that tube anemones secrete a toxic substance into the water that irritates the gills of even large fishes.

Ceriantharians will fall victim to a number of predatory molluscs and starfish. These obviously should be excluded from an aquarium housing tube anemones, as should large, active crustaceans. Small prawns, robust shrimps such as *Stenopus hispidus*, the banded coral shrimp, and small hermit crabs make suitable companions for these anthozoans. So do small brittle stars and representatives of other sessile filter feeding groups, such as sponges and tubeworms.

Order Scleratina  True or stony corals

*Plerogyra sinuosa* Bladder coral

True corals are colonial anthozians characterized by their massive calcreous skeletons, which form the backbone of tropical reefs. Marine aquarists have long made use of the bleached skeletons of true corals to provide a decorative backdrop for their tanks. With the exercise of a bit of care, it is now possible to maintain the living organisms themselves in the marine aquarium. Bladder coral is a conspicuous reef-building coral native of the Indo-Pacific region and the Red Sea. It occurs mainly in areas of moderate current on both the inner and outer reef faces at depths of 3.0–15.0 m (c. 10'–50'). In nature, colonies up to 2.0 m (c. 6') in diameter are not unusual, Aquarium specimens range from 3.0–15.0 cm (1.25"–6") in diameter. This is one of the true corals most frequently exported by Far Eastern collectors.

An unusual anthozoan, the bladder coral, *Plerogyra sinuosa*.

This species is probably the hardiest of the reef-forming corals. Bladder coral requires clean water and a moderate ammount of water movement to prosper. A temperature range of 20°–26° C. (70°–78° F.) is optimal. Temperatures in excess of 30° C. (86° F.) are lethal. It requires the same levels of illumination as green organ pipe coral for its zooxanthellae to function normally. During the day, the polyps are withdrawn inside of their distinctive bladders, whose beige to brownish coloration is caused by symbiotic algae. At night, they extend their 10 tentacles – which can measure up to 15.0 cm (6″) long – and feed upon planktonic organisms. If water conditions deteriorate or the tank is inadequately lit, individual polyps will detach themselves from their stony skeleton. They do not form a new skeleton but simply float about in the water for an indeterminate interval before dying.

Bladder coral must be fed regularly. It relishes the same types of food as true anemones, but should be offered smaller pieces. This species accepts TetraTips readily. It is best to initially offer food just before the tank lights are turned off. It suffices to place the morsel between two bladders. Bear in mind that *P. sinuosa* is a colonial organism. The food assimilated by one polyp benefits the entire colony, so it is only necessary to feed a single polyp at each feeding.

The tentacles of bladder coral are well furnished with nematocsysts capable of delivering an extremely toxic sting. This species will encroach aggressively on other colonial anthozoans and sting them to death. Specimens must thus be sited at least 20.0 cm (8″) from other coelenterate colonies if mishaps are to be avoided. Appropriate companions and unsuitable tank mates are as given for disk anemones. Bladder coral is sometimes attacked by parasitic flatworms that are apparently imported unnoticed with their hosts.

*Tubastrea coccina* Red cup coral

*Tubastrea aurea* Golden or yellow cup coral

*Tubastrea* are small true corals whose colonies range from 10. cm–15.0 cm (4″–6″) in dia-

The yellow cup coral, *Tubastrea aurea,* is one of the most beautiful anthozoan species available to marine aquarists.

meter. Thus though they have a calcareous skeleton, they are not regarded as reef-building corals. They are usually to be found over the same depth range as leather coral in dimly lit locations along the outer reef face characterized by a strong current. Both red and yellow cup coral are frequently exported from the Far East.

The vivid coloration of both cup coral species makes them a distinct asset in any invertebrate community. However, both are demanding subjects best left to the experienced aquarist. *Tubastrea* are extremely sensitive to the consequences of nitrogen cycle mismanagement and tolerate high nitrate levels poorly. They require strong water movement and must be kept under dim illumination to prosper. Cup corals are easily overgrown by filamentous algae, with predictably fatal consequences. The easiest way to ensure suitable lighting for *Tubastrea* is to house them in a dimly lit tank. However, they will usually do well if placed in the shadow of a coral overhang or just inside the mouth of a cave Both species do well over a temperature range of 20°–24° C. (70°–76° F.). Kept any warmer than this, they go into a decline and die.

*Tubastrea* must be fed daily. Offer the colony food only when the polyps are fully extended. Cup corals readily accept the same food items as true anemones, but must be offered them in smaller pieces. Remember that only a few polyps must be fed for the entire colony to derive nourishment from the meal. Most aquarists make it a practice to offer food to a different set of polyps each time they feed the colony.

Under optimum water conditions, *T. coccina* will reproduce by releasing free-swimming planula larvae into the water. The adult often dies thereafter. These larvae swim about in the aquarium for 2 to 4 days, then settle onto a suitable surface. Successful metamorphosis occurs only in dark sites swept by a strong current. After a few months, the appearance of numerous lentil-sized miniature colonies indicates successful reproduction has occured.

Butterflyfish, angelfish, carnivorous molluscs, including ovulid snails and many nudi-branchs, large, active crustaceans and predatory starfish do not make suitable companions for *Tubastrea*. Cup corals do well with the same mix of species that suits the needs of soft corals, but because of their extreme sensitivity to elevated nitrate levels, it is prudent to keep their tank's waste load well below the filter's capacity by keeping its mobile residents such as fish at a minimum.

**Phylum: Annelida**

Class: Aclitellata

The Aclitellata are exclusively marine worms characterized by external fertilization of the eggs and a free-living planktonic **trochophore** larval stage. The overwhelming majority of species belong to the subclass Polychaeta, which includes two orders of aquaristic interest, the featherduster worms (Terebellida) and the tube worms (Sabellida). The adult stage in both groups is a sessile plankton feeder that relies upon an elaborate crown of fine tentacles to strain food items from the water. The crowns are structures of great delicacy and are frequently brilliantly colored in the bargain. Hence the appeal of these marine worms to aquarists. The larger species of featherduster and tube worms are those generally exported and sold as specimens to invertebrate enthusiasts. The smaller species are among the most numerous and successful recolonizers of seasoned "living rock".

Both sabellid and terebellid worms are an important source of food for a wide range of marine fishes. Such popular coral reef dwellers as butterflyfish, angelfish, triggerfish, puffers and most wrasses prey efficiently upon these worms and are thus absolutely contraindicated as tankmates. So are carnivorous molluscs such as cone and murex shells, large, active crustaceans and predatory starfish. As long as care is taken to exclude such

**An Aggregation of feeding giant tubeworms, *Spirobranchus giganteus* (right). These spectacular sabellid worms make a striking display in an invertebrate aquarium.**

predators from their tank, both featherduster and tube worms are quite easily cultured and can be recommended for neophyte invertebrate fanciers. Indeed, several species have reproduced successfully without any encouragement on their keepers' part beyond reasonable attention to maintaining good water quality in their quarters.

Order Terebellida Featherduster worms

*Sabellastarte magnifica* Peacock featherduster worm

This spectacular terebellid worm enjoys a cosmopolitan distribution in the warm seas of the world. It constructs its mucilaginous tubes in coral rubble, between rocks and, less frequently, in sandy bottoms in shallow water 2.0–15.0 m (6°–50°) deep. It prefers areas of slight to moderate current, where its feeding mechanism can operate most effectively. This is a rather large species, whose tubes can reach 15.0 cm (6") in length. Crown diameter can range from 5.0–8.0 cm (2"–3.25"). Specimens are regularly exported from both the Caribbean and the tropical Indo-Pacific.

**The fully extended crown of *Sabellastarte magnifica*, the peacock featherduster worm.**

Peacock featherduster worms can either be attached to a tank's infrastructure or allowed to attach themselves to the substratum. They quickly secrete new tubes when placed in a novel environment. They dislike strong water movement and should be placed in a location well away from the filter's return flow. Lighting is not critical, although it often takes some time before newly introduced specimens feel sufficiently at ease to extend their crowns in a brightly lit environment. A temperature range of 20°–24° C. (70°–76° F.) suits this species well. Temperatures in excess of 28° C. (84° F.) are stressful and can cause individuals to shed their crowns. Such behavior can also occur as a result of a sudden change in water salinity, constant exposure to a strong current or harrassment by tankmates. Once the source of stress is removed, specimens typically regrow their tentacles.

In nature, these worms feed upon very fine plankton. In captivity, they will readily accept the same synthetic plankton formulations recommended for other sessile filter feeders as well as live *Brachionus* and *Artemia* nauplii.

Peacock featherduster worms do well in the company of other sessile filter feeding invertebrates, such as sponges and soft corals. Small brittle stars and sea cucumbers make suitable companions for them, as do small shrimp and hermit crabs. The latter tend to nibble on the worms' tubes if they become overgrown with algae, as do sea urchins. Only small, inoffensive fishes such as gobies, blennies, dottybacks and fairy basslets should be attempted as tankmates for these worms.

Order Sabellida Tubeworms

*Spirobranchus giganteus* Giant tubeworm

This spectacularly colored member of the Family Serpulidae occurs in appropriate habitats throughout the tropics. It is invariably found living upon live true corals, often encased by the calcareous skeleton of its chosen host. Corals of the large genus *Porites* are prefered substrata for this serpulid worm, as are the fire corals of the genus *Millepora*. The giant tubeworm is typically found in areas of moderate water movement to depths of 15.0 m (50'). As its crown tentacles measure only 2.0–3.0 cm (0.75"–1.25") in diameter, the common name of this species reflects the length of its calcareous tube, which can reach 12.0 cm (5"). The modest dimensions of the crown are compensated to a degree by the brilliant coloration of the tentacles. Aquarium specimens are typically of Far Eastern provenance.

Serpulid worms appreciate good water movement in captivity. They should be placed in a position where they enjoy a moderate current on all sides. If the base to which the worms are are attached at the time of purchase is living coral, the entire specimen must be placed in a very well lit tank. This species is particularly long-lived if the coral to which it is attached contains healthy living polyps. Conversely, it cannot be expected to prosper as its coral host declines and dies. Specimens attached to dead coral are not particular about lighting. Temperatures of 20°–24° C. (70°–76° F.) are acceptable. Those in excess of 28° C. (84° F.) are stressful and can eventually prove lethal.

The giant tubeworm will prosper on the same diet as *S. magnificus*. Although each worm can close off the entrance to its tube with a calcareous plug, the operculum, seruplids must contend with a large number of potential predators. Their companions must thus be chosen with as much care as would be the case for their larger – and presumably less well protected – relatives. With the exception of shrimps and spider crabs, the organisms recommended as tankmates for terebellids are suitable for these worms as well.

Great care must be taken to prevent the tubes of serpulid worms from drying out when moving them from one tank to another. The resulting damage to the tube does not seem ammenable to repair and usually results in the death of its inhabitant.

**Butterflyfish feed enthusiastically on both tube and featherduster worms both on the reef and in captivity.**

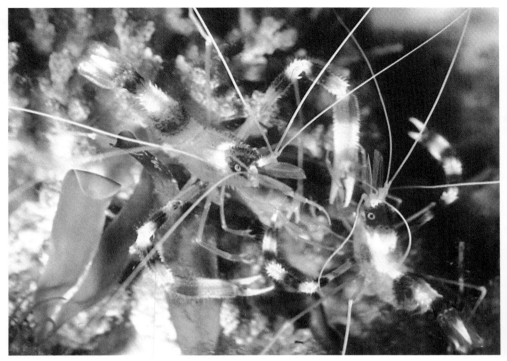

**A mated pair of banded coral shrimp,** Stenopus hispidus.

# Chapter 11.

# Mobile invertebrates in the Marine Aquarium

The phylla that constitute this group are sometimes known as the "higher" invertebrates because of their more complex body plans. As their description implies, these animals forage actively for food. From a practical standpoint, this means that their husbandry resembles that of fish more than it does that of the sessile taxa considered in Chapter 10. Like fish, they must be fed regularly and generate a waste load proportional to their mass. Their requirements for shelter must also be taken into account when setting up their quarters. With the exception of the tridacnid clams, which are more conveniently

grouped with other molluscs despite their sessile life style, none of these animals enjoys a symbiotic relationship with intracellular algae. Thus they will prosper in less intensely illuminated tanks than are required for many coelenterates. Furthermore, many of these invertebrates can hold their own successfully in the company of coral reef fishes. This recommends them highly to the aquarist who wishes to set up a mixed community tank.

The three phylla of mobile invertebrates of most interest to marine aquarists are the Mollusca (marine snails, nudibranchs, bivalves and octopi), the Arthropoda (mantis shrimps, true shrimps, prawns, coral lobsters and crabs) and the Echinodermata (sea urchins, starfish, brittle stars and sea cucumbers). As representatives of these major groups differ dramatically in overall appearance, life style and maintenance requirements, the remainder of this chapter will deal with each in turn. As in the previous chapter, the emphasis will be on representative species aquarists are most apt to encounter.

## Phyllum: Mollusca

Molluscs are unsegmented invertebrates characterized by a well-developed foot and a specialized organ, the mantle, that secretes a protective shell in most representatives of this group and functions as a propulsive organ in the others. Most molluscs have a well developed head and display bilateral symmetry. The exceptions to this pattern are the filter-feeding bivalves, which have lost a recognizable head and are secondarily asymmetrical as adults. Three of the phyllum's six known classes are of interest to aquarists. These differ so markedly in details of their anatomy and life style that each must subsequently be considered at greater length.

### Class: Gastropoda

The Gastropoda (Literally, "belly-foot"), include snails, which are protected by an external shell, and slugs, which carry a vestigal shell remnant internally. These animals have a well developed head, with eyes, sensory tentacles and a proboscis, or feeding organ equipped with a tooth-covered tongue-like structure known as a radula. As their name suggests, they propel themselves by means of a well-developed muscular foot. Most gastropods respire by means of gills; one subclass, the Pulmonata, which includes both terrestrial snails and slugs as well as all known freshwater gastropods, utilizes the mantle cavity as a lung.

The radula is an extremely efficient rasping structure that permits gastropods to utilize the widest range of food items of any molluscan class. Most terrestrial and freshwater gastropods are herbivorous, while most marine species feed upon other organisms. Many carnivorous snails, such as the numerous rock shells of the Family Muricidae can actually drill a hole right through the shells of other molluscs with their radulae. The most extreme example of radular specialization involves the cone shells. In *Conus*, the radular teeth are easily detached and have been modified to deliver a powerful neurotoxic poison that paralyzes the prey. This allows cone shells to successfully prey upon large, active animals such as fish. Because so many marine gastropods are predatory to a greater or lesser degree, great care must be taken when selecting their tankmates unless these are intended as a meal!

Two of the three gastropod orders of interest to marine aquarists, the Mesogastropoda and the Neogastropoda, are externally fertilizing **gonochorists**, each individual capable of functioning as either male or female, but not as both. The third order, the Nudibranchia, is characterized by Synchronous hermaphroditism, each individual capable of functioning as both male and female, and internal fertilization. Representatives of all three orders deposit their eggs in gelatinous egg cases, which may be guarded by the adult. The eggs develop into miniature version of the adult, by-passing the planktonic larval stage seen in some other molluscan groups. As this greatly simplifies the task of rearing the young, it comes as no surprise that a number of marine gastropods have been successfully bred by marine aquarists.

Order Mesogastropoda

Family Cypraeidae Cowries

Cowries have long been esteemed by shell collectors for their strikingly marked, porcelain-like shells. In life, the shell is almost totally covered by an extensive mantle that is often more colorful still. Cowries are usually inhabitants of shallow waters . They are often associated with algae-encrusted rocks and eel grass flats as well as reef habitats. Most are crepuscular or nocturnal feeders that usually take shelter under rocks or pieces of coral during the day.

*Cypraea tigris*, the tiger cowry and *C. mappa*, the map cowry are widely distributed throughout the Indo-Pacific region and can be considered as representative of this large assemblage of species. The tiger cowry is the larger of the two. Its shell measures up to 10.0 cm (4") long, and when extended, the

*Cypraea tigris,* the tiger cowry, is one of the commonest – and largest – Indo-Pacific cowry species.

An attractively marked Indo-Pacific species, the map cowry, Cypraea mappa.

head and mantle can add an additional 2.5 cm (1″) to these dimensions. The map cowry's shell rarely exceeds 8.0 cm (3.25″) in length, and its mantle is less voluminous than that of its larger congener. Both species are exported from the Far East, the tiger rather more often than the map cowry. The snake's head cowry, *C. caputserpentis*, is another Indo-Pacific species sometimes exported from Hawaii. The shell of this small cowry seldom exceeds 4.0 cm (1.75″) in length and the body of its inhabitant is scaled in proportion. *Cypraea cervus,* the deer cowry, is native to Florida and the Caribbean. Its slightly smaller

Pacific coast analog, *C. cervinetta,* is sometimes exported from the Gulf of California. Both are large cowries, with shells measuring 13.0 cm (5″) and 10.0 cm (4″) long respectively.

These are easily kept molluscs. Like all gastropods, they are rather massive animals and contribute significantly to a tank's waste load. Prudence thus dictates stocking them conservatively. As they tend to secrete substantial ammounts of mucus, an efficient protein skimmer greatly simplifies nitrogen cycle management in their aquaria. Tropical cowries prosper over a temperature range of

The snakehead cowry, *Cypraea caputserpentis,* a small species often exported from Hawaii.

20°–24° C. (70°–76° F.). Temperatures in excess of 28° C. (84° F.) quickly prove fatal. Subtropical and Mediterranean species should be kept a few degrees cooloer than their tropical analogs.

All cowries are essentially crepuscular/nocturnal organisms, but most will learn to feed during the day in tanks that are not too brightly lit. Their quarters should be well furnished with caves and overhangs to afford them daytime shelter. Though not as actively carnivorous as some other marine gastropods, they will graze on sponges, leather corals and other sessile invertebrates, particularly if encrusting algae are in short supply and their keeper happens to miss a few feedings. Cowries will also browse on *Caulerpa*. Their suitability for inclusion in Dutch minireef or similar systems that feature extensive growths of macroalgae and sessile invertebrates is thus at best debatable. Cowries should be offered fresh seafood regularly. Mussel meat on the half shell is particularly relished. They will also take TetraTips readily.

Although they are often found living as pairs in nature, there is no reason why these gastropods cannot be maintained as solitary specimens in captivity. Cowries are very suitable subjects for tanks dedicated to true and tube anemones. They also fit in well with shrimps, small hermit crabs and non-predatory echinoderms such as sea cucumbers, brittle stars and scavenger starfish. Large crabs, predatory molluscs and the larger, more voracious starfish will prey upon cowries. So will many large coral reef fish. Triggerfish, puffers and the larger wrasses can actually crack a cowry's shell with their formidable jaws. Large angelfish and small wrasses pick constantly at the mantle, effectively forcing the snail to remain withdrawn inside its shell as long as the tank is iluminated. Only small, inoffensive fishes, such as those recommended as suitable tankmates for sponges, should ever be kept with these gastropods.

If properly cared for, cowries will deposit their gelatinous egg cases in a sheltered spot in the aquarium. In nature, one or both parents often remain in the vicinity of the eggs, presumably to provide them with protection against predators. In captivity, the fate of the resulting larvae depends upon the availability of suitable food. In a Dutch mini-reef aquarium, the liklihood that its "living rock" will furnish a suitable food supply is sufficiently great that the survival of a few young would not be too surprising.

Family Ovulidae  Egg Shells or False Cowries

Ovulid snails superficially resemble cowries, to which they are closely related. All are carnivorous and most have very specialized feeding habits. The most frequently imported representative of this group is *Cyphoma gibbosum*, the flamingo tongue snail, a small mollusc whose shell rarely exceeds 2.5 cm (1") in length. This species feeds only on gorgonians. Its colorful mantle effectively camouflages it as it moves over the surface of its prey, providing it with considerable protection against its own predators.

The flamingo tongue has the same overall maintenance requirements as the cowries. However, it is much less suitable as an aquarium subject because of its specialized feeding habits. Contrary to popular belief, this snail will not graze upon algae. It **must** have access to live gorgonians or it will eventually starve to death. This process may take a while, as *C. gibbosum* can fast for long periods, but its outcome is inevitable. Unless he is prepared to sacrifice a thriving colony of

**Its attractive coloration nothwithstanding, the specialized dietary requirements of the flamingo tongue snail, *Cyphoma gibbosum*, make it a poor condidate for the marine aquarium.**

**A selection of Mediterranean murex shells, displaying a small range of the ornamentation that endears these gastropods to shell collectors and aquarists alike.**

these anthozoans to feed them, the aquarist should avoid purchasing these colorful trophic specialists.

Order Neogastropoda

Family Muricidae Murex, Rock or Purple Shells

The murex or rock shells are a large assemblage of carnivorous gastropods much prized by shell collectors because of their often elaborately sculpted shells The famous Tyrian purple dye of antiquity was made from the crushed bodies of several Mediterranean species, hence the third common name of purple shell applied to members of this group. Though some temperate zone species are known, muricids are most numerous in subtropical and tropical waters. Rock shells are in the main shallow water molluscs. The family has successfully colonized the full range of littoral habitats, from sand flats and eel grass beds through rocky shores to the reef itself.

Although specimens of such elaborately ornamented IndoPacific species as *Murex pecten*, the Venus' comb murex and *Hexaplex chicoreus* are sometimes exported from the Philippines, the rock shells most often available to North American aquarists are indigenous to the Gulf Coast and the Gulf of California respectively. *Phyllonotus pomum*, the apple murex, and *Chicoreus brevifrons*, the lace murex, can usually be had from Florida shippers, while the Gulf of California yields *Hexaplex erythrostoma*, the rosy murex and *Muriacanthus nigritus*, the back and white murex. Maximum recorded shell lengths for the apple and lace murices are 11.0 cm (4.5″) and 15.0 cm (6″) respectively. However, both have been exploited so heavily by shell collectors that it is unusual to find specimens more than half that size. The rosy murex and the black and white murex are both robust animals, with maximum recorded shell lengths of 10.0 cm (4″).

Rock shells prosper under the same conditions as do cowries, and like them, are fairly

The apple murex, *Phyllonotus pomum,* is a fairly common resident of the southern Atlantic and Gulf coasts of the United States.

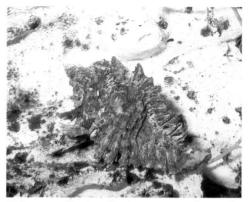

*Chicoreus dilectus,* the lace murex, shares the range of the apple murex.

straight-foward subjects for the invertebrate aquarium. Indo-Pacific species find a temperature range of 20°–26° C. (70°–78° F.) to their liking. Species from the Gulf of Mexico and the Gulf of California prefer somewhat cooler water and should not be kept warmer than 24° C. (76° F.). Most muricids are crepuscular feeders, so their quarters need not be brilliantly lit.

Murex shells are easily fed. Though all are highly efficient predators in nature, they will also feed upon carrion when the opportunity presents itself. Hence pieces of frozen shellfish or fish are eagerly taken in captivity.

TetraTips are also well received, and fresh clam or mussel on the halfshell are special treats. It suffices to offer muricids a small feeding every two or three days.

In nature, rock shells feed chiefly upon other molluscs. using their radulae to drill through the shells of their prey. Bivalves are the prefered food of most species, but in captivity, many species will also attack other gastropods – including conspecifics – and, when sufficiently hungry, will go after sabellid and terebellid worms as well. Unless they are intended as murex fodder, none of these animals should be housed in the same tank as

The rosy murex, *Muriacanthus fulvescens,* a large muricid native to the Pacific coast of Mexico and Central America.

*Fasciollaria lilium Phyllonotus pomum* feeding on *Melongena.*

The egg cases of several different murex species.

rock shells. The animals that prey upon cowries will also attack rock shells, so their presence in the same aquarium is also contraindicated. Sponges and coelenterates are ignored by these molluscs. They in turn are not usually bothered by the sort of small, inoffensive crustaceans and fishes that can be housed with the generality of sessile invertebrates.

Well-fed muricids will often deposit long strings of gelatinous egg cases. These yield substantial numbers of miniature rock shells whose rearing is a fairly straightfoward matter, as they will eat the same food items as their progenitors. They also eat one another with considerable relish, so it is unusual for more than one or two individuals to attain a reasonable size under aquarium conditions.

## Family Conidae Cone Shells

Cone shells are a primarily tropical assemblage of species with a few species penetrating subtropical habitats in both the northern and southern hemispheres. These predatory gastropods are famed both for their beautifully patterned shells and their remarkable feeding apparatus. The radula of a cone shell is modified not to rasp away at food but rather to pierce prey animals with a harpoonlike, venom-bathed tooth. All *Conus* produce an extraordinarily potent neurotoxin that paralazyes their prey and allows them to ingest it whole. Like rock shells, *Conus* have colonized a wide range of coastal marine

habitats. However, most of the species available to aquarists are found over rocky shores or on the reef proper in water less than 5.0 m (16′) deep.

Cone shells can be divided into three groups according to their feeding preferences. By far the largest number of species for which dietary data are available feed upon marine worms. Smaller numbers specialize upon other molluscs and fishes respectively. *Conus* are as a rule extremely specifc in their food preferences. This is the only factor that makes it possible to even consider keeping cone shells in a community aquarium. However, when extremely hungry, some piscivorous species have been onserved to attack marine worms. Thus even knowing a given

*Conus textile,* a beautiful and widely distributed Indo-Pacific species responsible for several documented human fatalities from stings provoked by careless handling.

154

**Prey capture and ingestion by *Conus purpurescens*, a piscovorous cone shell native to the Pacific coast of Mexico.**

species' trophic guild does not always allow one to predict with complete accuracy how it will behave toward's a tank's other residents. Of the Indo-Pacific species episodically imported, *C. abbreviatus, C. eburneus, C. generalis, C. imperialis* and *C. virgo* are vermivorous, *C. aulicus, C. marmoreus* and *C. textile* are mollusc eaters and *C. geographus, C. striatus* and *C. tulipa* are piscivorous. The three species available from Florida, *C. floridanus, C. regius* and *C. spurius* feed on worms. Of the *Conus* sometimes exported from the Gulf of California, *C. princeps* is vermivorous, *C. dalli* feeds on mol-luscs and *C. purpurascens* takes fish. The dietary preferences of only a few score of the 1500 nominal species of *Conus* are known. See the list of recommended readings for further sources of information.

Apart from the problems that their predatory life style poses their keeper in his selection of suitable tankmates, cone shells are easily maintained. Their overall maintenance requirements are like those of the other molluscs thus far considered, and as was suggested for rock shells, subtropical species should be kept a few degrees cooler than their tropical congeners.

*Conus marmoreus,* a robust mollusc-eating species native to the Indo-Pacific.

Most aquarists inadvertently wind up offering their cone shells live food. Given both that prey appear to be located exclusively by chemical cues and that *Conus* are sometimes taken in baited traps, there seems no reason not to try offering mollusc and fish eaters a diet of fresh clam, scallop and mussel flesh in the first instance and fish in the second. Aquarists living on the coast will find it easiest to satisfy the dietary needs of vermivorous species with the nereid worms sold in bait shops, but at present, there is no convenient substitute food for these cone shells available away from the sea.

*Conus* obviously should not be kept together with their prefered prey items unless these are intended as live food. The simple fact that a given mollusc or fish is too large for a given cone shell to ingest does not guarantee its safety. When very hungry, *Conus* will attack and kill fish or molluscs to large for them to eat. While it might appear that their venom apparatus would confer effective immunity from attack upon these snails in captivity, it would probably be unwise to try housing them with large crabs, predatory starfish or triggerfish. Cone shells do well in the company of coelenterates and sponges, and as carnivores, they pose no threat to *Caulerpa* or other macroalgae.

Cone shells can be dangerous to humans. This suggests that these otherwise easily maintained gastropods are best left to the attentions of experienced marine invertebrate keepers. Deaths have been attributed to the stings of *Conus aulicus, C. marmoreus, C. striatus, C. textile* and *C. geographus*. The last species alone is responsible for over a dozen fatalities. Strikes often followed attempts by shell collectors to scrape the protective periostracum, or outer coating of the shell away to secure a better view of their treasure. Other collecters were stung through the mesh of a canvas or cloth bag slung over their shoulder or hung from their waist. Both mollusc-eating (*C. aulicus, C. marmoreus, C. textile*) and piscivorous (*C. geographus, C. striatus*) species have demonstrated lethal abilities. It has been suggested that the less sharply pointed radular teeth of vermivorous species render them potentially less dangerous to humans. In view of the large size of many representatives of this trophic guild, a prudent person would be reluctant to put this hypothesis to the test.

In the light of current knowledge of the biology of cone shells, it is impossible to predict the potential of a given species to deliver a fatal sting on the basis of its feeding pattern. Nor is it always clear what factors elicit a strike. ALL *Conus* WITH A SHELL LENGTH IN EXCESS OF 5.0 cm (2″) SHOULD BE ASSUMED CAPABLE OF DELIVERING A FATAL STING AND HANDLED ACCORD INGLY! NEVER PICK UP A LIVE CONE SHELL BARE-HANDED! In the event of a sting, seek IMMEDIATE medical assistance.

A large fish-eating species form the Indo-Pacific, *Conus geographus.* This species has also killed a number of persons who mishandled living specimens.

Order Nudibrancha Nudibranchs or Sea Slugs

As implied by both their scientific and common names, these molluscs lack external shells and carry their gills externally. This somewhat unflattering description fails utterly to convey the extraordinary grace and dazzling coloration of these distinctive marine gastropods. The nearly 4500 described nudibranchs are divided into four suborders, of which the Doridacea furnishes the majority of aquaristically interesting species. The doridoid nudibranchs imported as aquarium subjects are representatives of two families, the Chromodorididae and the Glossodorididae.

These gastropods can be found in all the world's seas. Unlike many other marine molluscs, nudibranchs can boast an impressive assemblage of brilliantly colored cold-water species. The Pacific coast of North America is particularly blessed with beautiful nudibranchs. Nudibranchs can be found in just about any marine biotope, but the species commonly available to aquarists are shallow water inhabitants of eel grass beds, rocky shores and the coral reef proper.

It is possible that the vivid hues flaunted by these seemingly vulnerable gastropods are intended to advertise their extreme unpalatability. Most nudibranchs feed upon coelenterates. Not only do they manage this without getting fatally stung – in itself no mean feat – but in the process they manage to transport the intact nematocysts of their prey to their own dorsal surface. Thus armed with captured weaponry, these nudibranchs are very effectively protected against the attentions of most predators. Species that brows on algae, byrozoans or sponges defend themselves by producing copious quantities of unpalatable mucus.

Nudibranchs are somewhat fussier about water quality than the other gastropods discussed herein. They can be expected to prosper under the same conditions that satisfy the needs of soft corals. Water temperatures are particularly critical for nudibranchs. Tropical species will do well over a temperature range of 20°–24° C. (70°–76° F.). Subtropical species should not be kept warmer than 22° C. (74° F.). Higher temperatures seem to trigger spawning, which is followed by the death of the adult animal(s). This tendency precludes the successful maintenance of cold-water species in aquaria unless their keeper is willing to invest in a cooling unit or else follow the practice of many aquarists in California who collect specimens in the fall and maintain a "winter aquarium" of native nudibranchs.

The chief obstacle to the successful culture of nudibranchs is their specialized feeding behavior. Although a few species take a mixed diet of algae and minute rock-encrusting organisms such as byrozoans, the overwhelming majority feed upon live coelenterates. As with cone shells, nudibranchs can be

*Chromodoris quadricolor,* a sponge-eating nudibranch browsing upon its food of choice.

This lovely but unidentified representative of the family *Glossodorididae* is feeding on bryozoans.

*Chromodoris annulata*

**The exposed external tuft of gill filaments from which nudibranchs derive their name is clearly visible on this unidentified chromodoridid species.**

apportioned to one of a number of feeding guilds, whose members specialize in anemones, gorgonians, soft corals and true corals. As they are disinclined to switch to alternative prey, nudibranchs can be kept successfully only if the aquarist is willing to provide them with the appropriate prey items. It thus pays to ascertain a given nudibranch's feeding pattern from one's dealer before taking it home. There is little point in purchasing an animal merely to watch it slowly starve to death.

Providing a suitable diet for captive nudibranchs may entail nothing more than liberally furnishing a tank with "living rock" and allowing nature to take its course. Alternatively, it may be necessary to purchase the appropriate live foods for them. In the latter case, it makes sense to maintain only those nudibranchs that will feed on live anemones. These are readily available at a moderate

price, which is more than can be said for soft or true corals and gorgonians!

The suitability of any given nudibranch as a tankmate for coelenterates or sponges depends entirely upon its feeding pattern. It is obviously impractical to try keeping predator and prey together unless the latter is meant as a food supply for the former. Despite their formidable defenses, nudibranchs are themselves preyed upon by other molluscs and predatory echinoderms. Any fish that feeds upon coelenterates is also unlikely to be detered by a nudibranch's borrowed nematocysts from trying a few mouthfuls of sea slug sushi. Nudibranchs can be kept with featherduster and tube worms without incident and also appear to get along well with the smaller shrimps and prawns. Any fish that make suitable tankmates for sponges can probably be kept safely with nudibranchs.

As already noted, nudibranchs are hermaph-

**The psychedelic color pattern of many nudibranchs serves to warn potential predators of their distastefulness.**

**This beautiful chromodoridid species is another sponge eater.**

**The flamboyantly colored *Facelina iodinea* with its egg vases.**

todites. Each individual can function as both male and female, although only towards another individual of the same species. It does not appear to be anatomically possible for nudibranchs to fertilize their own eggs. Fertilization is internal and the ability of many species to deposit fertile eggs in isolation suggests that they can store sperm for considerable periods of time following copulation. Though nudibranchs often deposit egg cases in captivity, there are no reports of successful rearing of the resulting larvae. This probably is due to the unavailability of appropriate food. In a Dutch mini-reef set-up liberally furnished with "living rock" collected from their native habitats, nudibranchs might have a much better chance of completing their life cycle successfully.

Class Bivalvia

Bivalves have diverged greatly from the basic molluscan body plan. The body is laterally compressed, the head is absent and a greatly enlarged mantle hangs down on both sides of the internal organs. The body is enclosed by a hinged shell whose paired valves are connected by a ligament that tends to pull them apart. The animal can only close its shells by the exertion of specialized aductor muscles. The foot is greatly enlarged and used in the majority of species to burrow into soft substrata, although many familiar bivalves live attached to rocks or similar solid surfaces and both rock-boring and free-swimming species are known. Most bivalves are filter-feeders, using their greatly expanded gills to remove fine detritus and microplankton from suspension.

The majority of bivalves are gonochorists, but a few hermaphroditic forms are known. In most species, fertilization is external, but in some instances, the eggs are retained within a special pouch adjacent to the female's gill chamber known as the marsupium. Here they are fertilized and undergo their initial period of development. These bivalves bypass the trochophore larval stage of externally fertilizing species and expel clouds of more advanced veliger larvae instead.

Relatively few bivalves are maintained as aquarium residents. This probably reflects the preponderance of burrowing forms within the group. Most aquarists see little point in keeping animals that are never to be seen. Not suprisingly, the few species that are of interest to marine aquarists are either attached of free-swimming forms.

Order Filibranchia

*Lima scabra* Red file shell

The file shells of the genus *Lima* are found in all the world's warm seas. The group's common name refers to the rough exterior surface of the paired valves. The species most widely available to aquarists, *L. scabra*, is native to the Caribbean, where it can be found tucked away in crannies between colonies of sessile anthozoans, usually in well-shaded portions of the reef. File shells measure about 5.0 cm (2″) long and slightly less than that across their shell. They moor themselves in place with threads of an adhesive material known as byssus. However, in the face of danger, they can release these anchors and swim away, like the related scallops of the Family Pectenidae. The most striking feature of this mollusc are its magnificent red mantle filaments. These structures are covered with highly sensitive chemosensory cells that allow the file shell to "taste" starfish – their main predators – up to 30.0 cm (1′) away. This usually affords it plenty of time to cut loose from the bottom and swim out of danger.

**A fine specimen of the red file shell, *Lima scabra*.**

File shells require the same sort of water conditions as sponges and soft corals. A temperature of 20°–24° C. (70°–76° F.) suits them well. Temperatures of 28° C. (84° F.) or more must be avoided. *Lima* have no special light requirements. They prefer shady locations but can be kept in brightly lit tanks so long as they are afforded appropriate refuges.

Most *Lima* starve to death because aquarists do not appreciate the necessity of offering them regular feedings of either live microplankton or the sort of plankton substitute recommended for sponges and soft corals. For this reason, file shells are best kept in a comunity of sessile plankton feeding companions such as sabellid and terebellid worms, sessile anthozoans and sponges. Even small fish and shrimps will pick at their mantle filaments, so such companions are not recommended. Obviously, predatory molluscs, large crustaceans, predatory starfish and mollusc-eating fishes are totally unsuitable as tankmates.

Order Eulamellibranchia

*Tridacna maxima* Giant clam

Tridacnids are the largest living bivalves. Adults of several species can measure 1.5 m (c. 5°) across their shell and weigh almost half a ton. Fortunately for invertebrate enthusiasts, captive specimens grow slowly and seldom exceed 15.0 cm (6″) in width! They are restricted to the tropical Indo-Pacific, where they are typically found in shallow water on the reef top. They attach themselves this close to the surface in order for the symbiotic algae present in their mantle tissue to enjoy the brightest illumination possible. *Tridacna maxima* is native to the entire Indo-Pacific region, *T. squamosa* is restricted to the central Indo-Pacific, while *T. crocea* is native to the Indian Ocean. All three species are exported by Far Eastern collectors.

Giant clams should be sited no more than 20.0 cm (8″) from the surface of the water. Like soft corals, they should never be placed directly on the substratum of an aquarium, as they are susceptible to bacterial attack that causes them to rot from their lower side up. Depending upon the species, giant clams are attached to their substratum by a fleshy stalk or a cluster of byssus threads. They must never be forcibly detached from the substratum, as this can lead to injuries that easily become secondarily infected. Giant clams must have moderate to strong water movement in order to prosper. As with all other invertebrates with algal symbionts, tridacnids require this brightest possible illumination in captivity. They can be expected to do well under the same conditions that suite green organ pipe coral.

**The colorful mantle of this young *Tridacna* sp. owes its vivid hues to the presence of symbiotic zooxanthellae in its superficial cells.**

Despite the presence of zooxanthellae in their mantles, giant clams require regular feedings of live microplankton or plankton substitute to survive and proper in captivity. It is best to deliver food offerings directly to the siphons using the sort of feeding apparatus described in Chapter 10. Two or three light feedings weekly are recommended for hand-sized or smaller specimens.

With the sole exception of tube anemones, giant clams can be safely housed with all sessile anthozoans. They also mix well with sponges and sessile, filter feeding worms. Non-predatory echinoderms and small shrimps are suitable tankmates, although in the long run, shrimps other than the commensal *Conchodytes meleagrinae* seem to have a disturbing effect upon tridacnids. The fish that make suitable companions for sponges are likewise suited for a tank containing giant clams. Large coral reef fish, particularly those with powerful jaws such as triggerfish and the bigger wrasses, should never be kept with giant clams. Large crustaceans, carnivorous molluscs and predatory starfish are also inappropriate companions for these robust but vulnerable bivalves.

Properly cared-for giant clams will sometimes release numbers of veliger larvae into the aquarium. They are large enough to be visible to the naked eye and can be seen propelling themselves through the water with a specialized structure, the vellum. Though their size suggests that they might be reared successfully through metamorphosis and settling, efforts along these lines have not to date proven successful. Perhaps a more satisfactory outcome in aquaria result were tridacnids to be maintained in a Dutch mini-reef system.

## Class Cephalopoda

The literal translation of Cephalopoda is "head-foot" and refers to the most salient feature of this group of molluscs. The foot has migrated from its primitive ventral position and instead surrounds the head with a crown of manipulatory tentacles. The proboscis has been replaced with a powerful horny beak, but like gastropods, cephalopods have a well-developed radula. In comparison with other molluscs, cephalopods have extremely well-developed vision and a highly sophisticated central nervous system. Extant species are characterized by extremely complex behavior, including a capacity for learning from experience and a well-developed memory.

Most extinct cephalopods possessed external shells. The only extant member of the class so equipped is the chambered nautilus, *Nautilus macrophalus*, a deep-water Indo-Pacific species. The remaining living cephalopods either carry a vestigal internal remanant of the shell, the so-called pen (Order Sepiida, cuttlefish and squid), or totally lack any trace of a shell (Order Octopodida, optopi). All living cepahlopods are highly mobile. Squid can easily match even pelagic fish in swimming ability, and while octopi spend most of their time crawling agilely over the bottom, when the necessity arises, they too are capable of high-speed bursts of jet-propelled locomotion when they squirt the contents of their mantle cavity through their siphon tubes. Squid and octopi have two further peciliarities that help them to survive in a hostile environment. They can change their color to match their background, an ability that is also used to communicate in social interactions, and they can release a plume of dark ink that appears to fix a predator's attention while its intended victim slips away unnoticed. The second of these two defense mechanisms can complicate the husbandry of these molluscs in a closed system.

Cephalopods are all internally fertilizing gonochorists. In males, one of the arms has been modified into a specialized copulatory structure, the heterocotyle, which breaks off and remains inside the female with its sperm packet after intromission. The large, yolky stalked eggs are deposited on solid surfaces and develop directly into miniature versions of the adult. Neither nautiloids nor sepiids afford any care to their eggs, but all octopi are characterized by well-developed parental behavior.

Although cuttlefish and, more recently, chambered nautilus, are sometimes available through commercial channels, neither is a very satisfactory subject for any save the most experienced marine aquarist. Octopi, on the other hand, are quite easily kept, and unlike the generality of invertebrates, quickly learn to relate to their keeper in much the same manner as the generality of coral reef fish.

Order Octopodida  Octopi

*Octopus joubanii* Dwarf Octopus

This species lives up to its common name – it is unusual to find individuals with a tentacle spread in excess of 20.0 cm (8") and the great majority of specimens imported measure no more than 15.0 cm (6") across. The dwarf octopus is native to the Gulf Coast and the Caribbean. This factor, as much as its diminutive size, explains its ready avaialability to North American aquarists. It is typically found over rocky bottoms or on the reef proper in water less than 5.0 m (16') deep. The common octopus, *O. vulgaris*, which has a world-wide distribution in temperate and subtropical waters, is a considerably larger species, capable of attaining a tentacle spread of nearly a meter (c. 3") and an average weight of 5.0 kg (c. 25 lbs). This is the octopus most generally available to European aquarists, but specimens exported from the Gulf of California sometimes find their way into the tanks of North American hobbyists. Though juveniles make satisfactory aquarium residents, adult common octopus generate a waste load beyond the capacity of most home aquarium filtration systems to handle. They are thus best left to the attentions of public aquaria.

The dwarf octopus is no more demanding about water quality than the majority of coral reef fishes. In nature, these cephalopods are crepuscular or nocturnal feeders. However, they will quickly learn to feed in the daytime as long as their tank is not too brightly lit. A temperature range of 20°–24° C. (70°–76° F.) suits the dwarf octopus well. The common octopus prefers water a few degrees cooler.

Life all octopi, *O. joubanii* is adamant on the subject of suitable shelter. In nature, these cephalopods invest a great deal of time and energy in constructing a permanant burrow from which they emerge to forage. Deprived of the wherewithal to construct a comparable refuge in captivity, an octopus spends its entire time trying to escape from the aquarium or else has the cephalopod equivalent of a nervous breakdown. Such "bent" individuals often go into catatonic withdrawal, refuse to eat, and die.

As octopi prefer to construct their own shelters, the easiest way to satisfy this need is to provide a captive specimen with a few pieces of CPVC pipe or small clay flowerpots and a double handful of small rocks, shells and coral fragments. It will quickly select a suitable site and display remarkable skill in constructing its fortress from the materials at hand.

Once it feels secure in its shelter, an octopus will explore the full extent of its aquarium with great thoroughness. This curiosity often leads to tragedy, for an octopus is not likely to limit its explorations to the interior of the tank. Octopi are much given to leaving their quarters, behavior that more often than not leads to their premature demise. Because their beaks are the only rigid structures they possess, octopi can force their bodies through the minutest cracks and openings. Beside the ability of an octopus to escape what seems to humans a totally secure aquarium, the feats of Harry Houdini pale to insignificance.

**The Caribbean dwarf octopus, *Octopus joubanii,* adapts well to life in captivity.**

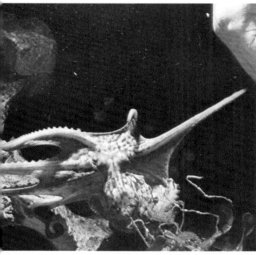
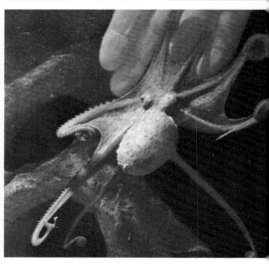
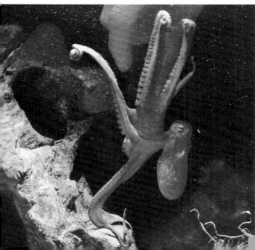

A young common octopus, *Octopus vulgaris,* interacting with its keeper. Octopi are extremely intelligent animals and make excellent pets.

The only way to prevent such outbreaks of octopodal wanderlust is to seal any openings between the cover and frame of an octopus tank with silicone elastic sealant. Comparable care must be taken to secure entry points for aquarium appliances and air lines, while the hinged section of the tank cover normally lifted at feeding time should be weighted down with a large rock or brick. To employ such elaborate security measures against a 15.0 cm long mollusc may seem a classic exercise in overkill. Nevertheless, the aquarist who neglects their implementation will sooner or later have to devise a use for a mummified octopus!

In nature, octopi are efficient predators, seizing prey with their tentacles and using their beaks to deliver an envenomed bite that quickly renders it immobile. The bites of most species are at the worst mildly irritating to humans, but the beautiful blue-ringed octopus, *Haplochlaena maculosa*, and its congeners can inject a potent neurotoxin that effectively paralyzes the respiratory muscles and can lead to death from suffocation unless the victim is promptly given artificial respiration. Octopi will also feed on carrion in the wild, so while periodic offerings of live crabs and shrimp, their favorite foods, are certainly relished, captive individuals quickly learn to accept small pieces of thawed shellfish or fish as dietary staples. It takes very little time for a captive specimen to associate its keeper with the appearance of food. With a little patience, it is quite possible for an aquarist to teach an octopus to take food from between his fingers. Compared to most marine invertebrates, octopi are quite active animals and should be given a small feeding daily.

The efficient predatory behavior of octopi severely limits the aquarist in his selection of suitable tankmates. First of all, these cephalopods are solitary and territorial in nature. They do not tolerate the close presence of other octopi. As the largest tanks customarily available to amateur aquarists barely meet the territorial expectations of the dwarf octopus, it is obviously not a good idea to try housing several specimens together. Crustaceans of any sort and shelled molluscs are simply treated as offerings of live food by a resident octopus. Small fish in an octopus tank are also poor risks for life insurance, while such large coral reef fishes as angels, triggerfish, puffers, groupers and morays are notably partial to octopus sushi. Octopi respond to such attacks by discharging a cloud of ink that can seriously pollute the tank's water. It is thus clearly in the interest of both its keeper and an aquarium's other inhabitants that a captive octopus be spared any harrassment. Apart from giant clams, sessile plankton-feeding invertebrates are ignored by octopi and along with echinoderms, seem to make the best companions for them.

A significant percentage of the *O. joubanii* collected for sale during the late winter and early spring are gravid females. Within a short time of their introduction to an aquarium, these individuals deposit several hundred eggs on the roof and sides of their shelter, thus affording their keeper the chance to observe the group's highly developed parental behavior. The female not only keeps predators away from the spawn, but cleans and aerates it continually. During the entire interval of brood care, the female will not accept food, grows steadily thinner, and immediately after her young have hatched, dies. This behavior is under direct glandular control and short of surgical intervention, is irreversible. Males are somewhat

**The bite of the blue-ringed octopus, *Haplochlaena maculosa*, can be fatal to a careless human. Attractive coloration notwithstanding, it cannot be recommended as an aquarium resident.**

longer lived, but their average lifespan is also quite short, a bare two years.

Newly hatched dwarf octopi are miniature versions of their parents and large enough to immediately go out and mug an adult brine shrimp for lunch. The aquarist who has on-going access to adult *Artemia* and who can supplement such offerings with small amphiopods or mysids, harvested either from the sea shore or from a tank with a well-established collection of "living rock" has a very good chance of rearing a few hatchlings to the point where they can take non-living foods. For additional information of rearing dwarf octopi in captivity, see the references cited in the final chapter.

Phyllum Arthropoda

Class Crustacea

The arthropods comprise a very large assemblage of invertebrates characterized by a segmented body plan, a chitinous exoskeleton composed of discrete plates and jointed appendages used for locomotion, feeding, sensory purposes and copulation. Some degree of the group's success can be obtained from the simple observation that over 80% of all living animals are members of the phyllum Arthropoda. Of the ten classes into which the living arthropods are divided, only one, the Crustacea, is of interest to marine aquarists.

Although both terrestrial and fresh water crustaceans are known, this class enjoys its greatest representation in marine habitats. All crustaceans have, at some point in their life history, two pairs of antennae, three pairs of specialized limbs that function as mouthparts, gills and a chitinous carapace. They are further subdivided into eight subclasses, largely on the basis of the degree of specialization displayed in their overall body plan and limb anatomy. While representatives of such subgroups as the Branchiopoda (brine shrimps, water fleas) and the Copepoda (copepods) play an important role in the diet of fishes and other marine organisms, only the Malacostraca is of direct concern to hobbyists. This large subclass comprises 19 orders, of which two, the Stomatopoda (mantis shrimps) and the Decapoda (shrimps, prawns, lobsters and crabs) provide subjects suitable for the marine aquarium.

A peculiarity of all crustaceans dictated by their anatomy is the necessity to molt, or shed their old exoskeleton, in order to grow. Copulation is only possible immediately after molting, a fact that may explain why so many sedentary crustaceans live as sexual pairs and the males of more active species attempt to sequester ready to molt females. Until their new carapace hardens, crustaceans are extremely vulnerable to predation. Thus most non-pelagic species seek out some sort of shelter when molting and the territorial behavior of stomatopods and many decapods appears to have evolved as a mechanism to secure a safe molting site. **Under aquarium conditions, it is absolutely essential to provide an abundance of shelter for its crustacean inhabitants lest they be literally eaten alive after molting by tankmates too small to normally pose them any threat.**

Order Stomatopoda  Mantis Shrimps

*Odontodactylus scyllaris* Peacock mantis shrimp

*Hemisquilla ensigera californiensis* Panamic mantis shrimp

Mantis shrimps derive their name from the resemblance between their highly modified forelimbs and those of the terrestrial praying mantises. These dactyls, sometimes known as the **raptorial**, or hunting appendages, are employed by stomatopods to capture their prey. Though a few species can be found in temperate and subtropical waters, the majority of mantis shrimps are inhabitants of the tropics. Although they exhibit a number of primitive structural features, these crustaceans are active and formidable predators that construct a permanant burrow from which they emerge to forage for food. Stomatopods can be found in a wide range of habitats, from sandy bottoms at depths of a hundred meters to rocky tidepools less than

The common name of *Odontodactylus scyllaris*, the peacock mantis shrimp, comes from the color pattern of its telson, or tail segment.

30.0 cm (1°) deep. Many tropical species find the transitional zone between sandy bottoms and isolated patch reefs an attractive place to excavate their retreats.

Mantis shrimps may be divided into two feeding guilds on the basis of how they capture their food. **Spearers** feed chiefly upon marine worms, other crustaceans and fish. As their name implies, they impale their prey with their raptorial apprendages, which are typically long, pointed and well barbed. The popular *Odontodactylus scyllaris* is a 30.0 cm (12″) long, brilliantly colored spearer widely distributed throughout the Indo-Pacific. **Smashers** feed upon such hard shelled prey as molluscs and large crabs. They employ the enlarged "heels" of the dactyls as hammers to smash open their prey. *Hemisquilla ensigera californiensis* is a colorful smasher native to the west coast of Mexico sometimes exported from the Gulf of California.

The strike of a stomatopod's raptorial appendage is one of the fastest movements in the animal kingdom. Velocities in excess of 10.0 m (34°)/second have been recorded for the larger spearers. The force behind such a blow is awesome. The impact of a strike by even a moderate-sized smasher is compar-able to that of a small-caliber bullet. A specimen no more than 10.0 cm (4″) in length can crack a panel of a glass aquarium with ease. The abilities of *Hemisquilla ensigera californiensis*, which grows to 25.0 cm (10″), can well be imagined! As captive stomatopods sometimes react to an overly inquisitive observer with a defensive strike, the merits of housing smashers in acrylic aquaria and moving them from tank to tank in polyethelyne containers are self-evident.

Mantis shrimp in general, and smashers in particular, are known to commercial shrimp fishermen, who frequently must remove them from their nets, as "thumb-splitters". Large specimens can even strike through a protective glove when provoked. Two practical instructions to stomatopod keepers follow from these observations. First of all, **ALWAYS** use a net and probe to capture mantis shrimp. These crustaceans invariably strike when cornered. Quite apart from the pain associated with alternative approaches, bleeding into the aquarium unnecessarily complicates nitrogen cycle management! Second, **NEVER** hand-feed stomatopods. Mantis shrimp have excellent eyesight and clearly represent the apex of crustacean intellection.

However, simple prudence suggests the question of whether their behavioral programming affords them sufficient motivation to discriminate between a morsel of food and the fingers that hold it is best left unanswered.

Like the other crustaceans covered herein, mantis shrimps are relatively straightfoward aquarium subjects provided care is taken to maintain high water quality. They go easily into shock if there is any difference in chemical make-up between the water of their old and new homes. Hence they should be acclimated to a new aquarium even more gradually than coral reef fish. They are indifferent to light intensity and prosper over a temperature range of 20°–26° C. (70°–78° F.).

Like octopi, stomatopods are compulsive in their drive to construct a secure refuge. They seem less inclined to accept flowerpots or similar artificial structures as the basis of their efforts, preferring to dig a burrow under a rock or coral head. The simplest means of satisfying this need for shelter is to offer a captive specimen a double handful of small rocks and empty shells and allow nature to take its course.

Mantis shrimp are not fussy eaters. While they obviously prefer live food, they quickly learn to take pieces of fish or shellfish as well as TetraTips. Established specimens soon learn to "beg" for food and when these efforts go unrewarded, often vent their frustration by striking the walls of their aquarium. This behavior affords yet another reason for keeping smashers in plastic tanks! Stomatopods are sufficiently active to warrant a daily feeding.

Stomatopods, like octopi, are poor community aquarium risks. Theoretically, spearers can be safely housed with hard-shelled tankmates and smashers will ignore fish. In practice, captive specimens often prove disconcertingly broad-minded in their selection of prey. Mantis shrimp ignore sessile anthozoans, sponges and filter-feeding worms and seem trustworthy towards echinoderms. **NEVER** try housing more than a single mantis shrimp per tank! The largest tanks available to amateur aquarists are too small to meet the territorial requirements of even a single large stomatopod.

Female mantis shrimps will often spawn large egg masses, which they carry beneath their walking legs. Such "berried" females are even more aggressive than usual and are best left strictly alone until the eggs have hatched. As stomatopods are gonochorists, the production of fertile eggs by such isolated

With its modified raptorial appendages, the Panamic mantis shrimp, *Hemisquilla ensigera californica,* can smash the densest of mollusc shells and annihilate any other crustaceans it might encounter.

specimens suggests an ability to store sperm for considerable periods of time. The nauplius larvae resulting from such spawns have not to date been cultured successfully in captivity.

Order Decapoda Shrimps, prawns, lobsters and crabs

Representatives of this order derive their name from the possession of five pairs of legs on the thorax, or middle body segment. The anteriormost pair is modified to permit the capture or manipulation of food, while the remaining four pairs are used in locomotion. The well-developed senses and nervous system of decapods permit considerable behavioral complexity. All marine species have complex life histories, characterized by several discrete larval stages. These often differ so markedly from the adult that many were originally described as separate species.

Decapods are divided into two suborders. The Natantia ("swimmers") comprises shrimps and prawns. These crustaceans have poorly developed **chelae**, or pincers, on their anterior pair of limbs, but well developed **pleopods** or swimming legs, on their abdomens. Prawns are somewhat more laterally compressed than shrimp and have a longer **rostrum**, the snout-like projection that juts foward between their stalked eyes. The Reptantia ("crawlers") are dorsoventrally flattened crustaceans with heavy body armor and well-developed chelae. Overall, they grow much larger than do shrimps or prawns, a fact that makes them poorer swimmers despite the presence of well-developed pleopods in many genera. In lobsters, the abdomen is as long as, or longer than the cephalothorax, whereas in crabs, it is much smaller. Both suborders are generously endowed with small, brilliantly colored representatives that make outstanding additions to any marine aquarium.

A behavioral peculiarity of many decapod crustaceans is extreme sensitivity to abrupt increases in ambient light levels. Many shrimps display an almost convulsive reaction if the lights in their aquarium are suddenly turned on after an interval of darkness. Such "light shock" can even result in mortalities. Always make a point of turning on the room lights a few minutes before illuminating a marine community containing these crustaceans. This courtesy will be appreciated by the tank's other residents too.

*Stenopus hispidus* Banded coral shrimp

The banded coral shrimp is the most widely distributed representative of the genus *Stenopus*, occuring in all the tropical seas of the world. Sometimes as boxer shrimps, because of the aggressive manner in which they hold their well-developed chelae, *Stenopus* are common inhabitants of the coral reef from depths of 2.0 m (6″) downwards. They live as pairs in caves or under overhanging ledges, with only their protruding, white, constantly waving antennae signalling their presence. Banded coral shrimp are one of a number of small crustaceans that make their living by removing parasites and dead tissue from reef fishes. Their conspicuously displayed antennae serve to advertise the presence of a cleaning station to potential customers.

With a body length of 7.5 cm (3″) and anterior limbs almost as long, the banded coral shrimp is one of the giants of the genus. The yellow backed coral shrimp, *S. scutellatus*, a species often exported from the Caribbean, in contrast, measures barely 3.5 cm (1.5″)

**Although differently marked, *Stenopus cyanoscelis* is quite as attractive as its better known congener, *S. hispidus*.**

An attractive Ind-Pacific coral shrimp, *Stenopus seutellatus*.

*Thor amboinensis,* another frequently exported Indo-Pacific coral shrimp.

long. *Stenopus cyanoscelis, S. devaneyi* and *S. earlei* are quite differently marked but equally attractive boxer shrimps imported from Hawaii and the western Indo-Pacific region. The maintenance of all *Stenopus* species are essentially the same, so the aquarist who encounters an unfamiliar boxer shrimp should not hesitate to purchase it.

Boxer shrimps require clean, well-aerated water to prosper. Nitrate levels in excess of 10.0 ppm are stressful and interfere with the normal molting process. Like all crustaceans, *Stenopus* are very sensitive to fluctuations in salinity. They should thus be acclimated very slowly to a new aquarium. The aquarist who pays due attention to maintaining high water quality in his tanks can look foward to the company of his pets for up to 6 years. In view of their habitat preference in nature, it should come as no surprise that newly imported specimens are quite retiring in brightly lit tanks and initially display a crepuscular pattern or activity. It is therefore essential to furnish their tank with a number of caves or overhangs to occupy. With the passage of time, these colorful shrimp will grow suffciently accustomed to their surroundings to leave their shelter and forage actively even under intense illumination. A temperature of 20°–24° C. (70°–76° F.) suits these shrimp well. Temperatures in excess of 28° C. (85° F.) lead to a highly stressful oxygen deficit in the tank and must be avoided at all cost. *Stenopus* require no particular attention at feed-

ing time. If kept in a mixed community, they manage quite nicely on scraps of food left behind by the fish. In an invertebrate community, they will clean up any food uneaten by its filter feeders with equal alacrity. If it appears that the boxer shrimps are not getting their share of food, it suffices to place a piece of a TetraTip tablet in their cave just before shutting off the tank lights to rectify the situation.

In nature, *Stenopus* live as mated pairs. The sexes are easily distinguished, as males are smaller and slimmer than females. Pairs will live happily together, but two individuals of the same sex will literally fight to the death if kept together in the same tank. While it is best to purchase *S. hispidus* or any other coral shrimp as pairs, a male and female purchased separately can usually be counted upon to pair successfully when introduced to one another. The male of a pair routinely brings pieces of food to his mate and indulges in an elaborate and quite pleasing courtship dance prior to copulation.

The banded coral shrimp is an active cleaner species in nature. In captivity, such behavior plays a less conspicuous role it its daily pattern of activity, which seems to center on scavenging over the substratum in search of food. Like most cleaner species, *S. hispidus* enjoys effective immunity from predation by most reef fish and therefore is a good candidate for the mixed community tank. Exceptions to this rule are large wrasses, triggerfish, smooth puffers and groupers. Larger crustaceans are also inclined to view boxer shrimps as fair game. The banded coral shrimp is not above harassing and sometimes killing smaller fish and crustaceans, although such behavior is much less likely from its smaller congeners. It has also been observed nibbling at tube worms and on the mantle of giant clams. When hungry, specimens may also pick at the tentacles of anthozoans. It is otherwise a good tankmate for both true and tube anemones.

If well fed, banded coral shrimp will molt every 6 to 8 weeks, each molt being followed by a spawning. The female carries the mass of greeish eggs between her pleopods until they hatch, about 3 weeks later. The larvae remain with the mother for another three weeks, then enter the plankton. The planktonic larvae can be reared through their third molt with *Artemis* nauplii. They then grow sluggish and die off one at a time untl the entire brood is lost. Presumably these mortalities are caused by a dietary deficiency. Hopefully further research by both scientists and serious invertebrate fanciers will to a breakthrough in rearing these delightful little shrimp in captivity.

*Lysmata amboinensis* White-striped cleaner shrimp

This is the most widely distributed representative of the genus *Lysmata*, found throughout the Indo-Pacific region. The very similarly colored *L. grabhami* replaces *L. amboinensis* in the Caribbean and tropical eastern Atlantic. Other popular congeners of more restricted occurence are *Lysmata debelius*, the cardinal or scarlet cleaner shrimp, native to the western IndoPacific region, *L. wurdemanni*, the Caribbean cleaner shrimp, whose range is defined in its common name, and *L. californica*, the Catalina cleaner shrimp, found, not as its specific name seems to imply, only along the California coast, but throughout the eastern Pacific.

Like the boxer shrimps, members of the genus *Lysmata* are rather small shrimps, their body length seldom exceeding 6.0 cm (c. 1.25″) inclusive of the rostrum. They also

A fine specimen of the white-stripped cleaner shrimp, *Lysmata amboinensis*.

are cave dwelling cleaner shrimps, characteristically found on tropical reefs from depths of 5.0 m (26′) downwards. Unlike *Stenopus*, these shrimps have a more flexible social system. Solitary or paired indviduals are most frequently encountered, but where the topography of the reef provides overhangs of suitable dimensions, assemblages of over a hundred individuals have been reported hanging upsidedown from the roof of their shelter. Perhaps the fact that unlike boxer shrimps, which are all gonochorists, *Lysmata* are hermaphrodites has something to do with this social plasticity. Be that as it may, it certainly makes it a simple matter for the aquarist to obtain a pair!

Like the preceeding species, *Lysmata* are easily maintained aquarium subjects as long as care is taken to keep nitrate levels below 10.0 ppm. Apart from the fact that their greater sociability makes it possible to keep

The cardinal cleaner shrimp, *Lysmata debelius,* is a striking addition to a marine invertebrate community.

**Lysmata wurdmanni, the Caribbean cleaner shrimp.**

reef fish. They should not be kept with larger crustaceans, including boxer shrimp, to whom they are fair game, nor is it wise to house them with the larger true sea anemones or tube anemones, as they are likely to be stung to death and eaten.

The white-striped cleaner shrimp spawns regularly in captivity. The larvae of both *Lysmata amboinensis* and *L. seticaudata*, the Monaco cleaner shrimp, have been successfully reared to adulthood. The chief obstacle to success is providing a 24 hour supply of living food and keeping water in the rearing tank scrupulously clean. For further information on the husbandry of this and other crustaceans, refer to the titles cited in the last chapter.

more than a single pair per tank, they should be handled identically to *Stenopus*. At certain times of the year, specimens of *L. amboinensis* are attacked by parasitic isopods. They give the armor of the head and thorax a misshapen appearance, but do not usually prove fatal to their host. The exoskeletal anomalies are not carried past the animal's next molt.

*Lysmata* solicit clients far more assiduously in captivity than do boxer shrimps and seem on the whole to do a better job as cleaners. Triggerfish and sharp-nosed puffers will eat them without any hesitation, and groupers can not always be trusted to honor the general immunity enjoyed by cleaner species. Wrasses will also attack newly molted females immediately before they spawn. These colorful cleaner shrimp can otherwise be kept safely with the entire gamut of coral

*Periclemenes* spp.  Anemone shrimps

As their common name suggests, these diminutive shrimps enjoy much the same sort of relationship with sea anemones as to the clownfish of the genera *Amphiprion* and *Premnas*. The two Caribbean species most often available to North American aquarists are *Periclemenes pedersoni*, which lives in association with the common anemones *Bartholomea annulata* and *Condylactis gigantea* or the false coral *Ricordea florida* and the clown anemone shrimp, *P. yucatanicus*, often found living with the Florida carpet anemone, *Stoichactis helianthus*. The two Indo-Pacific species most often imported are the Pacific clown anemone shrimp, *P. brevicarpalis* and the glass anemone shrimp, *P. holthuisi*. Both are frequent lodgers in carpet

**Its somewhat psychedelic color pattern explains the popularity of the Catalina cleaner shrimp, Lysmata californiensis.**

**The diminutive Caribbean anemone shrimp, Periclemenes pedersoni.**

*Periclemenes yucatanicus,* **the clown anemone shrimp.**

**The glass anemone shrimp,** *Periclemenes holthuisi.*

anemones of the genera *Radianthus* and *Stoichactis.* An unusual representative of the genus is *P. imperator,* a species that lives in the gill filaments and shares the scarlet coloration of a free-swimming nudibranch, *Hexabranchus sanguineus,* the Spanish dancer. The species associated with anthozoans typically live as sexual pairs, the female being the larger of the two partners, and function as symbiotic cleaners.

Anemone shrimps require the same care as do the cleaner shrimps of the genus *Lysmata.* With the exception of the rarely seen *P. imperator,* the species to date imported wild actively solicit the custom of the fishes with which they are housed. However, they are by no means exclusively dependant upon this source of food and once established, will leave the shelter of their anemone and forage actively over the tank's substratum for minute scraps of edible matter. They will also enthusiastically share any offerings of live or synthetic plankton given the tank's sessile residents.

Anemone shrimp should not be kept without a host anemone to take refuge in. These diminutive crustaceans rarely exceed 3.5 cm (1.5″) in length. Though their cleaning activities confer a degree of protection from many predatory fishes, there is no shortage of potential predators large enough to consider them a convenient mouthful. Thus it is hardly surprising that *Periclemenes* seem distinctly ill at ease when deprived of their habitual shelter. Those organisms that can be safely kept with *Lysmata* species make suitable tankmates for anemone shrimp. Though *Periclemenes* will often spawn in captivity, there appear to have been no instances in which the larvae were successfully reared.

*Rhynchocinetes* sp. Dancing or humpacked shrimps

As one of their common name suggests, these small shrimp have a decidedly humpbacked appearance. They also differ from all other shrimps in having a rostrum that can be moved up and down. Dancing shrimps are sexually dimorphic. Males have much larger chelipeds and chelae, which makes it a simple matter to distinguish between the sexes. This is rather important to the aquarist, for while females will live peacably in small groups, males tend to fight among themselves, though their encounters usually do not result in fatalities.

These large-eyed crustaceans seldom exceed 5.0 cm (2″) in length. They live in large

**A Pacific anemone shrimp,** *Periclemenes brevicarpalis.*

*Rhynchocinetes uritai,* **the rosy dancing shrimp.**

groups in caves and grottos on the reef proper and along rocky coasts. Dancing shrimps are deepwater species, rarely encountered at depths of less than 5.0 m (27°). The species most commonly available to aquarists is *Rhynchocinetes uritai,* the rosy dancing shrimp, native to the Indo-Pacific region and regularly exported by Far Eastern collectors. Considerably rarer and correspondingly more costly is a Caribbean species, the red dancing shrimp, *R. rigens.*

Dancing shrimps have the same maintenance requirements as the cleaner shrimps of the genus *Lysmata.* They are considerably more crepuscular in their pattern of activity, however. It is not unusual for newly imported specimens to be quite shy, and even well acclimated individuals tend to avoid areas of intense illumination. *Rhyncocinetes* do not engage in cleaning behavior. They accept the full range of live and prepared foods and make excellent scavengers for marine community tanks of 100.0 l or larger stocked small fish.

If hungry, dancing shrimps will nibble at the tentacles of sessile anthozoans, particularly those of true corals. There no reports of attacks upon echinoderms, but this possibility should not be ruled out, particularly if the shrimps are underfed by their keeper. They will otherwise live compatibly with any organisms that can safely be housed with cleaner shrimps. If pleased with their surroundings, dancing shrimps will breed regularly. There have been a number of successful efforts to rear the larvae.

### *Alpheus* spp. Snapping shrimps

These shrimps derive their common name from the explosive sound they can make by snapping an enlarged pincer shut. They are sometimes also called pistol shrimp because of the alleged similarity of this sound to a pistol shot. In actuality, the snapping of these shrimps sounds a lot more like an aquarium developing a pressure crack, a similarity that has come close to driving more than one unsuspecting aquarist to distraction before he identifies its real source! Most alpheids are nondescriptly colored, but pinkish-violet *Alpheus armatus,* a Caribbean species that lives as pairs in associaton with anemones of the genus *Bartholomea* makes a decorative addition to a marine community tank. A number of Indo-Pacific species of uncertain identity enjoy a symbiotic relationship with

**The red dancing shrimp,** *Rhynchocinetes rigens.*

*Alpheus armatus,* **a snapping shrimp frequently available from Florida exporters.**

A pair of gobies (*Cryptocentrus* sp.) sitting at the mouth of the burrow they share with an *Alphaeus* sp.

gobies of the genus *Cryptocentrus*. Both shrimp and gobies are quite often imported, though not, unfortunately, together.

Alpheids are very hardy. They will propser under the same conditions that satisfy the needs of cleaner shrimp. Taken with their small size, this would seem to recommend them highly for any marine aquarium. Unfortunately, snapping shrimp have two rather serious drawbacks as aquarium residents. First of all, most species are burrowers. Thus their first priority upon being added to an established tank is to dig a suitable shelter, from which they usually emerge only to feed. The aquarist is likely to see more of his specimens if he anticipates this behavior and places a few suitable slabs of rock or pieces of brain coral for the shrimp to burrow beneath near the front glass of their tank. This operation is eased if these shrimp are maintained over a substratum whose particle size falls between 0.5 and 1.0 cm.

Secondly, the pressure wave generated when one of these shrimps snaps its claw is powerful enough to stun other shrimps and small fish at a distance of several centimeters. On the balance, such behavior appears to be primarily a defense response provoked by a tankmate's overly close approach. However, alpheids are not averse to making a meal of imprudent companions. Prudence thus dictates keeping smaller crustaceans and fish away from snapping shrimp. As a rule, alpheids are more partial to the usual fare offered marine aquariums.

Snapping shrimp make nice companions for sessile filter feeding invertebrates. Assuming their tankmates are not too much smaller, they can be safely kept with a wide selection of small reef fish and crustaceans. Triggerfish, sharp-nosed puffers, large angelfish and groupers do not make good tankmates. Neither do large crabs, carnivorous molluscs or predatory starfish. Aquarists wishing to recreate the shrimp-goby symbiosis in captivity are more likely to be successful if the two participants are kept together in a tank of their own.

*Hymenocera picta* Harlequin or clown shrimp

This exquisitely marked species inhabits shallow waters on coral reefs throughout the Indo-Pacidic region. The similarly colored *H. elegans* is native to the western Pacific and Indian Oceans. Both species are found as pairs living in close association with the starfish that constitute their only food. These shrimp employ their characteristic flattened chelae to slip under the arms of a starfish and sever its tube feet, which are eaten. They are also used to tip a starfish over in order to expose its vulnerable lower surface to the shrimps' specialized pick-like **periapods**, or feeding legs. Notwithstanding an adult size that seldom exceeds 5.0 cm (2″), harlequin shrimps are quite capable of turning over a

The harlequin shrimp, *Hymenocera picta,* makes a colorful addition to an invertebrate community tank as long as its specialized dietary requirements can be met.

starfish 15.0 cm (6″) across, due in large part to the fact that both members of a pair will cooperate in such an undertaking.

The overall maintenance requirements of *H. picta* are identical to those of *S. hispidus*. The chief difficulty entailed in the successful husbandry of harlequin shrimps is providing them with an adequate food supply. These shrimps will eat only starfish. *Linckia, Fromia* and *Echinaster* are the genera prefered as food, but even temperate zone starfish will elicit a normal feeding response from *H. picta*. Aquarists living along the coast thus have the option of collecting suitable live food for these shrimps. Those dwelling inland should consider keeping harlequin shrimp only if they are ready to purchase the starfish necessary to meet their dietary needs. It should be noted that such species as *L. laevigata*, the blue starfish, abd *E. spinulosus* are readily available through commercial channels and relatively inexpensive. A 10.0 cm (4″) wide starfish will feed a pair of *H. picta* for 7 to 14 days.

It is not a good idea to try and keep more than a single pair of harlequin shrimp per aquarium. They cannot be safely housed with large predatory fish such as groupers, "beaked" species such as triggerfish and sharp-nosed puffers, wrasses of any size or larger, predatory crustaceans, a category that in this instance must be broadened to include hermit crabs. It is also unwise to try keeping them in the same tank as true or tube anemones. As long as they have a shelter to which they can retreat when molting, harlequin shrimps run no risk from the smaller coral reef fishes. Their depredations upon starfish notwithstanding, *Hymenocera* pose no threat to other echinoderms.

*Hymenocera picta* spawns freely in captivity if well fed. The planktonic larvae require 5 to 7 weeks to pass through the several intermediate stages to metamorphosis. They have been successfully reared to this point but only when their diet included planktonic copepods. The newly metamorphosed young are also extremely specific in their food preferences, demanding live *Linckia* for their initial meal. For further information, see the aposite references in the final chapter.

**The red reef lobster, *Enoplometopus occidentalis*.**

*Enoplometopus daumi,* the orange and violet reef lobster.

*Enoplometopus* spp.  Reef lobsters

With their well developed chelae and bold coloration, the reef lobsters look like psychedelic versions of the familiar freshwater crayfish. As they rarely exceed 15.0 cm (6″) in body length, they are far better suited for life in captivity than their more robust relatives, the spiny lobsters of the genus *Panulirus*. Reef lobsters are solitary, nocturnal crustaceans found mainly in caves on the coral reef at depths greater than 5.0 m (27°). Such a life style does not make them easy to collect, and taken with their overall rarity in any given patch of coral, it explains their rather stiff asking price. Three species are usually available commercially. *Enoplometopus occidentalis*, the Hawaiian or red reef lobster, is widely distributed in the Indo-Pacific. However, most of the specimens available in the trade are exported from Hawaii, hence their common name. The similarly colored *E. antillensis* is much more rarely exported from its Caribbean home. The violet and orange reef lobster, *E. daumi*, is regularly exported from the Philippines and Indonesia, together with its close relative, the violet-spotted reef lobster, *E. debelius*.

Reef lobsters are very hardy crustaceans.

The male (left) and the female of *Enoplometopus debelius*.

They require clean, well aerated water, but otherwise make no major demands on their keeper. They require a cave or similar shelter into which they can completely withdraw their bodies, but seem quite willing to accept artificial refuges such as pieces of CPVC pipe as well as more traditional grottos constructed of rocks or dead coral. Newly imported animals are strictly nocturnal and will never leave their caves while the tank lights are on. With the passage of time, specimens will learn to come out into the light when the tank is fed. They may even come to forage freely during the daylight hours, but always remain very wary and easily frightened by disturbances.

Reef lobsters eat just about anything. Fresh seafood cut into pieces suitable for feeding anemones suits them nicely, and they are quite partial to TetraTips. Regretably this combination of catholic taste and hearty appetite makes reef lobsters a real threat to many invertebrates. Over the years, aquarists have discovered that *Enoplometopus* will devour echinoderms – sea urchins are a particular favorite – as well as smaller crustaceans, molluscs and tube worms. It is also tempting fate to house reef lobsters with smaller, slow-moving fish.

Their size notwithstanding, reef lobsters must fear the attentions of triggerfish, sharp-nosed puffers and large wrasses like the harlequin tuskfish, while their robust claws are no deterent to an octopus. *Enoplometopus* make good companions for all but to most fragile anthozoans and can be expected to prosper in the company of most small to medium-sized coral reef fish. A word of warning: these solitary crustaceans come together only in order to mate. It is emphatically not recommended to attempt keeping more than one to a tank unless the animals can clearly be seen living together as a pair at the moment of their purchase. Once pairing has occured, spawning regularly follows. Regretably, efforts to rear the larvae have to date proven unsuccessful.

*Stenorhynchus seticornis* Caribbean arrow crab

This unusual crab is native to inshore habitats along rocky coasts and coral reefs. It is often found living commensally with large anemones of the genus *Condylactis*. While the Caribbean arrow crab is most commonly available to aquarists, its very similar Pacific coast cognate *S. debilis* is sometimes exported from the Gulf of California. Though their long legs give an impression of large size, arrow crabs are really quite small, their bodies never measuring more than 2.5 cm (1″) long and 1.2 cm (0.5″) across.

Arrow crabs are as hardy as they are bizzare. They are a good beginner's choice provided their companions are selected carefully. A temperature range of 20°–24° C. (70°–76° F.) suits them well. Like most Caribbean invertebrates, they should not be kept any watmer than 26° C. (79° F.). *Stenorhynchus* accept a wide range of animal foods, both living and dead. They seem notably partial to TetraTips. These crabs are unusual in that they do not molt after reaching adulthood. Thus they are not able to replace lost or damaged appendages, after the manner of other crustaceans. Hence the importance of housing them apart from potential predators, a category that includes triggerfish, sharp-nosed puffers, wrasses and large angelfish, as well as larger, predatory decapods like reef lobsters and true crabs. For their part, arrow crabs will use their apical spine as a weapon to impale prey. There are reports of *Stenorhynchus* thus attacking fish up to 2.5 cm (1″) long. Larger fish appear immune to such assaults. Arrow crabs will also use their apical spine in self defense and are capable of inflicting a

**The Baribbean arrow crab, *Stenorhynchus seticornis*.**

**A porcelain crab, *Neopetrolisthes maculatus*, amidst the tentacles of its host anemone.**

painful wound on a bare hand. They are thus best handled only with nets. Arrow crabs will also feed on tubeworms and sessile bivalves. This does not recommend them as residents for a mini-reef style aquarium. They can be kept safely with small crustaceans, echinoderms and most sessile anthozoans.

*Neopetrolisthes maculatus* Porcelain or anemone crab

These diminutive crabs are native to the tropical IndoPacific region, where they live in an obligatory commensal relationship with the large reef anemones of the genera *Radianthus, Gyrostoma, Stoichactis, Cryptodendron* and *Physiobrachia*. Both *N. maculatus* and the more irregularly spotted *N. oshimai* are frequently exported from the Far East.

This attractive species requires much the same attention as the smaller coral reef shrimps if it is to prosper in captivity. It will spend most of its time in hiding if the illumination of its tank is to bright, but otherwise the anemone crab makes no demands in this regard. A temperature range of 20°–24° C. (70°–76° F.) suits it sell. Water warmer than 28° C. (84° F.) is extremely stressful.

Anemone crabs are filter feeders, utilizing their highly modified third pair of maxillipeds to "comb" planktonic organisms from the water. Their dietary requirements are thus identical to those of filter feeding sessile invertebrates. Both live and synthetic plankton are readily accepted. Some captive specimens will learn to take minute morsels of food presented with a pair of tweezers. Newly pur-

chased specimens will only feed at night until they grow accustomed to their surroundings. They should therefore be fed immediately before the tank lights are extinguished.

Because their small adult size makes them very vulnerable to harrasment and outright predation by their tankmates, anemone crabs must always be kept together with an appropriate anthozoan host if they are to do well in captivity. Any of the anemone genera cited above will do in this regard. Leather and bladder corals are acceptable alternate hosts. Tube anemones are not. They will sting anemone crabs to death and consume them with no hesitation. *Neopetrolisthes* will share an anemone with clownfish. Their small size notwithstanding, they seem to have no difficulty holding their own in the face of their cotenants rather extroverted personalities.

Anemone crabs live together as sexual pairs in nature. Such relationships persist in captivity, so it is perfectly possible to keep a male and female together in the same aquarium. Individuals of the same sex are very agressive to one another. Attempts to keep them in the same tank lead to damaging and often lethal fights. As these crustaceans are not easily sexed, prudence dictates purchasing only couples that are already living together harmoniously in the dealer's tanks.

*Neopetrolisthes* should not be kept with large, invertebrate feeding coral reef fishes. The species recommended for life in a sessile invertebrate community can be counted on to leave anemone crabs in peace. Large crabs will prey upon their anemone-dwelling cousins given the chance, and there are re-

***Dardanus cadenati***, *a small hermit crab well suited to life in an invertebrate community tank.*

My home is my castle: *Paguristes ocellatus* with a sponge *Suberites domuncula* living in the Mediterranean Sea.

ports that banded coral shrimp will bully them badly. Other crustaceans are suitable companions for anemone crabs, as are the generality of echinoderms.

*Dardanus* spp. Reef hermit crabs

Hermit crabs are best known for their habit of using empty mollusc shells as portable shelters. Unlike other crabs, their abdomens are devoid of chitnious armor. It is instead modified in a manner that allows a hermit crab to grip the interior of its shell with such tenacity that it is impossible to forcibly extract a resident without doing it fatal damage. Reef hermits of the genus *Dardanus* are found worldwide in tropical and subtropical seas. They occur both on the reef proper and along rocky

*Darnanus venosus?* derive additional protection from predators by "cultivating" a stinging anemone on their shells.

shorelines from the subtidal zone to depths in excess of 5.0 m (17'). They range in size from *D. cadenati*, a commonly imported Carribbean species that only grows to 2.5 cm (1") in length to the spectacular red reef hermit crab, *D. megistos*, another Indo-Pacific species that can attain a length of 15.0 cm (6"). A number of *Dardanus* species regularly install stinging anemones of the genus *Calliactis* on their shells. The anemonegardeners most often available to aquarists are the Indo-Pacific *D. lagopus* and two Caribbean species, *D. venosus* and *D. fucosus*.

Reef hermit crabs are ideal beginner's subjects. They are far more tolerant of toxic nitrogen cycle byproducts than the generality of marine organisms. Indeed, many dealers recommend using a hermit crab as a tank's initial source of nitrogenous waste when running in its biological filter. Unlike most marine fish suggested for this dubious distinction, hermit crabs almost always emerge unscathed from the experience! They have no special lighting requirements and can tolerate temperatures in excess of 30° C (85° F.) for brief periods of time. Like most marine invertebrates, however, to prefer a temperature range of 20°–24° C. (70°–76° F.).

As they carry their shelter with them, reef hermits are not as dependant upon fixed refuges are other crustaceans. However, it is essential to have a good supply of empty shells of varying sizes available in their tank. Hermit crabs need progressively larger shelters as they grow. Many species have well-marked shell preferences in nature. Red reef hermit crabs, for instance, prefer to occuppy murex and triton shells. In captivity, they seem content with any shell large enough to accomadate them.

Reef hermit crabs will enthusiastically devour **any** food of animal origin, living or dead. They are very partial to tablet foods such as TetraTips. Individual specimens quickly learn to associate the appearance of their owner with the arrival of a meal and become accomplished beggars in captivity.

Regretably, the pronounced predatory tendencies of hermit crabs severely limit their desirability in a comunity tank situation. If one wishes to maintain a hermit crab in an invertebrate aquarium, the golden rule to follow is "Small is beautiful." Even small specimens will attack fanworms and tubeworms and are apt to nibble on the skeletons of gorgonians if these support any sort of algal growth. As a rule, individuals in the 2.0 cm – 3.0 cm size range can be kept safely with the larger shrimps, but bigger individuals are likely to attack newly molted crustaceans.

Small reef hermits do quite well in an anthozoan community tank and are very suitable companions for both true and tube anemones. They can also be expected to prosper in the company of small to medium-sized coral reef fishes, as long as specialized invertebrate feeders such as sharp-nosed puffers and wrasses are excluded from the tank.

Large reef hermits, such as *D. megistos*, are totally unsuited to the invertebrate community aquarium. They simply eat up everything in sight, even anemones whose stings are lethal to other predators! They seem particularly fond of snails, sea urchins and starfish. There is no objection to housing them with medium-sized to large fishes. Indeed, the red reef hermit can even be kept with triggerfish as long as it has a few caves it can retire too when harrassed.

However, the good they do as scavengers is often cancelled out by their tendency to undermine and knock over a tank's infrastructure as they lumber over the bottom. Large reef hermit crabs, like mantis shrimp, make amusing and interesting pets but are really best kept as isolated specimens in a tank of their own.

True crabs of the Families Portuniadae (swimming crabs), Grapsidae (stone crabs) and Xanthidae share the hardiness of reef hermits as well as all of their drawbacks as aquarium residents.

Many tropical species are brightly colored, but all are highly predatory and most are cannibalistic in the bargain. Any aquarist who wishes to become more familiar with one of these interesting crustaceans should plan on giving it a tank of its own.

## Phyllum Echinodermata

The Echinodermata (literally, spiny-skinned ones) are a distinctive group of strictly marine organisms characterized by radial symmetry somewhat reminiscent of that seen in the Coelenterata. However, the basic body plan of echinoderms is **pentamerous**, the number of arms surrounding the mouth based upon multiples of five. Furthermore, the fact that all species pass through a bilaterally symmetrical larval stage suggests that their radial symmetry is a secondarily derived condition. This contrasts markedly with the Coelenterata, for whom radial symmetry is clearly the primitive condition. The most distinctive feature of the echinoderms is their possession of a water vascular system, which is involved in respiration, locomotion, the capture of prey and the movement of foodstuff within the body. It is the water vascular system that generates the differences in hydrostatic pressure that allows the group's distinctive tube-feet to function.

The evolutionary relationships of echinoderms are obscure. However, all extant species pass through a free-swimming bipinnaria larval stage and share several other embryological features with the Phyllum Chordata. Few contemporary biologists regard the Echinodermata as in any sense ancestral to chordates. It rather seems the two phyla are sister groups that share a common ancestor. The extant echinoderms can be grouped into five very distinctive classes, four of which include species of interest to the aquarist. Their differences make it simplest to deal with each in turn.

## Class Echinoidea

The Echinoidea include sea urchins, heart urchins and sand dollars. Only true sea urchins are generally kept as ornamental subjects. While attractive enough, both heart urchins and sand dollars are burrowing forms that spend most of their time out of sight. This makes them less than satisfactory aquarium residents! True urchins have a spherical or flattened globular test, or body covered with spines of varying length, thickness and sharpness. Tucked in among the spines are numerous flexible arms, the pedicellariae, which allow the animal to remove any inert or living objects that settle onto the surface of the test. The mouth is located on the underside of the body. It is equipped with a five-part jaw structure, known as Aristotle's lantern, that allows urchins to browse such food items as encrusting algae and sponges from solid surfaces and in some instances, even bore holes in rock.

Sea urchins are **extremely** sensitive to fluctuations in salinity, to which they respond by shedding their spines and dying. This apart, they are hardy, easily maintained aquarium subjects. The very fine-spined species such as *Diadema*, the hatpin urchins, must be handled with care. Their spines are both pungent and brittle. They commonly break off in a wound, causing it to fester. Urchin punctures should be **immediately** swabbed with vinegar, which both disinfects the wound and works to dissolve any spine fragments within it. If the affected area is still tender and sore after a day or two, seek a doctor's care to cope with the resultant infection.

Order Echinoidea

*Phyllacanthus imperialis* Pencil urchin

This robust urchin is an inhabitant of the fore-reef most commonly found at depths greater than 3.0 m (10′). Aquarium specimens with

Hatpin urchins (*Diadema* spp.) must be handled with extreme care, for their fragile, needle-sharp spines can inflict painful wound upon careless aquarists and skin divers alike.

A fine specimen of the pencil urchin, *Phyllacanthus imperialis*.

an overall diameter of 15.0 cm (6″) are not uncommon. It is native to the Indo-Pacific region and commonly exported by Far Eastern collectors. Similar species are collected in Hawaii, the Gulf of California and the Caribbean.

If due attention is paid to water quality, the pencil urchin is easily maintained and long-lived. As a nocturnal species, it is effectively indifferent to light levels during the daytime. A temperature range of 20°–24° C. (70°–76° F.) suits it well. Temperatures in excess of 28° C. (84° F.) quickly prove lethal. Take care when setting up a tank intended to house these large urchins that its infrastructure is solidly emplaced. They can use their stout, mobile spines like crowbars to pry loose or otherise disrupt insecurely seated pieces of rockwork or dead coral.

This species is omnivorous with marked carnivorous tendencies. Captive specimens should be offered small morsels of shellfish and fish as well as food tablets. It is relatively easy to forget about feeding urchins due to their daytime immobility. Failure to satisfy their hearty appetites can lead to serious depredations upon a tank's sessile inhabitants.

The carnivorous tendencies of *P. imperialis* make it a poor choice for a tank of sessile anthozoans and sponges, for it will graze on such tankmates as enthusiastically as it will crop attached algae. It will get along well with true and tube anemones. Shrimps and small hermit crabs also make suitable companions.

Apart from triggerfish, it need fear nothing from coral reef fishes. Large hermit crabs, most carnivorous snails and predatory starfish have no difficulty making a meal of this or other urchins and should never be selected as tankmates for them.

*Echinometra lucunter* Caribbean rock-boring urchin

Its common name notwithstanding, this species is widely distributed in the tropical west Atlantic. It is a common shallow-water inhabitant of both rocky shorelines and the coral reef proper. Individuals typically excavate a depression for themselves in the rock to which they return daily after a night's foraging. Most aquarium specimens measure 6.0 cm (2.75") in diameter, but slightly larger individuals are sometimes encountered in dealer's tanks. The closely related *E. mathaei* is native to the tropical Indo-Pacific.

This is a very durable sea urchin, though like all echinoderms, prone to react adversely to any changes in water density. Specimens must be offered one or two pieces of soft limestone or tuffa rock from which to scrape a resting place. Otherwise, no particular attention need be given to setting up their quarters. Like other noctural species, it is indifferent to daytime light levels. The Caribbean boring urchin is comfortable over a temperature range of 20°–24° C. (70°–76° F.). At temperatures greater than 30° C. (85° F.), it sheds its spines and soon dies.

*Echniometra lucunter,* **the Caribbean rock-boring urchin.**

*Echinometra* is a strictly herbivorous sea urchin. It is particularly well suited to life in mini-reef set-ups, where it plays a useful role in the control of thread algae. If its natural food is not available, offer this species blanched lettuce and TetraTips.

Unlike the preceeding species, the Caribbean boring urchin makes an excellent addition to a community of sessile anthozoans and other plankton-feeders. It also does well in the company of true and tube anemones. It is vulnerable to predation by triggerfish, large crabs, carnivorous molluscs and predatory starfish. Other coral reef fish and mobile invertebrates make suitable tankmates.

Class Asteroidea  Starfish or sea stars

To most people, starfish are the quintessential marine organisms. They are certainly the invertebrate most novice marine aquarists think of first adding to a community aquarium. Their shape apart, starfish are characterized by a ventrally placed mouth and the arrangement of their tube feet in a series of distinct grooves, the **ambullacrae**, located along the lower surface of each arm. All starfish are carnivorous, differing only in the degree to which they exploit carrion or living prey. They feed by everting their stomach through the mouth and enveloping the food item to be digested. Depending on the species, digestion either takes place entirely outside of the body cavity or else stomach and prey are retracted and digestion takes place internally.

Starfish are capable of regenerating lost or damaged arms. Indeed, an entire new animal can develop from a detached arm as long as a portion of the central disk is torn loose with the fragment. As starfish reproduce sexually, this ability is best regarded as a repair mechanism rather than as an alternative mode of reproduction.

Order Valvatida

*Protoreaster lincki* East African starfish

Its common name notwithstanding, this colorful starfish is a common inhabitant of the shallow waters of coral reefs throughout the Indo-Pacific region. In the wild, it can

A colorful East African starfish, *Protoreaster lincki* (right).

*Culcita schmideliana*, (left) an unusually shaped starfish.

The blue starfish, *Linckia laevigata* (right).

measure up to 25.0 cm (10″) from arm-tip to arm-tip. Aquarium specimens seldom exceed a span of 15.0 cm (6″). Commonly exported from the Far East, it can be considered representative of a group of large, colorful and carnivorous starfish that includes such frequently imported species as *P. tuberculatus, Culcita schmideliana, Choiaster granulatus, Oreaster reticulatus* and *Pentaceraster mammillatus.*

As long as it is not exposed to changes in salinity, *P. lincki* is an extremely hardy species that can unhesitatingly be recommended to a beginner. It is indifferent to light levels and propsers over a temperature range of 20°–24° C. (70°–76° F.). Higher temperatures are stressful, while those in excess of 30° C. (85° F.) are swiftly fatal.

This carnivore must be offered small pieces of frozen fish or shellfish. It will also accept TetraTips or other food tablets and often will scavenge morsels left uneaten by an aquarium's other residents. The occaisional treat of a live clam or mussel is relished.

Regretably, the East African starfish can be kept safely with only a few other invertebrates. The only sessile species that can count themselves safe from its depredations are large sea anemones and tube anemones, whose potent stings afford them effective protection. Highly mobile invertebrates such as shrimp and small hermit crabs are also unlikely to fall victim to its appetite. However, small molluscs or those with a herbivorous feeding pattern are fair game. For its part, *P. lincki* is vulnerable to attack by many carnivorous snails, large crabs and, most improbably, the diminutive harlequin shrimp. Triggerfish and large angelfish are also not above taking a bite or two from a starfish if the opportunity presents itself. Small to medium sized coral fish otherwise make excellent tankmates for this starfish

### *Fromia milleporella* Red starfish

This strikingly colored starfish is a common inhabitant of shallow water reef habitats throughout the Indo-Pacific region. It is a small species, measuring a maximum of 6.0 cm (1.25″) across. Together with the the

*Fromia milleporella,* **the aptly christened red starfish.**

somewhat larger *F. elegans*, it is commonly exported by Far Eastern collectors. It can be considered representative of an assemblage of small, brightly colored shallow-water species that includes the popular blue reef starfish, *Linckia laevigata, Gomophia aegiptica*, and the Java starfish, *Nardoa variolata.*

The red starfish shares the sensitivity of all echinoderms to even small changes in water density. It is indifferent to light intensity. Indeed, it has been suggested that the intense pigmentation displayed by this and other shallow-water starfish has evolved as a protective mechanism against the effects of ultraviolet radiation. While it finds a temperature range fo 20°–24° C. (70°–76°F.) to its liking, the red starfish is more sensitive to overheating than the East African starfish. Temperatures in excess of 26° C. (78° F.) will cause it to shed its arms and die.

Unlike *P. lincki*, this species is a microphage, feeding exclusively on minute particles of food vacuumed from the reef surface. It does well on a diet of finely minced frozen seafood or pulverized food tablets. Its feeding habits make it an ideal scavenger for a comunity of sessile plankton-feeding invertebrates.

*Fromia milleporella* is suspected of browsing on sponges, but does not seem to do them any permanent harm. It otherwise poses no risk to other animals. Together with other microphagous starfish, it is thus a welcome addition to a mini-reef community tank. It is vulnerable to harrassment by large coral reef fish. Only those species recommended as tankmates for sponges should be housed with the red starfish. Large crabs, carnivorous snails and predatory starfish consider *F. milleporella* legitimate prey and should never be housed with it. This species is also vulnerable to the attacks of harlequin shrimp. Indeed, a pair of these colorful but rapacious little predators can eat a red starfish alive in a matter of days.

## Class Ophiuroidea  Brittle stars

Both the scientific and popular names of these distinctive echinoderms refer to distinctive morphological features. The extremely mobile arms of ophiuroids (literally, "snake tails") indeed have a serpentine appearance. Moreover, as the common name of brittle star suggests, they break off at the slightest pressure. Although they have the same five-armed body plan as starfish, brittle stars differ from them in having a sharp division between the arms themselves and the central disk. Their tube feet lack suckers and are arranged differently on the arms, which in most instances are covered with numerous well-developed but immobile spines.

All brittle stars are scavengers or detritus feeders. A number of diminutive species exist as obligate commensals of various sessile invertebrates. They often appear "spontaneously" in an invertebrate community after purchase of their host species or the addition of a new piece of seasoned living rock. They are quite harmless and add an agreable element of variety to the tank's make-up.

**An atytractively colored and easily maintained brittle star, *Orphiolepis superba*.**

Brittle stars have a reputation for fragility among marine aquarists. This seems to follow from the fact that exporters rarely make any effort to tailor their shipping techniques to meet their particular requirements. Those species that are available through the trade should be regarded as essential members of the clean-up squad in a mini-reef style aquarium.

## Order Ophiurida

### *Ophiolepis superba*  Banded brittle star

This widely distributed species can be found in the intertidal and shallow subtidal habitats of coral reefs throughout the Indo-Pacific region. Imported specimens rarely exceed an arm spread of 12.0 cm (5"), but larger specimens are sometimes to be had. The episodic appearance of this species in shipments of invertebrates from the Philippines and Indonesia seems due as much to the fact that the banded brittle star does not drop its arms at the slightest disturbance as to its handsome color pattern.

Like all echinoderms, the banded brittle star reacts adversely to sudden changes in salinity. This apart, it makes a good beginner's subject, for it is hardier than most starfish and fits far more smoothly into a community setting. Brittle stars should be afforded a selection of refuges empty clam shells are particularly appreciated but apart from this, they make no particular demands upon their keeper. Like most nocturnal feeders, *O. superba* is indifferent to daytime light intensity. A temperature range of 20°–24° C. (70°–72° F.) suits it well, although it will withstand water as warm as 28° C. (84° F.) before shedding its arms and dying.

Although they are efficient scavengers, banded brittle stars should be offered pea-sized morsels of fresh or frozen seafood two or three times weekly. They are quite partial to TetraTips. It is best to offer newly purchased specimens food immediately before turning the tank lights off for the night. Eventually, individuals of this species will respond immediately to the chemical cues released by newly introduced morsels of food and come out to feed in broad daylight.

The worst enemies of *Ophiolepis superba* in captivity are large crabs and predatory starfish, but both triggerfish and large wrasses will harrass any brittle star unmercifully. The banded brittle star is an ideal scavenger in a community of sessile, plankton-feeding invertebrates. It can be safely kept with both true and tube anemones and makes a good tankmate for small mobile invertebrates and coral reef fishes.

## Class Holothuroidea  Sea cucumbers

Sea cucumbers deviate most dramatically from the usual echinoderm body plan. The most immediate diffierence lies in the flaccid, elongate body, which lacks the heavy armoring characteristic of the other four extant orders of the phyllum. Equally important is the specialization of the tube feet in different parts of the body to perform specific functions. Only those along its underside are involved in locomotion. Those of the dorsal surface serve a respiratory function, while special clusters located around the mouth are modified as food-gathering structures. Only the arrangement of the mouthparts and their surrounding specialized food-gathering structures reveal the basic pentamerous echinoderm body plan.

Holothurians are for the most part benthic detritus feeders. As might be expected, they are found over soft bottoms and live their lives half buried as they slowly plow through the substratum in search of food. A much smaller number live in rock crevices and filter plankton from the water. The handful of species maintained as aquarium residents are drawn from this assemblage. A few genera, such as *Pelagothuria* and *Planktothuria* have – however improbably – evolved modifications that allow them to exist as pelagic plankton feeders.

Although they lack the armor and spines of their distant relatives, sea cucumbers are by no means defenseless. Most species possess specialized structures known as the Cuverian organs. When a holothurian thus armed is irritated, these organs discharge a mass of sticky, white threads. These serve to entangle many potential predators and are charged with a substance known as holothurin, distasteful to most invertebrates and absolutely deadly to fish. There are numerous reports of fish deaths following defensive discharge of the Cuverian organs under aquarium conditions. The observation that deaths did not occur in tanks with activated carbon filtration suggests a prudent preventive measure should one desire to house fish and sea cucumbers together. Most discharges follow efforts to handle holothurians. The simplest means of preventing them is to gently coax sea a cucumber into a vessel when the need to move it arises rather than to attempt netting it from the tank.

## Order Dendrochirotida

*Paracucumeria tricolor*  Sea apple, tricolor sea cucumber

This strikingly colored sea cucumber is a fairly common inhabitant of coral reefs throughout the Indo-Pacific region. It can grow to 20.0 cm (8″) in length, although most aquarium specimens measure from 10.0–12.0 cm (4″–5″) long. The sea apple is commonly exported by Far Eastern collectors.

This highly decorative sea cucumber displays the usual echinoderm aversion to sudden changes in salinity, but is otherwise a hardy and durable aquarium subject. It relishes strong water movement. Specimens will posi-

**The sea apple, *Paracucumaria tricolor*.**

tion themselves in the part of the tank with the strongest current and spread their oral tentacles wide in anticipation of finding a rich harvest of plankton. The sea apple has no particular light requirements and prospers over the same temperature range as the echinoderms previously considered. Temperatures greater than 28° C. (84° F.) are swiftly lethal.

Aquarists often complain that specimens of the sea apple literally shrink before their very eyes and eventually die for no apparent reason. The explaination of this phenomenon is quite simple: the animals are starving slowly to death! Appearances notwithstanding, *P. tricolor* is a plankton feeder and must be regularly fed the same diet offered such sessile anthozoans as soft corals and gorgonians. If an individual seems to be shrinking, simply feed it more frequently!

Sea apples and other aquaristically interesting sea cucumbers make an agreable addition to a community of sessile plankton-feeding invertebrates. Most mobile invertebrates leave them strictly alone. However, given the complications that can follow from a discharge of the Cuverian organs, prudence would dictate keeping specimens separated from large crabs, carnivorous molluscs and predatory starfish. The extreme sensitivity of fish to holothurin poisoning makes the sea apple and its ilk dubious tankmates for them. As discharges occur in response to provocation, small, inoffensive coral reef fishes stand in less danger when housed with sea cucumbers than do such species as triggerfish and wrasses. In any event, make a point of running an outside power filter charged with activated carbon on any aquarium housing both fishes and holothurians.

**A colorful tropical sea cucumber.**

# Chapter 12.

# Catalog of Fish for the Marine Aquarium

The coral reef supports an astonishingly diverse assemblage of fishes, ranging in size from giant sharks and groupers to miniscule gobies and blennies barely 2.5 cm (1″) long. A remarkably large percentage of the reef's fishes fall at the small end of the size distribution, and most of these are of potential interest to the aquarist. Close to to 300 species have to date been imported at least once, and each year sees the debut of brilliantly colored newcomers to the aquarium scene that bid fair to join the steadily growing list of salt-water staples.

A comprehensive catalog of the marine fishes exported as aquarium subjects is clearly beyond the scope of a work such as this Our object is instead to present an over-view of the principal aquaristically interesting families of coral reef fishes. The focus is on those characteristics common to its members that influence their aquarium husbandry. We will then fill out this narrative with a selection of species primarily chosen from among the families' hardier representatives. The selection of species favors to some extent fish native to the Caribbean, the Gulf of California and Hawaii. These species are readily available to North American aquarists, and because the distance they must travel from reef to retailer is relatively modest, most are relatively inexpensive. Furthermore, because the use of chemical agents as an adjunct to their capture is forbidden in all three locales, the buyer need not fear that fish from these sources will succumb to the delayed effects of cyanide intoxication after he takes them home. Because of the continuing liklihood that fish exported from the Philippines will be afflicted in this manner, we have attempted in our choice of Indo-Pacific species to select those available from alternative sources of supply.

**The sparkling blue waters of the Caribbean are home to many beautiful marine fishes.**

In order to convey relevant information about each species in the most economical manner possible, we have employed the following coding:

**Distribution (D):**
(1) Caribbean
(2) Gulf of California and the Pacific coast of Mexico
(3) Indo-Pacific
(4) Indo-Pacific exclusive of Hawaii
(5) Endemic to Hawaii
(6) Endemic to the Red Sea.
(7) Pantropical

**Adult size, measured from the tip of the snout to the base of the tail fin (SL).**

**Index of Hardiness (H):**
(1) Will survive minor management errors. Has no special dietary requirements. Good beginner's fish.
(2) Sensitive to water quality. Requires regular partial water changes to do well in captivity. Has no special dietary requirements. Best undertaken by aquarists with 8–12 months experience.
(3) Sensitive to water quality. Has special dietary requirements, e.g., live food, fresh vegetable matter, algae. Best undertaken by aquarists with > 12 months experience.
(4) Problem species. Listed special requirement(s) must be meet for successful maintenance.

**Index of Sociality (S):**
(1) Territorial. Extremely intolerant of conspecifics. Often attacks newly introduced fish, even of other species. Only one individual/tank. Best added last to a community aquarium.
(2) Territorial. Tolerates neither conspecifics nor other representatives of the same family. Only one individual of the family in question/tank.
(3) Territorial only towards conspecifics. Other fishes ignored. One individual/tank.
(4) Territorial, but more than one specimen can be kept per tank as long as each has its own shelter.
(5) Territorial towards conspecifics. Lives as pairs in nature and best kept as pairs in captivity. One pair/tank.
(6) Social. Best kept in groups of 3 or more.
(7) Indifferent to the proximity of conspecifics.

**Index of Predatory Tendencies (P):**
(1) Poses no risk to smaller fish.
(2) Preys opportunistically on smaller fish.
(3) Preys routinely on smaller fish.
(4) Preys routinely on fish its own size or larger.
(5) Preys routinely on sessile invertebrates.
(6) Preys routinely on mobile invertebrates.

A typical catalog entry would thus read:

*Eupomacentrus leucostictus* Beau Gregory. D: 1. SL: 15.0 cm (6"). H: 1. S: 2. P: 2.

Decoded, the entry states that the fish in question, the Beau Gregory, is native to the Caribbean, grows to 15.0 cm standard length, is hardy enough to be a good beginner's fish but is extremely territorial and apt to attack other species of damselfish. Thus it should not be kept with other damsels and a specimen should only be added after the community's other residents are well established. Though not a specialized predator, this damsel will eat smaller fish if the opportunity arises.

Family Pomacentridae – Damselfish and Clownfish

Pomacentrids are small to medium-sized fishes found in all the world's subtropical and tropical oceans. A few robust species like the Garibaldi, *Hypsipops rubicundus*, have even managed to colonize warm temperate coastal regions. Damselfish are superficially similar to cichlids and were once thought to be closely related. Contemporary anatomical studies suggest the relationship between the two families is more distant than originally believed, the similarities in question representing convergent adaptations to a similar life-style.

Damselfish occupy two feeding guilds on the coral reef. Members of the first are plankton feeders. These are moderate to highly social species that aggregate where local currents concentrate their prefered food. These damsels are only territorial when sexually active, the male defending a breeding site against others of his sex and vigorously protecting his clutch of eggs against predators. All *Chromis* and most *Dascyllus* species are members of the plankton-feeding guild. These damselfish are relatively unaggressive in captivity and it is usually possible and often desirable to keep several individuals in the same tank. Three seems to be the critical number of individuals required to elicit social behavior. Attempts to keep two specimens per tank usually end with a single survivor.

Representatives of the second guild are primarily herbivorous, although they will also take zooplankton when the opportunity arises. The guild's most specialized representatives systematically create algal "gardens" by killing off all the polyps in a patch of

The blue chromis, *Chromis cyanea,* (above) a colorful zooplankton feeding damselfish.

Zooplankton feeding damselfish like this *Dascyllus* species (below) usually live in large schools in nature. However, they do not always display a comparable fondness for the close company of conspecifics in captivity.

**Although they are zooplankton feeders, clownfish like this pair of *Amphiprion clarkii* are quite territorial and will defend their host anemone vigorously against invasion by congeners.**

coral. This affords filamentous algae a substratum to grow upon, and within a short time, the dead coral supports a vigorous carpet of green threads. The diligent "gardener" rigorously eradicates all algae save its prefered food species from the culture and ferociously defends it from the attentions of other herbivorous fishes, a category to which more than one snorkeler or SCUBA diver has found himself assigned! The genera *Pomacentrus, Stegastes* and *Microspathodon* are all herbivorous, though not all species are algal gardeners. Herbivorous damsels are all territorial towards conspecifics, and many extend their intolerance of intruders to a wide range of other fishes. No more than a single specimen of a given species should be kept per tank and its level of intolerance for heterospecific tankmates must be carefully considered before adding an individual to an established community.

The clownfishes of the genera *Amphiprion* and *Premnas* are, strictly speaking, representatives of the plankton-feeding guild. However, they are notable for their symbiotic

relationship with large carpet anemones of the genera *Radianthus* and *Stoichactis*. By carefully annointing themselves with the mucus on its tentacles that inhibits the anemone from stinging itself to death, clownfish borrow an imunity that permits them to cavort in the heart of some of the reef's most dangerous invertebrates. The value of such a shelter in an environment so well supplied with predators is self-evident. It is thus hardly surprising that feeding habits notwithstanding, clownfish are strongly territorial and defend their anemones against potential usurpers regardless of species.

It is possible to split clownfish into two subdivisions, based upon the degree to which a given species relies upon the protection of its anemone host when carrying out its daily activities. At one extreme are slender-bodied species like *Amphiprion ocellaris, A. percula, A. perideraion, A. polymnus* and *A. sandaracinos*. They are very poor swimmers that virtually never venture away from their anemones to feed. At the other extreme are deep-bodied species such as *Premnas bia-*

*culeatus, A. clarkii, A. ephippium, A. frenatus* and *A. sebae*. These damsels are strong swimmers that often forage considerable distances from their hosts and return to them only in the face of an immediate threat.

Representatives of the first group are relatively unaggressive towards other fishes and often find themselves on the receiving end of their tankmates' aggression. They seem most at ease in the presence of an anemone and cannot be expected to prosper in the company of more assertive tankmates unless they have access to a suitable host. Members of the second group appreciate the availability of an anemone but seem to do quite well in captivity without access to one. They are much more aggressive and will often bully less assertive or smaller companions mercilessly. Thus it is best to introduce them last to a community aquarium.

As a rule, it is tempting fate to try keeping more than a single species of clownfish in a community tank. Aquarists inclined to experiment in this regard are far more apt to succeed with two species of the first group than with two of the second. Under no circumstances should representatives of the two different groups be housed together, for the lives of individuals drawn from the first will be brief, brutish and nasty!

In nature, several clownfish share an anemone. The largest individual is female, the next largest her mate, and the smaller residents immature males. If the female is removed, her erstwhile consort changes sex and becomes a functional female, while the largest of the immature males develops functional testes and becomes her mate. This life history pattern, known as **protandrous hermaphroditism**, is relatively uncommon among coral reef fishes, where the usual rule is for individuals to change from female to male as they grow larger. It simplifies matters considerably for the aquarist who wishes to house a compatible group of clownfish in his aquarium. He need only select specimens that differ several centimeters in size to enjoy a reasonable liklihood of domestic tranquility in the anemone!

That damselfish are frequently used as the starter fish to run in a newly set up biological filter testifies eloquently to their hardiness. They are easily fed and will prosper on a diet of flake and frozen foods. Even the herbivores relish the occaisional treat of live *Artemia*, and all species should be offered fresh vegetable food at least once a week. Newly imported clownfish are somewhat susceptible to velvet and must be carefully quarantined before being added to an established community. Tank-reared specimens seem hardier in this regard.

**Damselfish deposit demersal eggs on a solid surface in a manner reminiscent of cichlids. *Amphiprion frenatus* is one of several pomacentrids successfully bred in captivity.**

Damselfish bellicosity is directly related to tank size. Attempts to house even relatively unaggressive species in tanks under 1.0 m (3') long invariably result in the harrassment of heterospecific tankmates. Providing the tank with a good selection of caves or similar shelters often goes a long way towards muting damselfish aggressiveness in captivity.

Assuming individuals of both sexes share quarters, it is not unusual for damselfish to spawn in captivity. A large plaque of demersal eggs is placed upon a meticulously precleaned surface and guarded ferociously by the male, or in the case of clownfishes, both parents. The eggs hatch the evening of the 5th day postspawning. This affords the larvae some protection as they rise into the plankton. Damselfish are among the very few coral reef fishes that have been successfully bred in captivity. As noted, tank-bred clownfish are regularly available commercially. Readers interested in attempting the task of rearing damsel larvae are refered to the aposite references in the final chapter for information on appropriate techniques.

Hardy and sociable, the sergeant-major, *Abudefduf saxatilis* in an exellent beginner's damselfish.

*Abudefduf saxatilis* – Sergeant-Major. D: 7. SL: 12.0 cm (5"). H: 1. S: 6. P: 2.

Though large by damselfish standards, the sergeant-major is quite peaceful towards other species. A trio of juveniles is as likely to survive the running-in of a new biological filter as a blue damsel and can be counted on to cause less grief to a tank's subsequent in-

habitants. The generally mellower tempraments of this species derives from its pelagic, plankton-feeding life style.

The unusual generic name of these damselfish is derived from Arabic rather than Greek or Latin. It translates as "full or fat flanked." Most *Abudefduf* species are mixed plankton and algae feeders.

*Chromis cyaneus* – Blue Chromis. D: 1. SL: 8.0 cm (2.25"). H: 2. S: 6. P: 1.

*Chromis viridis* – Green Chromis. D: 4. SL: 8.0 cm (2.25") H: 2. S: 6. P: 1.

The blue chromis, by virtue of its distribution, is usually available to North American aquarists on a more regular basis and at a lower price than its Indo-Pacific cognate. There is otherwise little to choose between the two as aquarium residents. Apart from their insistance on regular water changes, these are

The blue chromis, *Chromis cyanea* (above) and *C. caeruleus,* the green chromis (below).

undemanding, highly social damselfishes. This is one of the few coral reef fishes that seems to prosper only when kept in small groups. Both make good additions to a mini-reef set-up.

*Chrysiptera cyanea* – Blue Damsel, Fiji Blue Devil. D: 4. SL: 6.0 cm (1.25"). H: 1. S: 1. P: 1.

This very hardy damsel is often recommended as a starter fish. It is really not well suited for such a role, for several weeks of prior residence reinforces its already well-developed territorial tendencies to such an extent that it usually makes life miserable for subsequent additions to the tank. On the other hand, if added last to a community of less aggressive tankmates, the blue damsel usually settles in to become a reasonably good neighbor.

*Chrysiptera parasema* – Yellow-tailed Chromis. D: 4. SL: 10.0 cm (4"). H: 1. S: 6. P: 1.

Like the sergeant-major, the yellow-tailed chromis is a social species better suited as a starter fish than the commonly used blue damsel. This attractive species is sometimes cited in the aquarium literature under the names *Abudefduf parasema*, *Chromis xanthurus* and *Pomacentrus caeruleus*.

**The three-stripped damsel,** ***Dascyllus aruanus*** **(above) and the four-stripped damsel,** ***D. melanurus*** **(below).**

*Dascyllus aruanus* – Three-striped Damsel. D: 4. SL: 7.5 cm (3"). H: 1. S: 4. P: 1.

*Dascyllus melanurus* – Four-striped Damsel. D: 4. SL: 7.5 cm (3"). H: 1. S: 4. P. 1.

Three-striped and four-striped damsels live in small groups among and above highly branched heads of coral. The social relationships within each group are complex, which may explain why adult specimens brought together in an aquarium at random are more likely to fight than school amicably together. The best way to obtain a compatible group is to purchase the smallest specimens available and introduce them simultaneously to their new home. Alternatively look for two specimens acting like a pair in a dealer's tanks and purchase them. Both the humbug and the black-tailed humbug, as these damselfish are sometimes called, spawn freely in captivity and the young have been reared passed the larval stage.

**Dascyllus trimaculatus (above), the three-spot damsel, and the Hawaiin domino, Dascyllus albisella (below).**

*Dascyllus trimaculatus* – Domino or Three-spot Damsel. D: 4. SL: 12.0 cm (5"). H: 1. S: 6, but see below. P: 1.

*Dascyllus albisella* – Hawaiian Domino. D: 5. SL: 12.0 cm (5"). H: 1. S: 6, but see below. P: 1.

Juvenile Hawaiian dominoes have a larger white spot on the forehead than do three-spot damsels of the same size; adults lack the forehead spot but have a larger lateral spot. In nature, both species enjoy the same sort of relationship with stinging corals that the

various clownfish do with carpet anemones. In captivity, they seem to manage better without their hosts than do clownfish. The larger adult size of these spotted damsels complicates the task of maintaining them in a group. Fortunately, both appear to do quite well when kept as solitary specimens, although such individuals are often more belligerent towards thankmates than would be the case were they members of a group. In any event, adults are very intolerant of other damselfish species. Both three-spot damsels and Hawaiian dominoes spawn freely in captivity.

**The cloudy samselfish, Dascyllyus carneus (above) and D. marginatus (below), the striped damselfish.**

*Dascyllus carneus* – Reticulated or Cloudy Damselfish. D: 3. SL: 7.5 cm (3"). H: 2. S: 6. P: 1.

*Dascyllus marginatus* – Striped Damselfish. D: 4. SL: 5.0 cm (2"). H: 2. P: 1. S: 6.

The rule with these two damselfish is either four or more specimens or else only one per tank. Fortunately their small adult size makes it easier to house a small group without putting undue strain on a tank's filtration system. These two *Dascyllus* species do not tolerate other free-living damsels in their quarters, but do seem to get along well with clownfish.

**Juvenile Beau Gregory, *Stegastes leucostictus* (above) and bicolor damselfish, *S. partitus* (below).**

*Stegastes leucostictus* – Beau Gregory. D: 1. SL: 15.0 cm (6″). H: 1. S: 2. P: 2.

*Stegastes partitus* – Bicolor Damsel. D: 1. SL: 15.0 cm (6″). H: 1. S: 2. P: 2.

Were it not for their extreme territoriality, these two Caribbean species would be ideal aquarium residents. They should be purchased at as small a size as possible and added last to a community aquarium. As they grow larger, their coloration becomes

drabber, while their notion of adequate *lebensraum* expands markedly. As adults defend teritories almost 2 square meters in extend in nature, it should be obvious why they usually outgrow their welcome in the home aquarium. Housed in the large display tanks of public aquaria, which afford sufficient room for several individuals to hold territories, both species spawn freely. Both of these damsels are refered to in the older literature under the generic name *Eupomacentrus*, a junior synonym of *Stegastes*.

*Pomacentrus mollucensis* – Yellow or Sulphur Damsel. D: 4. SL: 8.0 cm (2.25″). H: 2. S: 4. P: 1.

The sulphur damsel is somewhat more delicate than the other pomacentrid species considered herein. Its behavior falls about midway between that of the blue damsel and the sergeant-major. Newly introduced specimens are often on the shy side, so their tank should be provided with plenty of cover.

*Pomacentrus melanochir* – Blue-finned Damsel. D: 4. SL: 7.5 cm (3″). H: 1. S: 2. P: 1.

This attractive damselfish resembles the blue damsel in most respects. However, it is more likely to attack heterospecifics, particularly if they possess a similar color pattern.

*Pomacentrus pulcherrimus* – Yellow-bellied Damsel. D: 4. SL: 6.0 cm (2.25″). H: 1. S: 1. P: 1.

Both the brilliant coloration and small adult

*Pomacentrus melanochir* (above), the blue-finned damselfish, and *P. pulcherimus* (below), the yellow-bellied damselfish.

size of this species make it a good community tank candidate. Sometimes written about under the name *P. pavo*.

*Paraglyphidodon oxydon* – Neon Damsel. D: 4. SL: 8.0 cm (2.25″). H: 2. S: 1. P: 1.

Similar in behavior to the blue damsel, the

neon damsel is slightly more demanding about water quality. As it grows larger, it also requires roomier quarters. A tank 1.3 m (4°) long suffices to meet its need for living space.

A common clownfish, *Amphiprion ocellaris* (above), comfortably established in a Florida anemone.

*Microspathodon chrysurus* – Marine Jewelfish. D: 1. SL: 15.0 cm (6″). H: 1. S: 1. P: 2, 5.

The marine jewelfish is yet another damsel whose spectacular juvenile coloration fades dramatically with adulthood. The yellow tail of mature specimens is poor recompense for the muting of the brilliant blue spots on the head and body. This species is an "algal gardener" that usually lives in close asociation with fire corals of the genus *Millepora* in nature. While not a good choice for a mini-reef set-up, the marine jewelfish makes an attractive addition to a more conventional community of coral reef fishes.

*Microspathodon chrysurus* has been successfully bred many times in captivity. Tank-reared young are often available commercially and are well worth their slightly higher price.

*Apmhiprion ocellaris* – Common Clownfish. D: 4. SL: 7.5 cm (3″). H: 1. S: 6. P: 1.

Common clowns should be kept either in sexual groups of one female and two or more males or as single specimens. They definately do better with a host anemone. As this species is not averse to taking up residence in an alien species such as the Florida anemone, it is not absolutely necessary to offer them a specimen of the somewhat more deli-

cate and always more expensive *Radian-thus*.

Common clownfish breed freely in captivity and are among the very few coral reef fishes reared in commercial quantities. Tank-bred specimens are more resistant to velvet, which can be a real scourge to imported specimens. They are thus a much better buy even if they cost a bit more than wild-caught fish.

**The orange skunk clown, *Amphiprion sandaracinos* (below).**

***Amphiprion perideraion* (below), the skunk clown.**

*Amphiprion perideraion* – Skunk Clown. D: 4. SL: 7.5 cm (3″). H: 4. S: 6. P: 1.

*Amphiprion sandaracinos* – Orange Skunk Clown. D: 4. SL: 11.0 cm (2.25″). H: 4. S: 6. P: 1.

Both of these look-alike species are a bit more sensitive to water quality than the common clownfish, as well as more dependant upon access to a host anemone if they are to prosper in captivity. They are easily bullied and should be housed only with small, un-aggressive companions.

*Amphiprion polymnus* – Saddle-back Clown. D: 4. SL: 12.0 cm (5″). H: 4. S: 6. P: 1.

The distinctive swimming behavior of this species as much as its striking coloration accounts for much of its appeal. The saddle-back clown is probably the weakest swimmer of the genus and certainly one of the most dependant upon access to a host anemone. Its large adult size notwithstanding, it is easily bullied and simply does not survive for any length of time unless kept with a suitable ane-mone. The saddle-back clown makes a nice addition to a mini-reef set-up but usually fares less happily in the usual community of coral reef fishes.

*Amphiprion clarkii* – Yellow-tailed Clown. D: 4. SL: 10.0 cm (4″). H: 1. S: 6, but see below. P: 1.

The yellow-tailed clown is one of the hardiest representatives of the genus. It lives well without a host anemone, but it is considerably more difficult to assemble a stable sexual group in the absence of such a common terri-torial focus. It can be kept as a single speci-men, but such isolated individuals often be-have aggressively towards other fishes and will sometimes attack and kill newly intro-duced specimens. It is thus prudent to add a yellow-tail clown last to a community tank.

*Amphiprion clarkii* (below), the yellow-tailed clownfish, amd the Sebae clown, *A. sebae* (below).

This species breeds freely in captivity. When available, tank-reared specimens are to be prefered over wild fish, particularly if the latter are of Philippine provenance.

*Amphiprion sebae* – Sebae Clown. D: 4. SL: 10.0 cm (4″). H: 1. S: 6, but see below. P: 1.

There is some question about the validity of this very variably marked species, which some authors treat as a synonym of *A. clarkii*. Certainly from an aquaristic perspective, the two fish are completely interchangeable.

*Amphiprion ephippium* – Saddle or cardinal clownfish. D: 4. SL: 8.0 cm (3.25″). H: 2. S: 6, but see below. P: 1.

Saddle clowns should be kept either as sexual groups in the company of a host ane-mone or as single specimens. Like other

The saddle clown, *Amphiprion ephippium*.

*Premnas biaculeatus,* the maroon clownfish.

deep-bodied clownfish, this species can be quite aggressive towards its tankmates and should be added last to a community aquarium.

*Amphiprion frenatus* – Tomato clown. D: 4. SL: 14.0 cm (4.5″). H: 2. S: 6, but see below. P: 1.

Tomato clowns should be handled in the same manner the preceeding species, but by virtue of their larger size, should be afforded larger quarters. Small specimens are more apt to settle easily into an established aquarium than are adults. Females turn black, white males retain their red coloratick.

*Premnas biaculeatus* – Maroon clown. D: 4. SL: 13.0 cm (5″). H: 2. S: 3, but see below. P: 2.

The maroon clownfish is the least dependant member of the group upon access to an ane-

mone, but the most choosy with regard to its host species. Unlike most *Amphiprion* species, *P. biaculeatus* will not usually take up residence in an exotic anemone. It seems to be very difficult to set up a sexual group of maroon clowns. Males are rarely more than half the size of females and are redder overall. Specimens chosen with these criteria in mind are more likely to settle in to a happy domestic life. Solitary specimens of the maroon clown can become extremely aggressive, attacking and killing newcomers to an established tank with grim efficiency. This species is best kept with tankmates its own size or larger and should always be added last to a community aquarium.

Family Labridae – Wrasses

Wrases are a remarkably diverse assemblage of fishes ranging in size from the diminutive cleaner wrasses of the genus *Labroides* to real giants like *Coris formosa* that can grow to nearly a meter in length. Most species go through a series of highly distinctive color patterns as they grow to maturity and many are strongly sexually dimorphic with respect to both size and coloration. Such a state of affairs makes life interesting for ichthyologists, who are frequently vexed to discover that two fishes originally described as different species are really only different life history stages of the same fish!

All wrasses are invertebrate feeders. Even species that rely chiefly upon zooplankton for

**Ontogenetic color change in the wrasse *Coris aygula*: juvenile (upper left), subadult (upper right) and adult (below).**

food are not above picking at tubeworms or making a quick grab for a small shrimp. Robust species like the harlequin tuskfish have the dental equipment to crack the shells of even large crustaceans like reef lobsters and most molluscs. Consequently, wrasses cannot be recommended as residents for a mini-reef set-up, although the great majority of species fare very well in a community of comparably sized coral reef fishes. Note that their formidable dental equipment can be used

with considerable effect on a careless aquarist. Handle any wrasse 10.0 cm (4") long or larger with care!

Many wrasses bury themselves for the night, emerging from their sandy bed at the break of dawn the next day. They will also dive for cover when introduced to new surroundings and display a preternatural ability to disappear from view as soon as their keeper approaches the tank net in hand. More than one marine aquarist has written off a newly purchased wrasse only to have the "deceased" reappear at feeding time a few days later. It is obviously much easier on such sand-divers if they are kept over a substratum with relatively smooth particles, such as Philippine coral gravel.

Although a few temperate Atlantic and Mediterranean species spawn demersal eggs that are guarded by the male, the tropical wrasses kept as ornamental fish scatter pelagic eggs. Many species are protogynous hermaphorodites. Wrasses of the genus *Thalassoma* complicate matters further by having **primary males**, individuals that are born male and remain so throughout their lives, and **secondary males**, individuals that begin their lives as females and subsequently change into males. Primary males are usually much larger thgan females and are strikingly different in coloration. Collectors and importers often refer to them as "supermales". Secondary males look just like females. These differences reflect different breeding strategies. Primary males defend display sites along the forereef from which a pair can make an easy ascent into the water column to spawn. Secondary males are not territorial, but rather swim about in groups and try to "mob" a ripe female and chase her up into the water column to spawn.

If due allowance is made for their size, wrasses are hardy, easily maintained fishes. They are heavy and unselective eaters. Most species appreciate the periodic treat of fresh mussel or clam meat while the larger wrasses should be offered small fish every 7 to 10 days. The only wrasses that are not easily fed in captivity are the cleaner wrasses. The dietary needs of these fish cannot be met with the foods available to aquarists. Their efforts to escape slow starvation translate to incessant solicitation of their companions that drives both their intended clients and their keeper to complete distraction. *Labroides dimidiatus, L. bicolor* and *L. phthirophagus* differ only in the rapidity with which they starve to death in captivity. No *Labroides* can be recommended as a resident of the home marine aquarium.

The Cuban hogfish, *Bodianus pulchellus* (above), and *B. rufus,* the Spanish hogfish (below).

*Bodianus pulchellus* – Cuban Hogfish. D: 1. SL: 30.0 cm (1′). H: 1. S: 3. P: 3, 5, 6.

*Bodianus rufus* – Spanish Hogfish. D: 1. SL: 30.0 cm (1′). H: 1. S: 3. P: 3, 5, 6.

It is impossible to satisfy the specialized dietary requirements of obligate ckeaner wrasses like *Labroides dimidiatus* in the home aquarium.

These hardy, colorful wrasses are a good beginner's choice. Their large size is their main drawback as aquarium residents. Both species grow substantially larger than 30.0 cm in nature, so it is hardly surprising thet they often outgrow their welcome in the marine aquarium. Juveniles 5.0 cm–7.5 cm (2″–3″) are readily available at reasonable prices and can be expected to settle into a newly run-in tank with minimum difficulty. Neither hogfish species is a burrower, so offer them plenty of caves and similar hiding places. The several Indo-Pacific representatives of the genus regularly imported are aquaristically equivalent to these two Caribbean wrasses.

**Primary male (above) and female (below) bird wrasse, *Gomphosus varius*.**

*Cirrhilabrus jordani* – Hawaiian Flame Wrasse. D: 5. SL: 10.0 cm (4″). H: 2. S: 3. P: 1.

This exquisite deep-water wrasse is not easily collected, which accounts for its fairly stiff price. However, after a period of initial shyness, the flame wrasse quickly becomes an active and highly visible member of a coral reef fish community. This is an unagressive, easily bullied species that should be housed only with inoffensive tankmates. Most damsels and large angelfish do not make suitable companions. This is one of the few wrasses that fits smoothly into a mini-reef set-up, although it would still be tempting fate to introduce a flame wrasse to a tank containing well-developed clusters of feather duster or tubeworms!

*Gomphosus varius* – Bird Wrasse. D: 3. SL: M: 30.0 cm (1°); F: 20.0 cm (8″). H: 2. S: 4. P: 3, 5, 6.

Dramatic sexual color differences characterize the bird wrasse. Bright green primary males were originally described as one species, brown females and secondary males as another. As a rule, such fully colored "supermales" are more expensive than putative females, possibly because these wrasses live in single male, multiple female groups. However, a certain percentage of the brown fish in any shipment are actually young primary males and can be expected to metamorphose away from the inhibiting presence of a fully mature male. It is thus not absolutely essential to pay the rather stiff asking price to have a fair shot at a primary male specimen.

It is not possible to house two primary males in the same tank. However, it is both feasible and desirable to keep one such male with a harem of two or more females. Large specimens will routinely eat tankmates up to 5.0 cm (2″) long, but can be expected to get along well with companions too large to make an easy meal. This very active wrasse has a reputation as a jumper. It should always be kept in a tightly covered tank. The bird wrasse is not a burrower. Handle this species with caution. Bizarre head shape notwithstanding, the bird wrasse has powerful jaws that can give a careless hobbyist a nasty bite.

The colorful clown wrasse, *Coris gaimard*, juvenile (above) and adult (below).

Juvenile (above) and adult (below) *Coris formosa*, the spotfin clown wrasse.

*Coris formosa* – Spotfin Clown Wrasse. D: 4. SL: 30.0 cm (1′) under aquarium conditions. Considerably larger in nature. H: 2. S: 3. P: 2, 5, 6.

*Coris gaimard* – Clown Wrasse. D: 3. SL: 30.0 cm (1′). H: 2. S: 3. P: 2, 5, 6.

**Secondary male or female (above) and primary male (below) bluehead wrasse, *Thalassoma bifasciatus*.**

*Thalassoma duperreyi* (above) – Saddleback Wrasse. D: 3. SL: M: 15.0 cm (6″); F: 10.0 cm (4″). H: 1. S: 6, but see below. P: 2.

*Thalassoma bifasciatus* – Bluehead Wrasse. D: 1. SL: M: 15.0 cm (6″); F: 10.0 cm (4″). H: 1. S: 6, but see below. P: 2.

These strikingly marked wrasses exemplify the rapid alternation of color patterns that characterize the life histories of many members of the family. Juvenile and adult specimens of *C. gaimard* were actually thought to represent two different species. Specimens less than 5.0 cm (2″) long often have difficulty adjusting to captivity, but larger individuals are gratifyingly hardy. The clown wrasse is somewhat the more colorful of the two and is available from Hawaiian collectors in the bargain. Less expensive Philippine-caught specimens of both clown wrasses usually succumb to the delayed effects of cyanide poisoning and should be avoided at all cost. Both species are skillful burrowers.

**Secondary male or female (above) and primary male (below) rainbow or Cortez rock wrasse, *Thalassoma lucasanum*.**

*Thalassoma lucasanum* – Rainbow Wrasse (females and secondary males), Cortez Rock Wrasse (primary males). D: 2. SL: M: 15.0 cm (6″); F: 10.0 cm (4″). H: 1. S: 6, but see below. P: 2.

**Female or secondary male *Thalassoma lutescens*.**

*Thalassoma lutescens* – Banana Wrasse (females and secondary males), Lime Green Wrasse (primary males). D: 3. SL: M: 20.0 cm (8″); F: 12.0 cm (5″). H: 1. S: 6, but see below. P: 2.

Wrasses of the genus *Thalassoma* are among the commonest of all coral reef fishes. They are highly social in nature, typically living in assemblages of a single primary male and a large number of females and secondary males. Two primary males will fight to the death under home aquarium conditions, but it is quite feasible to keep these wrasses in harems of a single "supermale" and two or more females. As in the case of the bird wrasse, primary males often command a higher asking price than do juveniles or females. However, the aquarist who purchases a group of 4 or 5 juveniles has a better than even chance of eventually obtaining a primary male. The aquarist who cannot adequately house a group of three or more individuals is advised to make do with a single specimen.

Juveniles of all four species are facultative cleaner fishes in nature. They will continue to pursue such activities in captivity, but unlike the obligate cleaner wrasses of the genus *Labroides*, never make nusiances of themselves. These wrasses are in large measure plankton feeders in nature. The risk in introducing small specimens to a mini-reef tank is thus tolerable. As adults will feed on sessile invertebrates and hunt out molting crustaceans, they are best restricted to more conventional community settings.

All *Thalassoma* species are active swimmers, constantly on the move in search of food. A tank at least 1.0 m (3′) long is a prerequisite for their successful maintenance. With the exception of *T. lucasanum*, these are burrowing wrasses. Each individual has its own patch of bottom to which it retreats each night and from which it emerges the following morning.

*Leinardella fasciata* – Harlequin Tuskfish. D: 4. SL: 30.0 cm (1′) under aquarium conditions. H: 1. S: 3. P: 3, 5, 6.

Specimens of this robust wrasse imported from other parts of the Pacific are hardy, easily acclimated aquarium residents. Cheap Philippine specimens are usually dead within a month of purchase from delayed cyanide poisoning. Net-caught specimens may cost nearly $100.00, but can look foward to a life expectancy of over 5 years in captivity.

Though harlequin tuskfish are death both on shelled invertebrates of any sort and marine worms, they rarely use their impressive dentition on tankmates too large to make an easy mouthful. Though they are not burrowers, these wrasses are large and strong enough to rearrange a tank's infrastructure to their liking. Hence it is important to place any rockwork or dead coral securely on the filter plate or bottom of their tank. If their quarters are furnished with a selection of shelters, harlequin tuskfish will sometimes forgo the satisfaction of redecorating them to their taste.

Family Pomacanthidae – Angelfish

Pomacanthids have earned the name angelfish because of their graceful movements and beautiful coloration. Juveniles and adults of many species differ dramatically in coloration, a state of affairs that often confused early ichthyologists but that usually delights the aquarist. Differences in color pattern aside, the feature that most obviously distinguishes the Pomacanthidae from the closely related butterfly fish of the family Chaetodon-

The spectacular harlequin tuskfish, *Leinardella fascita*.

tidae is their possession of a strong pre-opercular spine. Mishandled specimens can deal their keeper a nasty puncture wound with this weapon. Thus even the dwarf angelfish of the genus *Centropyge* should be handled with great care. The easiest way to capture and transport an angelfish is to steer it into a glass or plastic container of the appropriate dimensions, which can then be removed from the tank.

In nature, the larger angelfish live either solitary lives or else are found in harems of a single male and several females. In captivity, it is impossible to recreate the conditions that permit the emergence of complex social systems for representatives of the genera *Holocanthus* and *Pomacanthus*. Furthermore, these robust angelfish seldom tolerate the presence of congeners, particularly those who sport a similar color pattern. They are thus best kept one to a tank. As these angelfish can grow quite large, the aquarist should not consider adding even a juvenile specimen to an aquarium of less than 300 l (75 U.S. gallons) capacity.

All the dwarf angelfish studied to date live in harems. Histological evidence suggests that they are protogynous hermaphrodites. The liklihood of several conspecific *Centropyge*

Pygmy angelfish such as this *Centropyge ferrugatus* begin their lives as females and eventually change sex, becoming functional males.

living amicably together is a function of the species in question, the sex ratio and aquarium size. Some species, like the flame angel, seem extremely intolerant of conspecifics in captivity regardless of circumstances. Most other dwarf angelfish are less contentious, but even among these, males fight continually if kept together. Since few of these fish are cooperative enough to sport obvious secondary sexual characteristics, the only option open to a prospective buyer is to purchase several specimens of different sizes

**Both juvenile (above) and adult (below) rock beauties live up to their name. However, the dependance of *Holocanthus tricolor* upon sponges for a significant portion of its diet seriously complicates its successful aquarium husbandry.**

and hope for the best. In any event, success is most likely in very large tanks [> 400 l (100 U.S. gallons)]. Happily for aquarists with less spacious facilities, most dwarf angelfish do quite well as solitary specimens.

Angelfish are all sessile invertebrate browsers that include a considerable ammount of fresh vegetable matter in their diet. The larger species are also quite adroit at picking off most of the crustaceans kept as ornamental subjects as fast as they molt. Needless to say, they are unsuited for life in a mini-reef tank, for they will simply graze its rockwork bare of invertebrates in a matter of days.

*Centropyge* species are not above taking a swipe at tubeworms or sponges when the opportunity presents itself. However, the scale of their depredations keeps their impact on the system as a whole within acceptable limits.

A given angelfish species's ability to adapt to captivity seems correlated to the degree to which sponges figure in its diet. The more it relies upon sponges as food, the less the liklihood that the fish will prosper in the aquarium.

The most extreme example of this phenomenon is the rock beauty, *Holcanthus tricolor*, which feeds almost exclusively upon sponges in nature. This magnificent angelfish invariably starves slowly to death in captivity unless its keeper provides it with a continuous supply of its staple food.

As a rule, very small angelfish [< 4.0 cm (1.5″)] are more dependant upon specific – and often hard to supply – food items than are older individuals. Consequently they adapt less readily to the dietary changes that inevitably follow their capture than do larger specimens.

Such very small specimens also quickly show the symptoms of malnourishment. Two or three days without regular feedings are sufficient to starve small angelfish past the point of no return. Baby *Holcanthus* and *Pomacanthus* are extraordinarily appealing in a retailer's tanks, but represent a poor risk unless their buyer can provide them a continual supply of living rock.

Angelfish are susceptible to vitamin deficiency blindness unless they are afforded ample access to fresh vegetable food in captivity. At least a third of their diet should consist of marine algae, leaf vegetables or blanched zucchini, a third of fresh or frozen shellfish and krill, and the remainder of flakes or tablet foods such as TetraTips.

The opportunity to work over a chunk of living rock is a treat appreciated by all pomacanthids. Angelfish should have at least three and preferably four or five small feedings daily. The larger angelfish are adroit beggars and quickly learn to take food from between their keeper's fingers.

Angelfish spawn by releasing pelagic eggs into the water, usually at dusk. Several Caribbean angelfish and a number of *Centropyge* species have been induced to spawn in captivity, but these efforts have not been crowned with the same degree of success as attempts to breed damselfish commercially. The smaller size of the larvae and the greater length of the larval interval greatly complicate efforts to rear them through metamorphosis. Research on techniques for rearing pelagic larvae continues apace, so perhaps the day will soon come when marine enthusiasts will routinely be able to purchase tank-reared angelfish for their tanks

*Holocanthus bermudensis* – Blue Angel. D: 1. SL: to 30.0 cm (1″) in captivity. H: 3. S: 2. P: 2, 5, 6.

*Holocanthus ciliaris* – Queen Angel. D: 1. SL: to 30.0 cm (1″) in captivity. H: 3. S: 2. P: 2, 5, 6.

Adult specimens of these two closely related species are easily told apart. Juveniles, to the contrary, are virtually indistinguishable. Indeed, given the frequency with which 5.0–7.5 cm (2″–3″) specimens purchased as the one prove when grown to be the other, one wonders whether collectors even make a serious effort to do so! To further complicate matters, naturally occurring hybrids of the blue and queen angelfish occur with some degree of regularity.

Adult *Holocanthus bermudensis.*

Juvenile (above) and adult (below), queen angel, *Holocanthus ciliaris.*

These extremely attractive animals were formerly thought to represent a third species, *H. townsendi*.

By virtue of the short distance they must travel to market, these angelfish are usually available to North American hobbyists in excellent condition. If one makes an effort to meet their dietary needs, both the blue and queen angelfish prove quite hardy in captivity. Regretably, large specimens sometimes turn into real bullies whose actions force their keeper to either set up a separate angelfish tank or else find them a new owner. The larger the tank in which they are housed, the less likely that these angelfish will develop anti-social tendencies in captivity.

*Holcanthus passer* – King Angel. D: 2. SL: to 30.0 cm (1″) in captivity. H: 3. S: 2. P: 2, 5, 6.

**Holocanthus passer, the king angelfish, juvenile (above), and adult (below).**

This strikingly marked angelfish is the Pacific coast cognate of the blue and queen angels. Specimens in the 5.0–7.5 cm (2″–3″) size range adapt readily to life in captivity and prove just as hardy as their Caribbean counterparts. Like them, the king angel is a good choice for marine aquarists with no prior experience of the family.

*Holocanthus arcuatus* – Blackband Angel. D: 5. SL: 20.0 cm (8″). H: 3. S: 2. P: 2, 5, 6.

The blackband angelfish is the only large representative of the family regularly found in Hawaiian waters. It is most common at depths > 20.0 m (c. 60″), which complicates the collector's task and contributes to its rather high price. However, no blackband is ever taken with cyanide, which is more than can be said of most Indo-Pacific angelfish species. Add to this the fact that *H. arcuatus* adapts well to captivity and the blackband angel comes across as a pretty good buy for the money.

*Pomacanthus arcuatus* – Black Angel. D: 1. SL: to 25.0 cm (10″) in captivity. H: 3. S: 2. P: 2, 5. 6.

*Pomacanthus paru* – French Angel. D: 1. SL: to 25.0 cm (10″) in captivity. H: 3. S: 2. P: 2, 5, 6.

Juvenile (above) and adult (below) black angelfish, *Pomacanthus arcuatus.*

*Pomacanthus paru,* adult.

The somewhat understated adult coloration and large size of these two closely related species causes many aquarists to overlook them in favor of their gaudier Indo-Pacific cousins. Specimens in the 5.0–7.5 cm (2″–3″) range are attractively colored, quite hardy and reasonably priced. They also act as facultative cleaners of other fish, a further reason for welcoming them to a community aquarium. Both the black and French angels are good beginner's angelfish.

Juvenile Cortex angelfish, *Pomacanthus zonipectus.*

*Pomacanthus zonipectus* – Cortez Angel. D: 2. SL: to 30.0 cm (1°) in captivity. H: 3. S: 2. P: 2, 5, 6.

Juvenile French angelfish, *Pomacanthus paru.*

Juvenile Cortez angels are easily distinguished from their Caribbean cognates by the combination of narrow blue and yellow bars on the flanks. Young specimens of this species are also facultative cleaner fish. The Cortez angel is usually somewhat higher priced than either of the two preceding species, but this aside, it is an equally good choice for the aquarist with no prior experience of the family.

*Pomacanthus annularis* – Blue-ring Angel. D: 4. SL: 20.0 cm (8″). H: 3. S: 2. P: 2, 3, 5.

*Pomacanthus imperator* – Emperor Angel. D: 3. SL: to 30.0 cm (1°) in captivity. H: 3. S: 2. P: 2, 3, 5.

*Pomacanthus semicirculatus* – Koran Angel. D: 3. SL: to 30.0 cm (1°) in captivity. H: 3. S: 2. P: 2, 3, 5.

*Pomacanthus xanthometopon* (below) – Blue-faced Angel. D: 3. SL to 30.0 cm (1″) in captivity. H: 3. S: 2. P: 2, 5, 6.

*Pomacanthus zonipectus,* adult.

Juvenile (above) and adult (below) emperor angelfish, *Pomacanthus imperator*.

Juvenile (above) and adult (below) Koran angelfish, *Pomacanthus semicirculatus*.

This quartet of Indo-Pacific dazzlers embodies every aquarist's fantasies about what coral reef fish ought to be like. All its component species have a reputation for extreme delicacy. As most specimens reaching North American markets are of Philippine provenance, the difficulties hobbyists have encountered with these angelfish probably have been due to the delayed effects of cyanide poisoning rather than to any inherent fragility of the animals themselves. European aquarists, who draw upon a wider spread of collecting sites in the Indian Ocean for Indo-Pacific fishes, report that if due attention is given to water quality in their tanks and their dietary requirements are met, these angelfish do quite well in captivity. The coloration and general well-being of all four species are enhanced if they are regularly allowed to browse the surface of a chunk of "living rock". Unfortunately, all of these fish grow quite large and often become very aggressive towards heterospecific tankmates in the bargain. None can be recommended unless their keeper is prepared to provide them with a tank of 400 l (100 U.S. gallons) or larger.

**Female Potter's angelfish, *Centropyge potteri*.**

*Centropyge argi* – Pygmy Angel, Cherubfish. D: 1. SL: 5.0 cm (2″). H: 3. S: 7. P: 5.

The pygmy angelfishes of the genus *Centropyge* have been described as God's gift to marine aquarists with limited tank space! Single specimens can be expected to do well in tanks as small as 80 l (20 U.S. gallons). By virtue of its distribution, *C. argi* is the species perhaps most readily available to North American aquarists. It is certainly among the lowest-priced and well in the running for first place in overall hardiness. Add striking coloration and the cherubfish emerges as the ideal beginner's angelfish. Though fairly mellow by the standards of the family, it is best to introduce this species last to an established comunity. If the intent is to house more than one specimen in a given tank, the exercise is more likely to succeed if the specimens selected differ somewhat in size and are all introduced simultaneously to their new home.

*Centropyge potteri* – Potter's Angel. D: 5. SL: 10.0 cm (3″). H: 3. S: 7. P: 5.

This Hawaiian species grows somewhat larger than the cherubfish, but like it, combines brilliant coloration with overall hardiness and a fairly placid temprament. Unlike many of its congeners, this species can be sexed reliably. Males have a darker, more extensive pattern of dark blue markings in the midportion of the flanks than do females.

Potter's angel has spawned several times in captivity, so serious marine aquarists might find it well worth the effort to put together a harem of these colorful little fish. Bright gold oligomelanic specimens of Potter's angel are very rarely collected. Their intense golden overlay slowly fades in captivity, suggesting that environmental factors and genetics both play a role in the production of this aberrant phenotype.

***Centropyge loriculus,* the spectacular flame angel.**

*Centropyge loriculus* – Flame Angel. D: 3. SL: 15.0 cm (5″). H: 3. S: 1. P: 5.

The flame angel is one of the most brilliantly colored coral reef fishes and makes a fine addition to a marine aquarium. Its one shortcoming is a distinctly peppery disposition.

This species does not tolerate conspecifics, frequently attacks other fishes with a red or orange-based color pattern and will often bully or even kill newly introduced tankmates regardless of species. A flame angel should always be added last to an established community tank and is least likely to cause future problems if its companions are all slightly larger than it is. This species maintains the full intensity of its coloration best if allowed to browse regularly over the surface of living rock, although regular access to vegetable food also aids this cause. Net-caught specimens from Hawaii are somewhat more expensive but are far more likely to adapt well to aquarium life than are cheaper Philippine exports.

*Centropyge bicolor* – Bicolor Angel. D: 4. SL: 10.0 cm (4″). H: 4. S: 6. P: 5.

*Centropyge flavissimus* – Lemonpeel Angel. D: 4. SL: 10.0 cm (4″). H: 4. S: 6. P: 5.

These spectacularly colored dwarf angels both have a reputation for extreme delicacy among North American aquarists. Australian aquarists, who are not dependant upon cynanidepoisoned Philippine fish, have a somewhat more positive view of both the bicolor and lemonpeel angels as aquarium subjects. Netcaught specimens from the Great Barrier Reef and elsewhere in the Pacific adapt well to life in captivity. Apart from plenty of fresh vegetables and the occasional opportunity to browse over the surface of a piece of living rock, neither species makes any special demands on its keeper. Both lemonpeel and bicolor amgels are easily intimidated and seem to do better kept in small groups. If circumstances make this impractical, single specimens do best when kept with relatively mellow tankmates such as dottybacks, social damsels, gobies and the smaller wrasses.

Family Chaetodontidae – Butterflyfish

Like angelfish, butterfly fish embody the essence of the coral reef for casual observers and experienced aquarists alike. Any diver who has watched these jewels of the sea flutter about the reef will attest that they are most aptly named. The Caribbean and the Pacific coast of North America are rather poorly endowed with butterfly fish. While these species are generally hardy and make good aquarium residents, their colors are not especially vivid. The Family Chaetodontidae enjoys its richest representation in the tropical Indo-Pacific region, where dozens of brilliantly colored species can be found.

Many butterfly fish have a reputation for fragility and inability to adapt successfully to life in captivity. In some instances, this is entirely justified. Many butterfly fish are obligate feeders on live coral polyps. They will not accept alternative foods and can only be maintained in captivity if their usual food can be provided them on a regular basis. These species are often sold under the catch-all tag of "mixed" or "assorted" butterflyfish. Their low price tempts many aquarists to buy a specimen or two for their tanks. However, such purchases are an exercise in futility, for the inevitable lot of these fish is death by slow starvation. The following species all feed heavily upon coral polyps: *Chaetodon bennetti, C. capistratus, C. melanotus, C. meyeri, C. ornatissimus, C. plebius, C. speculum, C. trifascialis, C. trifasciatus* and *C. quadrimaculatus*. The time may someday come when aquarists have convenient means to satisfy the nutritional demands of these admitedly beautiful fishes, but until then, they are better off left to embellish their natural surroundings.

The want of hardiness attributed to less specialized feeders stems in considerable measure from the fact that a substantial percentage of the butterflyfish available through commercial channels are exported from the Philippines. The fact that netcaught specimens of a given species from Hawaii adapt well to captivity while drugged specimens from the Philippines do not suggests that this apparent lack of hardiness stems from the technique of capture the fish than any inherent fragility. For this reason, we have concentrated heavily on those butterflies that are available from Hawaiian exporters. Though net-caught specimens from Hawaii and other parts of the Pacific where the use of cyanide to collect fish is prohibited are more expensive than drugged Philippine fish, they are always the better buy.

Butterflyfish are sensitive to any deterioration in water quality. They should thus only be introduced to a tank after the biological filter is fully run in. Maintaining them in an aquarium with a flourishing growth of green algae may stretch out intervals between water changes somewhat, but the key to successful butterfly fish husbandry is a program of frequent partial water changes.

Butterfly fish are social animals in nature, living either as mated pairs that forage together over an extensive home range or in

Like these *Chaetodon arabicus*, many butterfly fish live as mated pairs in nature.

loose schools. They can be succesfully kept as single specimens in a marine community tank, but the aquarist who so chooses will miss out on a great deal of interesting social behavior. Relatively few aquarists have tanks large enough to house a school of these medium-sized fish successfully. However, apart from the degree of compatibility of the two individuals in question, there are no obstacles to keeping these fish as pairs. Matters are most apt to go smoothly if the aquarist selects two individuals that seem fond of one another's proximity in the dealer's tank. Failing that, purchase two juvenile specimens, introduce them simultaneously to their new home and hope for the best. The fact that individuals brought together at random so frequently pair up successfully suggests either that pre-pubescent behavioral interactions influence the ultimate sexual identity of a given individual or that butterfly fish simply enjoy one another's company regardless of their sex!

Juvenile butterfly fish share the predeliction of their near relatives, the angelfish, for acting as facultative cleaners. A few species, like *Johnrandallia nigrirostris*, continue such behavior into adulthood, hence its vernacular name of **barbero**, or barber, along the Pacific coast of Mexico. Butterfly fish are much less likely than angelfish to become bullies as they grow older. This gratifying absence of bellicosity does not mean that they are in any sense shy. After an initial period of adjustment, butterfly fish spend most of the time swimming actively about their tank's open spaces. Only severely stressed individuals are given to hiding out of sight.

The species presented herein are all known to adapt more or less readily to the usual selection of live, fresh and prepared foods. Newly captured specimens may take some time to learn that food flakes are edible. The process can be accelerated by incorporating one's prefered flake food into the recipe for making feeding stones presented in Chapter – and introducing it to the fish in that manner. Very small chaetodontids – < 5.0 cm (2″) in size – have greater difficulty adjusting to a new diet in captivity and are best bypassed in

favor of larger specimens. All butterfly fish feed enthusiastically upon sessile invertebrates. Tube and featherduster worms are particular delicacies, while several species will even pick at the stinging tentacles of sea anemones!. This hardly recommends most of them for life in a mini-reef set-up. The corollary to this behavior is that all butterfly fish do better in captivity and display more vibrant coloration if offered a piece of "living rock" as a treat every 4 to 6 weeks.

Contrary to the case among the angelfish, butterfly fish are not hermaphroditic. All butterfly fish are pair-spawners, shedding their pelagic eggs into the water column as dusk. Their extremely spiny **tholichthys** larvae were once thought to represent an entirely different group of fishes. The larval interval can be several months long. This does not bode well for efforts to breed butterflies in captivity, but as techniques of larval fish husbandry grow in sophistication, so does the hope that tank-reared specimens of even these "problem" species will someday be available to marine aquarists.

Both of these Caribbean butterflies are frequently available to North American aquarists at reasonable prices. Because they have a relatively short distance to travel from their native haunts, specimens usually arrive at

*Chaetodon sedentarius* – Reef Butterfly. D: 1. SL: 13.0 cm (5″). H: 3. S: 5. P: 1, 5.

*Chaetodon striatus* – Banded Butterfly. D: 1. SL: 13.0 cm (5"). H: 2. S: 5. P: 1, 5.

the retailer's in good condition. This makes it easier for them to quickly adapt to aquarium life. Specimens of either the reef or the banded butterfly thus qualify as excellent beginner's butterfly fish.

The lemon butterfly is a common resident of shallow inshore habitats throughout the

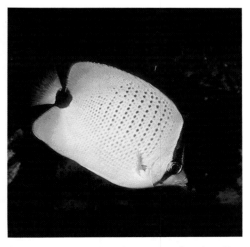

*Chaetodon miliaris* – Lemon or Crochet Butterfly. D: 5. SL: 15.0 cm (6"). H: 2. S: 7. P: 1, 5.

Hawaiian archipelago. This species continues as a cleaner fish into adulthood in nature. It is considerably more colorful than its distant Caribbean cousins, but shares their hardiness. A good first butterfly.

*Roaops tinkeri* – Tinker's Butterfly. D: 5. SL: 15.0 cm (6"). H: 2. S: 5. P: 1, 5.

This strikingly marked species is the unquestioned aristocrat of the Hawaiian butterfly fish. Its gratifying hardiness as much as its beautiful coloration make it a welcome addition to a community of coral reef fish. However, like most deep-water living species, it is not easily collected. Thus when specimens are available, the asking price is likely to be high.

*Chaetodon semilarvatus* – Yellow Butterfly. D: 6. SL: 15.0 cm (6"). H: 3. S: 6.

Red Sea fishes are rarely available to North American aquarists and are usually quite expensive when they can be had. Thus the yellow butterfly is not as well known on this side of the Atlantic as it is in Europe. This is one of the most social of all *Chaetodon* species. It definately seems to do better when kept in small groups. Adults are very picky eaters and seldom come to accept prepared foods. Half-grown specimens are considerably more flexible in this regard. Once

**The yellow butterfly fish.** *Chaetodon semi-larvatus.*

*Chaetodon ephippium,* **the saddleback butterfly.**

they begin eating in earnest, yellow butter-flies are no more difficult to maintain than any other representative of the family.

*Chaetodon auriga* – Threadfin Butterfly. D: 3. SL: 20.0 cm (8″). H: 2. S: 5. P: 2, 5.

*Chaetodon ephippium* – Saddleback Butter-fly. D: 3. SL: 15.0 cm (6″). H: 2. S: 5. P: 1, 5.

*Chaetodon lunula* – Racoon Butterfly. D: 3. SL: 18.0 cm (7″). H: 2. S: 7. P: 2, 5.

*Chaetodon unimaculatus* – Teardrop Butter-fly. D: 3. SL: 15.0 cm (6″). H: 2. S: 5. P: 1, 5.

**The racoon butterfly,** *Chaetidon lunula.*

**The threadfin butterfly,** *Chaetodon auriga.*

*Chaetodon unimaculatus,* **the teardrop butterfly.**

The members of this foursome of species are widely distributed throughout the Indo-Pacific region inclusive of Hawaii. The liklihood that an aquarist will have a happy experience with them is a function of their point of origin. Philippine specimens are poor insurance risks. Net-caught specimens from elsewhere in the Pacific prove gratifyingly hardy and long-lived in captivity. Any of these fish is a good choice for the aquarist without previous experience of the family. Both the racoon and saddleback butterflies have a reputation for browsing on anthozoans over and above the family norm, so choose their companions accordingly.

*Chaetodon xanthurus* – Pearl-scale Butterfly. D: 4. SL: 12.0 cm (5″). H: 3. S: 7. P: 1, 5.

As is the case with the preceding quartet of species, specimens exported from the Philippines are to be avoided at all cost. Even net-caught fish often prove difficult to acclimate to life in captivity and are usually very picky eaters when first purchased. As a rule, half-grown specimens are more easily taught to accept prepared foods than are either juveniles or adults. Once they have learned to accept the usual fare offered marine fishes, they can be expected to do quite well as aquarium residents.

*Chaetodon collare* – Red-tailed Butterfly. D: 4. SL: 12.0 cm (5″). H: 3. S: 7. P: 1, 5.

*Chaetodon vagabundus* – Vagabond Butterfly. D: 4. SL: 15.0 cm (6″). H: 3. S: 5. P: 1, 5.

*Hemitaurichthys zoster* – Pyramid Butterfly. D: 2, 3. SL: 17.0 cm (7″). H: 2. S: 6. P: 2, 5.

This widely distributed butterfly is highly gregarious in nature. Though usually found in large schools, the pyramid butterfly sometimes also lives as mated pairs and can be so maintained in captivity. Like the lemon butterfly, this species will clean other fishes as an adult, but does not make a pest of itself in captivity. A good beginner's butterfly fish.

*Chelmon rostratus* – Copperband Butterfly. D: 4. SL 12.0 cm (5″). H: 4. S: 3. P: 5, 6.

This striking butterfly fish has probably caused marine aquarists greater frustration than all other members of the family Chaetodontidae combined. Newly captured specimens take only live food and can only with difficulty be persuaded to accept fresh or frozen seafood substitutes for their usual diet of small crustaceans and marine worms. Featherduster and tube worms apart, copperband butterflies pose no risk to sessile invertebrates. They are thus good candidates for a mini-reef tank, whose fortuitously acquired microcrustacean fauna affords them an essential dietary supplement.

*Forcipiger flavissimus* – Long-nosed Butterfly. D: 3. SL: 15.0 cm. H: 2. S: 3. P: 5, 6.

Delicate appearance notwithstanding, net-caught specimens of the long-nosed butterfly fish are gratifyingly hardy and adapt well to life in captivity. They are good eaters and soon learn to take prepared foods in addition to their prefered fare of live and frozen foods. While they will eat featherduster and tube worms, long-nosed butterflies usually ignore

**The exotic-looking longnosed butterfly fish, *Forcipiger flavissimus*.**

anthozoans. They are thus suitable candidates for residence in a mini-reef aquarium. The very similarly colored *F. longirostris* occurs together with *F. flavissimus* over much of its range. The easiest way to tell the two apart apart is to count the number of spines in the dorsal fin: 10–11 in *F longirostris*, 12 in *F. flavissimus*.

*Heniochus acuminatus* – Wimplefish, Heni. D: 3. SL: 15.0 cm (6″). H: 1. S: 7. P: 2, 5.

Sometimes known as the "poor man's moorish idol", *H. acuminatus* is a strikingly attractive aquarium subject in its own right. Net caught specimens are probably the hardiest of all butterfly fish. The heni is certainly the only commonly available representative of the family Chaetodontidae that could in any sense be described as a beginner's

Wimplefish are quite social in nature. Like these *Heniochus acuminatus,* they are ususally found in large schools on the reef.

fish. Wimplefish are highly social in nature. Their schools are often the foci of intense grooming activity, for this species actively cleans other fishes as an adult.

*Johnrandallia nigrirostris* – Cortez Wimplefish, Barbero. D: 2. SL: 15.0 cm (6″). H: 2. S: 7. P: 2, 5.

The barbero is another butterfly fish that continues to clean other fish as an adult. It is almost as hardy as the heni and just as social, although it will live well as a solitary specimen in a coral reef community tank.

Families Acanthuridae and Siganidae – Tangs, Surgeonfish, Moorish Idols and Rabbitfish

These fishes are all herbivores. As such they can play a important role in controling the growth of filamentous algae in the aquarium. However, most aquarists base their decision to purchase a specimen less on its utility than its beauty. Tangs are brilliantly colored even by the unrestrained standards of the coral reef. Furthermore, their habit of swimingly boldly about in the open makes them ideal display fishes.

The siganids, or rabittfishes, are not, for the most part, coral reef fishes. They usually occur over sandy bottoms within the lagoon proper, often in beds of turtle grass. A number even regularly enter fresh water as adults. Though most siganids are hardy and attractively marked as juveniles, their rapid growth rate and large adult size make them poor candidates for the home aquarium. The only member of the family Siganidae usually kept as an ornamental subject is the foxface, *Lo vulpinus*.

Most members of the Acanthuridae possess one or two pairs of sharp, blade-like spines on the caudal peduncle. The Moorish idols are an exception to this rule. They were formerly placed in a family of their own, the Zanclidae. However, recent anatomical studies have revealed that they share a suite of specialized characteristics with the surgeonfishes and are thus best considered rather aberrant members of the Acanthuridae.

In the smaller surgeonfish species, the caudal spines fold back into a special groove and are erected only in the face of danger. Usually lighter in color than their surrounding background, they are easily visible at a distance. Many species advertise possession of these "switchblades" by surrounding them with a patch of brilliant color. The Achilles tang provides a dramatic instance of such an **aposematic**, or warning color pattern. Other

fishes have a healthy respect for these weapons and usually leave their bearers strictly alone. The prudent aquarist will cultivate a similar respect and handle tangs with extreme caution. Even a 10. cm (4") long specimen can inflict a nasty, painful, slow-healing wound. Should such a misadventure occur, refer to Chapter 9 for appropriate first aid measures.

Though many species of surgeonfish are highly social in nature, the rule is one tang per tank in captivity. Tangs are known for their intolerance of heterospecific representatives of their family. Several species will even attack unrelated fishes with a color pattern similar to their own. These foibles apart, acanthurids make good neighbors and can be recommended for both mini-reef and conventional community tanks, although their appetite for fresh greens conflicts with efforts to cultivate a profuse growth of macroalgae in the former.

Tangs do not prosper unless at least half of their diet consists of fresh vegetable foods. They prefer filamentous algae, but will also take *Caulerpa*, blanched leaf vegetables and thinly sliced zucchini eagerly. The remainder of their diet should consist of flake foods with

**Many tangs share the social tendencies of these *Paracanthurus hepatus* on nature, yet prove intolerant of conspecifics in captivity.**

a high vegetable content, such as Tetra Conditioning Food, or tablets such as TetraTips. Tangs are accustomed to graze continually in nature and thus require at least 4 small feedings daily to do their best in captivity. The importance of such a feeding schedule cannot be overemphasized. Tangs simply starve to death on the one or two daily feedings that suffice to keep most fish happy. Like most fish with robust appetites, they quickly associate the appearance of their owner and that of food. Specimens soon learn to take food from their keeper's fingers.

Tangs and rabbitfishes are not hermaphrodites. They spawn either as single pairs or in groups, shedding pelagic eggs into the water at dusk. Tangs have a specialized, very spiny larval form, the **acronurus**, which spend a long time in the plankton. This bodes ill for eventual captive rearing. Several siganids, on the other hand, have been bred and reared past the larval stage many times by mariculturists. Regretably, the foxface is not among them, but there is no reason to think it would prove any more challenging to breed than any other rabbittfish.

*Acanthurus leucosternon* – Powder Blue Tang. D: 4. SL: 20.0 cm (8″). H: 3. S: 2. P: 1.

Net-caught specimens of this stunning surgeonfish settle in quickly to captive life and prove quite hardy. This species is very intolerant of other tangs and often behaves aggressively towards other blue fish. Best added last to a community tank.

*Acanthurus achilles* – Achilles Tang. D: 3. SL: to 30.0 cm (1°) in captivity. H: 3. S: 2. P: 1.

*Acanthurus olivaceous* – Red-shouldered Tang, Olive Surgeonfish. D: 3. SL: to 30.0 cm (1°) in captivity. H: 3. S: 2. P: 1.

The reputation these species have earned as difficult aquarium subjects is largely based upon the short life-span of cyanide poisoned Philippine specimens. Hawaiian collectors have found that both adapt well to life in captivity. Their chief disadvantage as aquarium residents is their large adult size, which mandates a tank of at least 400 l (100 US gallons), and their insatiable appetites, which mandate with equal urgency an extremely efficient filtration system. On both counts, prospective purchasers without the option of donating outsized specimens to a public aquarium should think carefully before purchasing either the Achilles or the orange-shouldered tang.

Juvenile (above) and adult (below) blue tang, *Acanthurus caeruleus.*

*Acanthurus caeruleus* – Blue Tang. D: 1. SL: 20.0 cm (8″). H: 3. S: 2. P: 1.

Blue tangs undergo such a dramatic color change from juvenile to adult that one could be forgiven for assuming the two to be different species! Apart from its specialized feeding requirements, this is a hardy, easily maintained tang. A good choice for the aquarist with no prior experience of the family.

*Paracanthurus hepatus* – Yellow-tailed Blue Tang, Palette Tang, Hippo Tang. D: 4. SL: 18.0 cm (7″). H: 3. S: 2. P: 1.

Sometimes called "the bluest thing on earth",

**As it bears no resemblance whatsoever to a hippopotamus, the peculiar common name of *Paracanthurus hepatus* probably derives from a long-standing mispronunciation of its scientific name.**

this relatively small tang is easily one of the most popular members of the family. This is yet another species whose reputation for delicacy apparently owes more to the delayed results of cyanide poisoning than to any inherent fragility. Net-caught specimens adapt well to aquarium conditions and display healthy appetites. This tang is particularly efficient at cropping green hair algae and less inclined than most to munch on *Caulerpa*. It is very susceptible to *Oodinium*. Hence the importance of a lengthy quarantine period before introducing it to an an established aquarium.

*Zebrasoma flavescens* – Yellow Tang. D: 5. SL: 15.0 cm (6″). H: 3. S: 2. P: 1.

If the preceeding species is the bluest thing on earth, then this tang is surely one of the yellowest! This is another good beginner's surgeonfish. Its relatively small size simplifies the task of housing it properly, while its provenance guarantees the buyer his purchase is net-caught. Regretably, most specimens are inadvertently starved to death by owners unaware of the need to offer their pride and joy four or five feedings daily.

*Zebrasoma veliferum* – Zebra Sailfin Tang. D: 4. SL: 25.0 cm (10″). H: 3. S: 2. P: 1.

This magnificent tang shares the tendency of *A. leucosternon* to go after other fishes with a similar color pattern. Adults make a magnificent display, but like the Achilles and orangeshouldered tangs, require very large aquaria to prosper in captivity.

*Zanclus canescens* – Moorish Idol. D: 2, 3. SL: 18.0 cm (7″). H: 3. S: 6, but see below. P: 1.

The moorish idol is also virtually synonymous with the coral reef to most people. Regretably, it is a delicate species that requires plenty of fresh vegetable foods to prosper. Moorish idols are susceptible to flukes, and heavy infestations will often depress their appetites. If a specimen goes off of its feed for no apparent reason, give it a freshwater dip as described in Chapter 9, then try tempting its appetite with fresh or frozen filamentous algae. Net-caught specimens from Baja California or Hawaii are always to be prefered over cheaper specimens from the Philippines.

*Lo vulpinus* – Foxface. D: 3. SL: 25.0 cm (10″). H: 2. S: 3. P: 2, 4.

Given proper attention to its dietary requirements, the foxface is a hardy, long-lived aquarium resident. Like all siganids, its venomous spines can deliver a nasty puncture wound that can be a long time healing. Hence it should be handled with care.

Families    Lutjanidae    and    Serranidae Snappers, Groupers and their Allies.

The snappers of the family Lutjanidae are medium-sized to large fish-eating predators. The more pelagic representatives of the family are cruise predators, actively chasing down their prey. Many are quite social in

**A magnificent specimen of the red argus grouper, *Cephalopholis miniatus* (right), also known as the coral trout.**

nature and hunt in schools. Species that live in closer contact with the bottom tend to rely more upon ambush to capture their prey and are usually solitary. Juvenile snappers are a regular fixture of mangrove swamps. The young of several species display considerable tolerance for fluctuations in water density and often penetrate into fully freshwater biotopes. While these important food fish are not particularly difficult to maintain in captivity, only a few species sport sufficiently attractive coloration to merit the interest of marine aquarists. They should be treated in the same manner as true groupers.

The family Serranidae is much more difficult to concisely characterize. Ichthyologists recognize three subfamilies. At one extreme are the true groupers of the subfamily Epinephellinae. These are large, sedentary ambush predators capable of preying on fish their own size or larger. The sea basses and hamlets of the subfamily Serraninae are smaller, more active predators. They rarely exceed 30.0 cm (1″) SL and feed on smaller fishes and inveretebrates. The coral perches of the subfamily Anthianae are medium-sized, highly social plankton feeders. Finally, there remains a residue of species of uncertain taxonomic status. These include such aquarium residents as the voracious goldline grouper, *Grammistes sexlineatus*. sometimes placed in a family of its own, the Grammistidae, and the diminutive basslets of the genus *Liopoproma*, colorful invertebrate feeders that rarely exceed 10.0 cm (4″) in length.

True groupers, operationally defined as the epinephillines and *G. sexlineatus*, suffer from two serious drawbacks as aquarium residents. First, they are large fish, most species growing to about 1.0 m (c. 3″) long in nature, with a few real monsters attaining lengths of nearly 3.0 m (10″). In captivity, groupers **routinely** grow to 30.0 cm (1″) long and will keep right on growing as long as their keeper continues to satisfy their ever increasing appetites. The waste load they generate is proportional to their size. They thus require large tanks equipped with efficient filtration systems that include both mechanical and biological elements. Two hundred liters (50 U. S. gallons) of water barely suffices for single specimen of the snowy or blue-dot grouper; a 400 l (100 U. S. gallon) tank comes closer to the ideal for long-term maintenance.

Their second shortcoming is their seemingly preternatural ability to devour virtually any other fish with which they are kept. Most grouper keepers begin their careers by placing 10.0 cm (4″) specimen in a coral reef community containing an assortment of larger tankmates. Within a surprisingly short time, the tank has only one inhabitant, a much larger and obviously well-fed grouper! Even relatively small species like the six-lined grouper can overcome deep-bodied prey their own length. Greater size affords slender-bodied fish no immunity from predation. A grouper simply grabs such prey by the head and swallows it in slow stages! Not even the caudal switchblades of surgeonfish and tangs assures their safety. The only coral reef fish that have not been reported victims of grouper gluttony in captivity are cleaner wrasses, moray eels, porcupine puffers and lionfish! No mobile invertebrate is safe from their appetites either. Even cleaner shrimp run a serious risk from these insatiable predators.

Their shortcomings aside, groupers are hardy, easily maintained aquarium residents. They have all the vices and virtues of large predatory cichlids, and like them, are best maintained as single "pet fish". True groupers do not appreciate intense light. They adjust more readily to life in captivity if their quarters are provided with one or more caves to which they can retire and from which they can survey their surroundings. These fish have, for reasons known best to themselves, the habit of "basking" in a column of air bubbles. Such behavior does not indicate respiratory distress and ought not provoke an immediate treatment for gill flukes!

Although they clearly prefer live fish or crustaceans, groupers can be easily taught to take pieces of fish or shellfish from their owner's fingers. They are the ideal pet for the marine aquarist who lacks the time to feed his

fish several times each day. Groupers are acustomed to infrequent large meals and do quite well if fed once every other day. These fish are incorrigible and highly persuasive beggars. However, it is worth remembering when being importuned by a frantic specimen that growth rate is proportional to food intake. The aquarist who wants to enjoy the company of a pet grouper for as long as possible thus will harden his heart at feeding time!

Epinephellines are protogynous hermaphorodites that spawn as single pairs or in single female, multiple male groups, depending upon species. Like most reef fishes, they shed pelagic eggs into the water column at dusk. After spending 30 to 40 days in the plankton, the larvae metamorphose and settle onto the reef. Several species of grouper have been reared through metamorphosis in captivity, but none are currently bred for sale as aquarium subjects.

Sea basses share the hardiness of their monster relatives but are much more easily managed in captivity. The hamlets in particular are somewhat shyer in new surroundings than are groupers and should be provided a choice of shelters. While all are predators, they restrict their depredations to smaller fish and crustaceans. Assuming one chooses their companions carefully, there is thus no reason why either sea basses or hamlets cannot be kept in a coral reef community tank. Sea basses and hamlets often live as pairs in nature. They can be so maintained in captivity, but solitary specimens seem to do equally well.

Like groupers, serranines prefer live food but quickly learn to take pieces of fresh or frozen fish or shellfish. Many specimens also develop a taste for tablet foods. Serranines can make do on a single feeding daily, but clearly prefer several smaller meals to one large one.

All serranines are **simultaneous hermaphrodites**, each individual capable of functioning as either a male or a female, though not of fertilizing its own eggs. They are pair spawners, shedding their pelagic eggs at dusk. Each member of the pair alternates as male or female. The larval interval is as in the

Serranines like this *Serranus tortugarum* are simultaneous hermaphrodites and have sex lives noteworthy even by the rather unusual standards of many coral reef fishes!

true groupers. The hamlets in particular would probably repay the attention of marine aquaculturists. Obtaining pairs clearly is no problem, and freshly-caught specimens will spawn regularly if well-fed.

The coral perches are so named from their habit of living in schools among the branches of large coral formations. They have a reputation for greater fragility than either true groupers or sea basses. This may in part reflect that fact that most specimens available to North American aquarists are of Philippine provenance. Certainly net-caught Hawaiian animals adapt satisfactorily to life in captivity. These plankton-feeders make excellent additions to either a standard community of coral reef fishes or to a mini-reef set-up. Coral perches are easily bullied and should not be housed with belligerent tankmates such as damselfishes. *Dascyllus* species in particular seem inclined to harrass anthianines, possibly because they are competitors for the same refuges and food supply in nature. Coral perch prosper on the same diet as planktivorous damselfishes in captivity.

Coral perches are protogynous hermaphrodites. Each school comprises a single functional male and his harem of females. In the event of his demise, the dominant female undergoes a rapid sex change and takes his place. The pelagic eggs are shed at dusk. There is no information available on the nature of the larval stages or their duration.

The taxonomic placement of the basslets of

the genus *Liopoproma* is uncertain. Some ichthyologists consider them to be somewhat unusual sea basses, others place them in a separate family. Regardless of their systematic status, they are colorful, little fishes, identical in their maintenance requirements to the grammas. They should not be kept with aggressive tankmates, but this aside, are well suited to life in either a conventional or a mini-reef community. Their one disadvantage is their episodic availability and relatively stiff price. Both reflect that fact that basslets are solitary deep-water fishes and as such, not easily collected in quantity.

Basslets are gonochoristic. In this respect, they differ from other serranoids. They are known to spawn as pairs, shedding their pelagic eggs at dusk, but nothing further is known of their reproductive biology. Their small size and brilliant coloration suggest that they would amply repay the attention of mariculturists.

*Lutjanus sebae* – Emperor Snapper, Government Bream. D: 4. SL: 60.0 cm (2"). H: 2. S: 3. P: 4, 6.

This magnificently colored snapper retains its attractive markings even into adulthood. However, few aquarists are equipped to house specimens over 30.0 cm (1") in length. Specimens from Sri Lanka have a better chance of survival in captivity than those of Philippine provenance. They are thus a better buy, notwithstanding their higher price.

**A juvenile emperor smapper, *Lutjanus sebae*.**

*Sympherichthys spilures* – Threadfin Snapper. D: 4. SL: 60.0 cm (2"). H: 2. S: 7. P: 3, 6.

The most striking feature of this snapper, the bright yellow soft dorsal filaments, are best developed on specimens 7.5 cm (3") – 15.0 cm (6") long. As specimens grow larger, the relative length of the dorsal filaments decreases and the intensity of their coloration tends to fade. This species is an active swimmer. Half-grown specimens require a tank at least 2.0 m (6") long to feel comfortable in captivity.

*Cephalopholis argus* – Blue-spotted Grouper. D: 3. SL: 45.0 cm (18"). H: 2. S: 2. P: 4, 6.

*Cephalopholis miniatus* – Red Argus Grouper, Coral Trout. D: 4. SL 45.0 cm (18"). H: 2. S: 2. P: 4, 6.

The blue-spotted grouper is one of the few marine fishes whose range has been artificially extended by direct human intervention. This Indo-Pacific species was successfully introduced to Hawaiian waters in the 1950's. Like the red argus, the blue-spotted grouper is widely distributed in the IndoPacific region. It is considerably more abundant than its red-bodied look-alike, which accounts for the considerable difference in both the availability and the asking price of these two groupers. Neither species is particularly difficult to maintain, although large tanks and plenty of shelter are an absolute must for both.

*Variola louti* is another large, red-bodied Indo-Pacific grouper marked with regular blue spots. It differs from *C. miniatus* in having a lunate rather than a rounded tail fin. It is equally hardy and makes a very desirable aquarium resident.

*Epinephelus summana* – Snowy Grouper. D: 4. SL: 55.0 cm (22"). H: 2. S: 2. P: 4, 6.

This handsome grouper is entirely representative of the numerous other species of its genus. Its maintenance requirements are as outlined for the subfamily. There are reported cases of snowy groupers going blind because their tanks were either too brightly lit or illuminated 24 hours a day. The schedule of lighting in its quarters should reflect this sensitivity. A good beginner's grouper.

*Plectropomus maculatus* – Saddleback Grouper. D: 4. SL: 1.0 m (3°). H: 2. S: 2. P: 4, 6.

The saddleback grouper displays considerable variability in the disposition of its distinctive black dorsal blotches. It makes a strikingly handsome aquarium resident. Speci-

*Cromileptes altivelis* – Panther Grouper. D: 4. SL: 60.0 cm (2°). H: 2. S: 3. P: 4, 6.

Sometimes called the polka-dot grouper, *C. altivelis* is probably the most popular representative of the subfamily Epiniphellinae. It is certainly the most generally available. The relatively small, pointed head of the panther grouper often leads aquarists to underestimate the capacity of its mouth, with predictably final consequences for its tankmates.

**The saddleback grouper, *Plectropomus maculatus*.**

mens very quickly learn to associate their keeper with the appearance of food and become real "pet fish". The only real disadvantage of the saddleback grouper as an aquarium resident is its large adult size. Even the most dedicated grouper enthusiasts are usually forced to find their pets more spacious quarters once they exceed 30.0 cm (1") in length.

*Grammistes sexlineatus* – Goldline Grouper. D: 4. SL: 25.0 cm (10"). H: 1. S: 3. P: 4, 6.

Sometimes placed in a family of its own, the Grammistidae, the goldline grouper is a strikingly marked species whose hardiness and small adult size make it an excellent aquarium subject. Its voracity is quite disproportionate to its size. A 20.0 cm (8") specimen is quite capable of devouring an angelfish or butterfly 15.0 cm (6") long by the simple expedient of seizing it head first and slamming its protruding body against the tank wall or a similar resistant object until its victim is literally rammed down its throat! Interestingly, goldline groupers can be kept safely with other epinephillines because their body slime renders them distasteful to other predators. Reports that these secretions can also poison other fish under aquarium conditions appear to be unfounded.

*Hypoplectrus gemma* – Blue Hamlet. D: 1. SL: 12.5 cm (5"). H: 1. S: 5. P: 3, 6.

The color pattern of this attractive hamlet strongly resembles that of the sympatrically

Hypoplectrus gemma, *the blue hamlet.*

occurring *Chromis cyaneus*. It has been suggested that this is an instance of mimicry, although it is not immediately evident what benefit obtains to either species from resembling the other so closely. The blue hamlet is readily available to North American aquarists and makes a good beginner's fish. However, it does not pay to forget that it is a predator, and size notwithstanding, a surprisingly efficient one, when selecting its tankmates.

*Hypoplectrus guttavarius* – Shy Hamlet. D: 1. SL: 12.5 cm (5"). H: 1. S: 5. P: 3, 6.

The common name of this variably colored serranine is something of a puzzle. While clearly more comfortable in a well-furnished aquarium, *H. guttavarius* is no more retiring than any of its congeners. The yellow hamlet,

*Hypoplectrus gummigutta*, is a uniformly golden yellow species found at depths of 30.0 m (c. 100°) or more. In view of the variable expression of the dark blotch in the shy hamlet, it has been suggested that the yellow hamlet is at best a color morph of *H. guttavarius*. Be that as it may, the depth distribution of the yellow hamlet explains why it is seen less frequently than its more common relative and commands a much higher price when available.

*Hypoplectrus indigo* – Indigo Hamlet. D: 1. SL 15.0 cm (6"). H: 1. S: 5. P: 3, 6.

The aptly named indigo hamlet is one of the largest, as well as among the most attractive, species of the genus. Like the forgoing species, it is easily maintained and readily

available to North American aquarists at a reasonable price. All hamlets make good residents for an aquarium featuring sessile invertebrates, provided their keeper does not loose sight of their predatory tendencies when adding other fishes or small crustaceans to the tank.

*Serranus tigrinus* – Tiger Basslet. D: 1. SL: 12.5 cm (5"). H: 1. S: 5. P: 3, 6.

The tiger basslet is representative of many other *Serranus* species of like size and handsome coloration that make good aquarium residents. All should be treated in the same manner as hamlets.

**The indigo hamlet, *Hypoplectrus indigo* (above).**

***Serranus tigrinus* (below), the tiger basslet.**

*Anthias pleurotaenia* – Coral Perch. Royal Anthias Squar-kads Anthias D: 4. SL: 12.5 cm (5"). H: 3 S: 6. P: 2.

Females of this graceful species lack the elegant caudal filaments and hot pink lateral blotch of males. The latter are often sold at a higher price, but a thrifty aquarist need only buy a number of females and exercise a bit of patience to obtain a fully developed male specimen. It sometimes takes newly imported specimens a while to learn that non-living foods are both edible and tasty, so be prepared to offer them live *Artemia* for their initial few meals. Flake-foods are not us usually accepted by any anthiines in captivity.

*Mirolabrichthys tuka* – Purple Queen. D: 4. SL : 15.0 cm (6"). H: 4. S: 6. P: 1.

The aquarist who takes the trouble to secure net-caught specimens of this lovely anthia-

prefer the company of other sedentary fishes, such as grammas and hawkfish. All make lovely additions to a mini-reef set-up.

nine will find it to be an easily maintained species. Regretably, most of the specimens available to North American aquarists are exported from the Philippines. This goes far towards explaining the purple queen's reputation for fragility in captivity. This and the preceeding species make splendid additions to a sessile invertebrate tank. Possibly because invertebrate enthusiasts take care to exclude most highly aggressive fishes from such a set-up, anthiines often do much better in a mini-reef tank than they do in a more conventional community of coral reef fishes.

*Liopoproma rubre* – Swiss Guard Basslet. D: 1. SL: 10.0 cm (4″). H: 2. S: 7. P: 1.

The Swiss Guard basslet is the most generally available species of this genus of brightly colored, deep-water serranoids from the Caribbean and the Pacific coast of Mexico and Central America. They do not appear to be particularly abundant even in their prefered habitat. This factor, taken with the difficulties entailed in collecting fish as depths of 20.0 m (c. 60″) or more, accounts for both their sporadic availability and high price. Basslets are slow-moving, easily intimidated fishes that do not appreciate aggressive or highly active tankmates such as damselfishes and most wrasses. They appear to

Families Grammidae, Pseudochromidae and Calloplesiopidae

These three families are more or less closely related to the family Serranidae. Unlike most serranids, all are comprised of small, non-predatory fishes that make splendid additions to either a mini-reef set-up or a conventional community of coral reef fishes.

The fairy basslets or grammas of the family Grammidae are all of Caribbean provenance. They are typical reef front inhabitants, where they can be found, often in large numbers, lurking in the shelter of caves and overhangs. They occupy a depth range of 2.0 to 100.0 m (6″–320″), but are usually found in substantial numbers only at depths of 20.0 m (63″) or more. The amount of working time a collector enjoys at such depths is limited, a fact that complicates their capture. This accounts in part for the often high price tags on these living jewels. Grammas are moderately social little fishes. There is evidence that like most serranids, grammas are **protogynous hermaphrodites**, all individuals beginning their lives as females and becoming males as they grow older and larger. Grammas are mouthbrooders, the male carrying the zygotes until hatching.

The dottybacks of the Family Pseudochromidae are restricted to the Indo-Pacific region, where they appear to function as the ecological counterparts of the Grammidae. A fair number of species occur in the immediate subtidal zone, and are thus more easily collected than are some of their Caribbean analogs. This probably accounts for their moderate prices, notwithstanding the greater distance they must travel to market. Dottybacks are territorial and many species will attack heterospecifics with a similar color pattern. Like damselfish, dottybacks spawn demersal eggs, which are guarded by the male. Although there are no accounts of successful spawning in captivity, the group would probably repay the attention of marine fish breeders.

*Calloplesiops altivelis*, the coral comet or marine betta, is the only representative of the small family Calloplesiopidae kept as an aquarium resident. This slow-moving species spends most of its time drifting slowly across its tank with its spectacular finnage fully spread. The marine betta is a moray eel mimic. When threatened, it takes shelter in the nearest cave or coral crevice, taking care to leave its fully spread tail, whose markings bear an uncanny resemblance to the head of a moray, in full view at its entrance. Though admitedly unconventional, this tactic seems to discourage most predators from pursuing the matter further.

Representatives of all three families do well on a diet made up of equal portions of flake and frozen food. A weekly treat of live *Artemia*, either nauplii or adults, is greatly appreciated. While none of these fish is herbivorous, it is not a bad idea to slip in the occasional feeding of Tetra Conditioning Flakes soaked in clam juice onto the menu. Newly captured specimens sometimes require a bit of coaxing to induce them to take prepared foods. This aside, their maintenance is quite a straightfoward matter.

*Gramma loreto* – Royal Gramma, Fairy Basslet. D: 1. SL: 6.0 cm (2.25″). H: 2. S: 4. P: 1.

*Gramma melacara* – Blackcap Gramma. D: 1. SL: 6.0 cm (2.25″). H: 2. S: 4. P: 1.

As long as due attention is paid to maintaining water quality in their tank, these two basslets are undemanding aquarium residents. It

*Gramma loreto,* the royal gramma.

The black-capped gramma, *Gramma melacara.*

is essential to offer them an abundance of cover and choose their companions with care, as they are quite easily intimidated by more assertive tankmates. While a small group of individuals makes an attractive display, neither the royal gramma not the blackcap fairy basslet seems to require the presence of conspecifics to feel at ease. So long as their quarters afford them shelter, single specimens can be expected to settle in and do quite well in either a mini-reef or a conventional community setting. The royal gramma has spawned in captivity, although no young were raised past the larval stage.

*Pseudochromis diadema* – Red-capped Dottyback. D: 4. SL: 6.5 cm (2.5″). H: 1. S: 2. P: 1.

**Pseudochromis diadema,** the red capped dottyback.

*Pseudochromis paccaguellae* – Bicolor Dottyback. D: 4. SL: 6.5 cm (2.5″). H: 1. S: 2. P: 1.

**Pseudochromis fridmani**, the purple dottyback.

*Pseudochromis fridmani:* – Purple Dottyback. D: 6. SL: 6.5 cm (2.5″). H: 1. S: 2. P: 1.

All three dottybacks are gratifyingly hardy little fishes that make nice additions to a sessile invertebrate community tank. While their territoriality extends to other representatives of the family Pseudochromidae, they do not usually trouble other fishes. Nevertheless, given their overall similarities in color pattern, it might not be a good idea to try keeping dottybacks and grammas together.

*Calloplesiops altivelis* – Marine Betta, Coral Comet. D: 4. SL: 15.0 cm (6.0″). H: 2. S: 7. P: 2.

The tail of this strikingly colored species is almost as long as its body, hence the common name of marine betta. Its size notwithstanding, this is a slow-moving, unaggressive fish, often bullied by more assertive tankmates regardless of size. It is also easily outcompeted at feeding time. Neither the generality of damselfish nor the more aggressive angelfish make suitable companions for the coral comet, though it gets along well enough with slender-bodied clownfish such as *A. ocellaris*. Like all the representatives of this group, *C. altivelis* is well suited for life in a community of sessile invertebrates.

**Like other holocentrids, the squirrelfish, *Adioryx ruber*, (right) is markedly social in nature.**

Families Holocentridae, Apogonidae and Cirrhitidae –

Squirrel or Soldierfish, Cardinalfish and Hawkfish

These three families are not particularly closely related, but do share a preference for low levels of illumination in captivity that correlates well with a crepuscular or nocturnal pattern of activity in nature. Hence representatives of all three should be kept in rather dimly lit tanks set up to provide a number of spacious caves or overhangs of whose shelter they can avail themselves. Because they are at something of a disadvantage during the daytime, none of these fish should be housed with extremely aggressive, diurnal foragers such as damselfish, large angelfish and wrasses and triggerfish.

Squirrel or soldierfishes of the family Holocentridae are highly social, crepuscular or nocturnal predators. Groups typically shelter in a cave or under an overhang during the day and emerge to forage at dusk. Like hamlets and sea basses, they pose no threat to any tankmates too large to make a convenient mouthful, but it is unwise to underestimate their capacity in this regard. Although they are quite abundant in their prefered habitats, nothing is known about their pattern of sexuality, mode of spawning, eggs or larvae.

Getting holocentrids to feed in captivity can prove something of a challenge. Like most crepuscular fishes, they are initially very reluctant to come out and eat during the day. They are more likely to settle down to normal feeding if kept in small groups with slow-moving, unaggressive heterospecific tankmates. The best way to start newly purchased specimens feeding is to introduce a few salt-water acclimated guppies to the tank immediately after the shutting the tank lights off for the night. A few days later, add the guppies immediately before turning the lights off. As soon as the fish are seen to feed on live food under normal tank lighting, cut back on the feeder guppies and begin offering the tank a small feeding of frozen krill or mysids immediately before putting thelights out.

Once a squirrelfish or soldierfish learns to recognize the frozen crustaceans as food, the battle is won. After the fish have made the association between the appearance of their keeper and food, they can be offered small strips of fresh fish or shellfish impaled on the tip of a prove. So me individuals will even learn to eat tablet foods such as TetraTips.

Cardinalfish are equally social, but by virtue of their generally smaller size, their predatory tendencies are not as apt to cause problems under aquarium conditions. Equally significant to the marine aquarist, a number of very attractive apogonids are either diurnal in nature or else quickly learn to feed during the day in captivity. Cardinalfish are not partial to prepared foods, but will readily accept frozen foods and small strips of fresh fish or shellfish. Specimens that prove initially reluctant to feed should be treated in the manner recommneded for holocentrids.

Most marine aquarists unknowingly sin against these extremely interesting little fish by attempting to keep them as solitary specimens. Most cardinalfish simply do not do well away from others of their own kind. They are among the very few marine species that should either be kept in a group or else not kept at all. As long as this requirement is met and care is taken in selecting suitable tankmates for them, cardinalfish can be expected to do quite well in captivity. The smaller species make lovely additions to a mini-reef set-up.

All the species of the family Apogonidae studied to date are paternal mouthbrooders that spawn as pairs. The eggs are fertilized internally up to 24 hours prior to oviposition. The egg mass is taken up by the male as soon as the female expels it and carried until hatching, 7 to 9 days later. The larvae are typically released at dusk and remain in the plankton for about 2 months. This may account for the fact that frequent reports of aquarium spawnings notwithstanding, there are no accounts of larvae being reared through metamorphosis in captivity.

Hawkfish are rather droll little creatures that spend a great deal of time sitting motionless among the branches of a coral head or in rocky crevices waiting for small crustaceans or similar prey to wander within striking range. The sudden dash that follows has earned the numerous species of the family Cirrhitidae their common name. In captivity, they are unselective and enthusiastic eaters that quickly learn to take food from between their keeper's fingers. Although they are colorful and adapt readily to aquarium life, hawkfish have never enjoyed the popularity they deserve, probably because their sedentary life style makes them the odd fish out in the hustle and bustle of the usual community of coral reef fishes. However, their "hurry up and wait" approach to life suits them admirably to life in a sessile invertebrate aquarium. If due account is taken of their predatory behavior, hawkfish are also highly desirable candidates for life in a mini-reef set up featuring mobile invertebrates.

The few hawkfish to date studied are protogynous hermaphorodites that live either as monogamous pairs or in harems of a single male and two or more females. They have been observed to spawn at dusk, rising into the water column to shed their pelagic eggs. There are no data on either the subsequent larval stages or their duration.

*Sargocentron diadema* – Flame Squirrelfish. D: 4. SL: 18.0 cm (7″). H: 3. S: 6. P: 3, 6.

These strikingly marked squirrelfish should be kept in small groups in a well-aerated tank of at least 300 l (c. 75 U.S. gallons) capacity. Once the challenge of getting them to eat during the day has been overcome, their maintenance is a straightfoward matter of making regular partial water changes.

*Adiorx xantherythrus*, the Hawaiian stripped squirrelfish is a very similarly colored species often seen on the price lists of Hawaiian collectors. Its characteristics and maintenance requirements are identical to those of *S. diadema*.

*Myripristis jacobus* – Blackbar Soldierfish. D: 1. SL: 20.0 cm (8″). H: 3. S: 6. P: 3, 6.

The extremely large eyes of this soldierfish betray its nocturnal life style. A large tank with plenty of hiding places is a must for this retiring species. Regular partial water changes are absolutely essential to the successful maintenance of this or any other holocentrid.

*Apogon cyanosoma* – Candystriped Cardinalfish. D: 4. SL: 12.5 cm (5″). H: 2. S: 6. P: 2, 6.

*Apogon maculatus* – Flame Cardinalfish. D: 1. SL: 7.5 cm (3"). H: 2. S: 6. P: 2, 6.

*Apogon erythrinus* – Red Cardinalfish. D: 3. SL: 7.5 cm (3"). H: 2. S: 6. P: 2, 6.

All three of these brilliant red cardinalfish are usually available to North American aquarists. Prospective buyers should plan on purchasing at least a pair, for like most of the smaller apogonids, they adjust much more rapidly to life in a new tank in a small group. It is essential that their tank be well furnished with caves and their tankmates be unaggressive. Like other small cardinalfish, they are easily intimidated and unlikely to feed properly when bullied. In congenial surroundings, they loose much of their shyness and spend a great deal of time in the open.

*Sphaeraia nematoptera* – Pyjama Cardinalfish. D: 4. SL: 10.0 cm (4"). H: 2. S: 6. P: 3, 6.

This deep-bodied, boldly marked cardinalfish is more likely to adjust to a solitary life than the generality of apogonids. Its larger size

240

also makes it less vulnerable to intimidation by heterospecific tankmates. Conversely, it also increases the threat it poses to smaller companions. The pyjama cardinal adapts well to captivity and is seldom shy at feeding time. This species would probably respond well to serious breeding efforts. Unlike many cardinalfish, it is easily sexed, males having longer fin filaments than females.

*Neocirrhitus armatus* – Flame Hawkfish. D: 4. SL: 7.5 cm (3″). H: 1. S: 7. P: 3, 6.

The red-spotted hawkfish is a good beginner's subject, although the prudent aquarist should take its sizeable mouth into consideration when choosing its companions. While it seems to have no objections to a solitary life in captivity, its life history pattern makes it a relatively simple matter to assemble a compatible group. Large specimens are invariably males, smaller ones females.

*Oxycirrhites typus* – Long-nosed Hawkfish. D: 2, 3. SL: 13.0 cm (5″). H: 1. S: 5. P: 2, 6.

This droll little fish is probably the most popular member of the family Cirrhitidae. Its admittedly bizarre appearance underlies most purchases, but its outgoing behavior and shameless begging quickly earn it the status of a favored pet. Like other hawkfish, *O. typus* has a much reduced swim bladder and thus

has difficulty holding position in midwater. The sight of a longnosed hawkfish "dog-paddling" just below the water surface in frantic anticipation of a pinch of flakes has to be one of the most improbable sights ever to grace a marine aquarium!

By virtue of its highly modified jaws, the long-nosed hawkfish poses the least threat to either vertebrate or invertebrate tankmates of any cirrhitid. It is thus least likely to outgrow its welcome in a mini-reef set up.

*Paracirrhites arcatus* – Arc-eyed Hawkfish. D: 3. SL: 12.5 cm (5″). H: 1. S: 7. P: 3, 6.

This short-snouted hawkfish is frequently offered for sale by Hawaiian collectors. Like the red-spotted hawkfish, *P. arcatus* is a harem-dweller in nature but does not seem to mind living alone in captivity. Small specimens can be safely kept with most ornamental shrimp species, but as they grow larger, they are apt to make a meal of their companions.

Families Gobiidae, Callionymidae and Opistognathidae –

Gobies, Dragonets and Jawfish

This assemblage of species represents another purely operational grouping of unrelated families. However, their members' shared behavioral and ecological characteristics make it practical for the marine aquarist to approach their husbandry in an identical manner. These are for the most part small fish that live in intimate association with the bottom. They are at best indifferent swimmers, and in consequence, tend to be sedentary, rarely moving any great distance from shelter. These are easily bullied fish. They should **never** be housed with larger, aggressive companions. All make excellent additions to a sessile invertebrate aquarium or a mini-reef set up containing mobile invertebrates.

Even in more congenial surroundings, no representative of this group ever feels completely at ease unless it has an assured refuge near at hand. Most will defend their shelter vigorously against conspecifics. However, such territorial behavior seldom extends beyond the immediate vicinity of their chosen refuge. It is thus quite feasible to keep several specimens together as long as the tank provides sufficient cover for each specimen to hold a suitable territory.

The Gobiidae comprise more species than any other single family of spiny-fined fish. Most of these are less than 10.0 cm (4″) overall length, and of these, the majority are attractively colored and gratifyingly easy to maintain under aquarium conditions. Yet only a handful enjoy any sort of popularity as aquarium fish. As with the hawkfishes, this seems largely due to their sedentary lifestyle. Although the subfamily Eleotrinae comprises a few mid-water dwelling species like the firefish, most gobies spend the bulk of their lives sitting on the bottom or in the mouth of a cave waiting for prey to move within striking distance. This behavior does not endear them to the average aquarist, who prefers his fish to be up and doing.

Furthermore, many gobies do poorly in the company of more active companions, simply because their limited swimming abilities make it very difficult for them to compete effectively for food. However, the very behavior that puts gobies at a disadvantage in a conventional marine community tank make them ideal residents in a mini-reef set up. Their sedentary lifestyle particularly recommends them for life in a sessile invertebrate tank. As interest in these alternative approaches to marine aquaristics increases, it seems safe to predict that gobies will at last begin to enjoy the popularity as aquarium fishes they have long deserved.

Most gobies seem to be gonochoristic, but there is reason to suspect that some representatives of the genus *Gobiodon* are protogynous hermaphorodites. Regardless of how they manage their sex lives, gobies deposit demersal eggs on the roof and sides of

*Nemaptereleotris magnificus,* an aptly names midwater-dwelling goby.

a cave or similar enclosed space. The male then defends the spawn until hatching, at which point the young rise into the plankton. The larval interval is usually less than a month long, which greatly simplifies the task of rearing the young through metamorphosis. Neon gobies have been bred successfully many times in captivity and are among the few marine fish produced in commercial quantities. There seems no reason why the other representativess of the family would not respond in a comparable manner to serious breeding efforts.

Superficial similarities notwithstanding, the Callionymidae are not closely related to gobies. The dragonets comprise a small family of primarily deep-water fishes. Most species are characterized by dramatic sexual dimorphism in fin development and a number have stunningly beautiful breeding coloration. The mandarin fishes of the genus *Synchiropus* are the only callionymids to enjoy any degree of popularity as aquarium residents. They are not inhabitants of the coral reef proper, but rather occur in shallow, rubble-strewn inshore habitats. They fare very poorly in the traditional community setting, for they are quite incapable of holding their own in the face of more agile and aggressive companions. Mandarin fish are best kept by themselves or in the company of other sedentary fishes in an invertebrate aquarium. Dragonets are gonochoristic. They spawn in pairs, the two sexes rising in an embrace to shed their pelagic eggs into the water column. It is not known how long the larval interval lasts.

Strictly speaking, the jawfish of the family Opistognathidae are not inhabitants of the coral reef either. These compulsive builders construct their elaborate burrows in sandy bottoms asdjacent to patch reefs or rocky outcroppings. Jawfish are hardy, easily maintained aquarium residents, but they must he housed over a substratum at least 10.0 cm (4″) and preferably 15.0 cm (6″) deep. Otherwise they will be unable to build a proper burrow. It is also important to provide them with a selection of pebbles of varying size to reinforce its sides and roof. Otherwise, the fish will attempt often with considerable success to undermine and tip over pieces of dead coral in an attempt to construct a stable shelter for themselves.

Jawfish are gonochoristic paternal mouth-brooders. A male and female will usually construct their burrows adjacent to one another. The ripe female visits the male in his burrow, where spawning occurs. The male carries the spawn until the young hatch, 7 to 9 days post-spawning. At this point, they enter the plankton, where they remain as pelagic larvae for 17 to 18 days. The pearly and dusky jawfishes have been successfully bred several times in captivity.

**Female (above) and dominant male (below) yellow goby, *Gobiodon citrinus*.**

*Gobiodon guinguestrigatus* – Red clown Goby. D: 4. SL: 7.5 cm (3″). H: 2. S: 7. P: 1.

The red clown goby is the most regularly imported *Gobiodon* species. All of these laterally compressed gobies are strikingly colored, and there is little difference between them with regard to maintenance. In nature, red clown gobies live among the branches of coral heads in harems. The largest individual is the male. In captivity, his removal from a similar group of individuals results in the next largest individual developing typical male coloration. This species would probably respond favorably to efforts to induce captive spawning. Regretably, most red clown gobies available to North American aquarists are exported from the Philippines and usually succumb to delayed cyanide poisoning so soon after their arrival that any hope of getting them to spawn is quite illusory. Net-caught specimens from elsewhere in the Indo-Pacific region prove quite hardy and are well worth their higher asking price.

*Gobiosoma evelynae* – Bicolor Neon Goby. D: 1. SL: 5.0 cm (2″). H: 2. S: 6. P: 1.

*Gobiosoma oceanops* – Neon Goby. D: 1. SL: 5.0 cm (2″). H: 2. S: 6. P: 1.

These delightful little fishes make their living in part as symbiotic cleaners. Unlike their Indo-Pacific analogs of the genus *Labroides*, they are not entirely dependant upon such activities for their food. Thus they do not make a nusiance of themselves in captivity, as cleaner wrasses do, and can be trusted to live harmoniously while practicing their trade in a community aquarium. While they seem to prefer group living, it is possible to keep neon gobies either as pairs or single specimens. As long as their keeper makes the effort to guarantee them sufficient food, neon gobies can be kept successfully in a community of larger fishes, for their role as cleaners protects them from predation.

Neon gobies are easily sexed. Females are somewhat less brightly colored and much fuller bodied than males. Interested readers are refered to aposite references in the last chapter for detailed information on breeding *Gobiosoma* species and rearing their larvae in captivity.

A pair of bicolor neon gobies, *Gobiosoma evelynae.*

*Gobiosoma oceanops,* the neon goby.

*Lythrypnus dalli* – Bluebanded or Catalina Goby. D: 2. SL: 5.0 cm (2″). H: 2. S: 4. P: 1.

As the common name Catalina Goby suggests, these colorful little fish have an essentially subtropical distribution. They thus seem to live longer if kept no warmer than 20° C. (70° F.), although they can tolerate brief exposure to higher temperatures. As they are not symbiotic cleaners and live in association with rocky bottoms rather than fire coral and sponges, bluebanded gobies do not enjoy the degree of immunity from predation enjoyed by *Gobiosoma* species. It is thus important to both choose their tankmates carefully and take care that each individual has its own shelter. Their maintenance requirements are otherwise very similar to those of the neon gobies.

Bluebanded gobies are easily sexed. Males have a taller first dorsal fin than do females, while the latter are much fuller bodied. This species would probably respond well to serious attempts at captive propagation.

**Juvenile (above) and adult (below) white-stripped eel goby, *Pholidicgthys leucotaenia*.**

*Pholidichthys leucotaenia* – White-stripped Eel Goby. D: 4. SL: 20.0 cm (8″). H: 1. S: 6 (juvenile), 4 (adult). P: 2.

This hardy goby undergoes a remarkable color transformation asit grows older, trading its silvery midlateral stripe for a crisp pattern of black and white bars. Juveniles are quite active and thus make a more satisfactory display than do the rather sedentary adults. The latter quickly learn to recognize their keeper and make very satisfactory "pet" fish.

*Nemateleotris magnifica* – Firefish. D: 4. SL: 7.5 cm (3″). H: 2. S: 6. P: 1.

These exquisite midwater-living gobies are not strictly speaking coral reef fishes. Like the madarin fishes, they occur in shallow, rubble-strewn inshore habitats. Though reasonably hardy little fishes, they are easily bullied. Hence their companions must be chosen with considerable care. Like all the gobies considered herein, the firefish makes an excellent addition to a mini-reef tank.

Firefish are easily sexed. Males are larger and have a much taller first dorsal than do their fuller-bodied consorts. Rather surprisingly, in view of its hardiness and general availability, there are no reports of spawnings in cpativity. This is another species that would probably respond positively to serious attempts at captive breeding.

*Syncheiropus splendidus* – Mandarin Fish. D: 4. SL: 6.5 cm (2.5″). H: 2. S: 7. P: 1.

These colorful little dragonets have a reputation for extreme fragility due in large measure to the fact that most specimens available to North American aquarists have been cya-

**The magnificent mandarin fish, *Syncheiropus splendidus*.**

nide-poisoned fish of Philippine provenance. Net-caught specimens are not at all difficult to keep as long as they are not housed with more aggressive, faster-moving tankmates. Newly imported specimens should initially be offered live *Artemia* to start them eating, but once they have settled in, mandarin fish quickly learn to take frozen and prepared foods.

Male mandarin fish have larger fins and are somewhat more boldly patterned than are females. The mandarin fish has spawned several times in captivity, but the larvae have not been raised through metamorphosis.

*Opistognathus aurifrons* – Pearly Jawfish. D: 1. SL: 10.0 cm (4″). H: 2. S: 4. P: 1.

Although its lovely pastel coloration makes the pearly jawfish a desirable addition to a community of like-sized fishes, most aquarists are initially attracted by its complex burrowbuilding behavior. As long as it is housed over a substratum at least 15.0 cm (6″) deep and provided with a supply of varioussized pebbles, this species will willingly demonstrate its engineering abilities in the home aquarium. Apart from an insistance on regular partial water changes, the pearly jawfish makes no additional demands on its keeper.

Males grow slightly larger than females and have longer fins. Ripe females are also very full bodied. If well fed, pearly jawfish will spawn regularly in captivity. Males are usually excellent parents. Repeated failures to carry the egg mass to hatching usually indicate poor water quality. The larvae are likewise extremely sensitive to water quality, but with due attention to nitrogen cycle management, they can be successfully raised past metamorphosis.

**Displaying male pearly jawfish, *Opistognathus aurofrons*.**

## Families Antennariidae and Scorpaenidae – Anglerfishes and Scorpionfishes

Anglerfishes are the ultimate ambush predators. Many such fishes exploit efficient camouflage to conceal their presence from potential prey, but most members of the family Antennariidae go one step further in bringing their meals within striking distance. They possess a highly mobile, modified dorsal fin ray, the **illicium**, they they use as a lure. The illicium can resemble a marine worm, a shrimp or in the most extreme instance, a small fish. By moving this structure in an appropriate manner, an anglerfish has no trouble luring smaller fish within range of its jaws. Then, one lightening snap and the hapless victim is history!

As might be expected in the practitioners of such a life style, anglerfish are poor swimmers, In most species, the swim bladder has atrophied completely, making it a major effort for these fish to lift themselves off the bottom. By way of compensation, anglerfish can walk very effciently, using their modified pectoral and ventral fins to move about the bottom. The sargassum fish, *Histrio histrio*, can even clamber quite freely through the branches of its leafy home.

Sometimes known as frogfish because of their enormous mouths, antennariids are hardy, easily maintained aquarium residents. Many species are quite vividly colored in the bargain. Before concluding that these fish are anything but cryptically colored, bear in mind that a fish that stands out like a ripe banana in a smokehouse under aquarium conditions may completely vanish against a garish background of coralline algae and soft corals in nature! Anglerfish are totally unsuited to life in a community aquarium. They are capable of swallowing fish larger then themselves and display a persistance in stalking prey that is positively chilling. Fortunately for the aquarist, most specimens quickly learn to take strips of fish or shellfish dangled immediately in front of their mouths on a pointed stick. Their highly sedentary character recommends them for life in a sessile invertebrate aquarium, but their presence precludes keeping any other fishes and most mobile inveretbrates therein.

Anglerfish are gonochoristic pair-spawners that produce a large, floating "egg raft". Nothing is known of the length of the larval interval. Well-fed specimens often spawn regularly in captivity, but there appear to be no instances in which the resulting larvae have been reared to metamorphosis.

Scorpionfishes, as their popular name implies, possess well-developed venom glands at the base of the dorsal fin spines. The consequences of a puncture wound from one or more of these spines can therefore be quite serious. There are no documented instances of scorpionfish envenomation causing human fatalities, contrary to the case of the stonefishes of the related family Synjaceidae. However, more than one victim has described the pain associated with a lionfish "sting" so excruciating that at the time, death actually seemed a preferable alternative! **Always handle scorpionishes with capacious nets and bear in mind that venom potency is not automatically a function of adult size.**

The venom delivery system of scorpionfishes is essentially defensive and affords its bearers considerable protection against larger predators. However, several aquarists have learned the hard way that **defensive** should not be confused with **passive**. When it feels threatened, a lionfish will raise its dorsal fin, tilt its body foward and advance more or less rapidly towards the perceived source of danger. In captivity, this is often their keeper's hand, engaged in routine maintenance of their quarters. Not all specimens react in this manner, and there is some reason to believe that long-established lionfish are less likely to so respond to their regular keeper than to a stranger. Nevertheless, given the severity of the possible consequences, simple prudence dictates keeping one's hands out of aquaria housing lionfish or any other reasonably mobile representative of the family Scorpaenidae.

Their venomous spines aside, scorpionfish are hardy, easily maintained aquarium residents. Lionfish can be used to run in a biological filter, although most aquarists display a preference for less costly alternatives! As none of these fish are very active, they can be maintained in smaller tanks than many other fish their size, so long in due attention is given to providing them with an efficient filtration system. Like most predators, they also get along quite nicely with a single feeding every other day. While they clearly prefer live fish, they learn quickly to take strips of fish and shellfish from the end of a pointed stick.

Their only real shortcoming as aquarium residents is their persistance in stalking and devouring their tankmates. Most scorpionish can manage prey their own size or slightly larger without any difficulty at all, as more than one disbelieving aquarist has learned to his sorrow. Large groupers or moray eels seem to make satisfactory long-term companions for scorpionfishes, but it is more practical for most aquarists to offer them a tank of their own. Like most other slow-moving species, scorpionfishes make satisfactory additions to a sessile invertebrate display tank.

Scorpionfishes are pair-spawning gonochorists. Many species practice internal fertilization of the eggs, and a number, the lionfishes among them, produce large floating egg rafts similar to those of the anglerfishes. Though there are numerous reports of captive lionfish spawning, there are no known instances of the resulting larvae being successfully reared through metamorphosis.

*Antennarius ocellatus* – Ocellated Frogfish. D: 1. SL: 15.0 cm (6″). H: 1. S: 7, but see below. P: 4, 5.

Like the generality of anglerfishes, this species closely matches its surroundings. Hence the existence of individuals whose base colors range from pale saffron and rusty brown through black. Hardy and easily maintained, if something less than lively, this species should never be kept with any fish not intended as live food, a category that can include smaller conspecifics.

***Antennarius hispidus*** (above), the Indo-Pacific anglerfish.

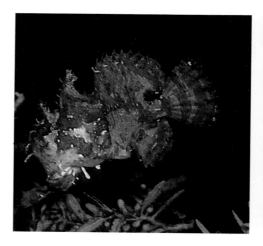

*Histrio histrio* – Sargassumfish. D: 1. SL: 15.0 cm (6″). H: 1. S: 7, but see below. P: 4, 5.

The elaborate tassled appearance of this species affords it almost complete invisibility in the sargassum beds to which it is endemic. All anglerfish can walk over solid substrata, but the sargassumfish is the only species that can actually climb along the fronds of its free-floating home. Its droll appearance notwithstanding, the sargassumfish is a voracious predator that will routinely stalk and devour substantially larger tankmates. It is also an opportunistic cannibal, whose tendencies to dine within the family are held in check only by a full stomach.

*Pterois sphex* – Hawaiian Lionfish. D: 3. SL: 25.0 cm (10″). H: 1. S: 7. P: 4, 5.

Although it occurs elsewhere in the Indo-Pacific basin, *P. sphex* is the only species of the genus native to Hawaii and thus the only one offered for sale by Hawaiian exporters. Hence its somewhat misleading common name. Net-caught specimens make hardy, long-lived aquarium residents.

**The Hawaiian lionfish, *Perois sphex*.**

*Pterois volitans* – Common Lionfish. D: 4. SL: 30.0 cm (12″). H: 1. S: 7. P: 4, 5.

This is the most readily available – and least expensive – of the half dozen or so *Pterois* species exported from the Indo-Pacific region. Philippine specimens are apt to have a short life expectancy. Net caught specimens can live for over a decade in captivity. Their longevity may have a lot to do with their far from active life style. Lionfish of any description come across as 17 rpm fish living in a 78 rpm world! For this reason, many aquarists find their behavior somewhat boring, although none can deny the beauty of their coloration and finnage.

*Dendrochirus biocellatus* – Fu Manchu Lionfish. D: 4. SL: 15.0 cm (6″). H: 1. S: 7. P: 4, 5.

The common name of this highly prized lionfish derives from the fancied resemblance of its pendant maxillary barbles to the drooping mustache of Sax Romer's infamous villain. The asking price for this species tends to be high. As this species is not native to Hawaii, the possibility that a given specimen has been taken with cyanide cannot be absolutely ruled out. Thus it is only prudent to ask for a demonstration of its willingness to take food before making a purchase.

*Dendrochirus brachypterus* – Dwarf Lionfish.
D: 3. SL: 17.5 cm (7″). H: 1. S: 7. P: 4, 5.

**The powerfull jaws and massive teeth of this *Pseudobalistes fiscus* allow it to make short work of hard-shelled invertebrate prey.**

Readily available, hardy and reasonably priced, this species is the ideal beginner's lionfish. Inexperienced aquarists are often tempted to add juvenile specimens to an existing community tank. They quickly learn that the dwarf lionfish's relatively small size simply means that its ability to prey upon other fish is somewhat curtailed, not its inclination to do so. Their shorter spines notwithstanding, *Dendrochirus* species are just as venemous as their larger relatives and should be handled as carefully as any *Pterois* species.

## Family Balistidae – Triggerfish

Triggerfish have a reputation as the "bad boys' of the marine aquarium. It is not undeserved. For a start, triggers are sure death to any mobile and many sessile invertebrates. Their admitedly peculiar appearance reflects a suite of adaptations that allows them to dispose tidily of any hard-shelled prey they might encounter in nature or in captivity. Secondly, while not specialized piscivores, triggerfish will make a meal of smaller tankmates whenever the opportunity presents itself. Third, they are extremely territorial. Triggerfish do not tolerate the proximity of conspecifics in nature. In captivity, this intolerance extends routinely to other triggerfish and less predictably to other tankmates. Individuals vary considerably in their behavior towards other species, and it must be noted that the likelihood of aggression towards heterospecifics is influenced by tank size. A triggerfish that displays all the social graces of a axe murderer in a 200 l (50 U.S. gallons) aquarium often proves a good neighbor in a 400 l (100 U.S. gallons) tank. However, a triggerfish can do so much damage so quickly with its powerful jaws that even a well-behaved specimen must always be treated as a potentially lethal threat to its companions.

Moving from the realm of social interactions to that of environmental manipulation, triggerfish frequently drive their owners to distraction by re-arranging their tank's infrastructure to their liking. They are large enough to move even substantial pieces of dead coral adroitly, and most species are efficient excavators in the bargain. Captive specimens spend a good deal of time on these landscaping projects and defend their handiwork vigorously against disturbance. More than one aquarist has received a nasty bite as a result of his efforts to restore the *status quo ante* in a triggerfish's tank! Of somewhat greater urgency to the well-being of an aquarium's inhabitants, triggerfish also display great curiosity about such fixtures as air lines, intake siphons and heaters. When, as often happens, such investigations extend to giving these objects a brisk exploratory nip, the results can be disastrous. Plastic and glass do not stand up well to jaws that can open up a sea urchin as effortlessly as a human peels an orange.

To their credit, triggerfish are extremely hardy. It is perfectly feasible to use them to run in a tank's biological filter. Most species are strikingly marked and display themselves without reservation in the open spaces of their tank. They are voracious, unselective feeders that quickly become shameless beggars. Aquarists find it a simple matter to train a triggerfish to take food from their fingers, notwithstanding the element of risk entailed in the practice. Like large groupers, triggerfish quickly assume the status of a household pet. Goggle eyes, nutcracker jaws and belligerance notwithstanding, aquarists who have once kept a triggerfish rarely find their tank complete without one.

Triggerfish husbandry is considerably simplified if the aquarist follows a few simple guidelines. First and foremost, provide these fish with plenty of room. A 200 l aquarium barely suffices to house a single specimen; 400 l comes a lot closer to providing one of these fish with adequate living space. Secondly, keep all aquarium appliances out of a triggerfish's reach. The easiest way to accomplish this is to cut a piece of plastic egg crate diffuser grating to fit the inside dimensions of the tank. Before filling the aquarium. fasten it in place with silicone sealant in such a manner that it leaves a free space some 5.0 cm – 7.5 cm wide at one end. All heaters, air lines and siphons should be **behind** this protective barrier. Thirdly, buy only a specimen smaller than an established tank's smallest resident and always add a triggerfish last to a community of fishes when setting up a new aquarium. Finally, use common sense in selecting tankmates for a triggerfish. Groupers, snappers, lionfish and the larger angelfish and wrasses usually run little danger from a trigger.

Triggerfish derive their common name from a peculiarity of their first dorsal fin anatomy. When pursued by a predator, these fish will dive into a hole or crevice in the reef and

**Like most triggerfishes, *Balistes carolinensis* grows quite large, a factor that must be taken into account before adding a specimen to an established community tank.**

erect their first dorsal fin. The large anterior spine is locked into place by the smaller second spine, which when depressed acts as a trigger to release the mechanism. It is virtually impossible to pull a triggerfish from cover once the first dorsal fin has been erected. While it is theoretically possible to release the lock by manipulating the trigger spine, aquarists faced with this tactic of avoiding capture should simply transfer coral and triggerfish to the latter's intended residence and allow the fish to come out on its own. More direct intervention runs the risk of injury to the fish in the case of an unsuccessful effort or to its keeper from the snapping jaws of an irate triggerfish should he succeed.

Triggerfish are gonochoristic substratum spawners. Though they spawn as single pairs, they are not necessarily monogamous. A harem-like social system has been reported for a number of species, among them the popular black trigger, *Odonus niger*. Many triggerfish defend their demersal eggs against predators. In all species for which the sex of the custodial parent has been determined, this role is carried out by the female. Parental triggerfish are extremely aggressive and will attack much larger fish without hesitation. There are even reports of divers in the Red Sea suffering serious injuries after inadvertantly swimming too close to a spawn-tending female. Both the inherent difficulties in inducing such extremely territorial animals to pair off under aquarium conditions and their prolonged larval stage work powerfully against successful captive propagation of triggerfish.

*Balistes conspicillum* – Clown Trigger. D: 4. SL: 50.0 cm (20″). H: 1. S: 1. P: 2, 5, 6.

The clown trigger is one of the most strikingly marked of all fishes. It appears to be relatively uncommon in nature, and in consequence, demand by aquarists far exceeds supply. The result is a stiff asking price. In the light of this, it is all the more regretable that so many of the specimens available to North American aquarists are cyanide-poisoned fish exported from the Philippines. The aquarist who makes the effort to secure an admitedly more expensive net-caught specimen can look foward to many years of pleasure from the presence of a clown trigger in his tank.

The clown triggerfish, *Balistes conspicillum,* makes a striking addition to a large marine community tank.

*Balistes vetula* – Queen Trigger. D: 1. SL: 50.0 cm (20″). H: 1. S: 2. P: 3, 5, 6.

This elegant species is one of the triggerfish most commonly available to North American aquarists. Though it is both colorful and reasonably priced, the queen trigger has some serious disadvantages as a aquarium resident. Size apart, this is one of the most aggressive triggerfish species known. Even small individuals have been known to totally disrupt a community of larger fishes. Kept in its own quarters, a queen trigger makes a highly responsive pet.

*Odonus niger* – Black Trigger. D: 4. SL: 45.0 cm (18″). H: 1. S: 2. P: 3, 5, 6.

The protruding teeth of this species account for its second common name of red-toothed trigger. Like those of all triggerfish, they grow

rapidly. It is thus important to offer these fish hard foods on a regular basis to keep them worn down. Black triggers receive mixed reviews as community tank residents. Most specimens get along well with other large fish, but some individuals prove to be holy terrors and have to be given separate quarters in order to keep the peace. Like many triggers, this species seems to have a particular dislike of tangs.

*Rhinecanthus aculeatus* – Picasso Trigger. D: 3. SL: 20.0 cm (10″). H: 1. S: 2. P: 2, 5, 6.

Its Hawaiian name, *humu humu nuku nuku apua'a* ("the hogsnouted fish that fits things together") perfectly describes both the appearance and the behavior of the Picasso trigger. Readily available from Hawaiian exporters, this colorful triggerfish is a fairly good community risk in tanks of 300 l (75 U.S. gallons) or larger. As its Hawaiian name suggests, *R. aculeatus* is much given to rearranging its quarters, but despite such tendencies, it is a good choice for the aquarist with no prior experience of the group.

*Sufflamen bursa* – Whiteline Triggerfish. D: 3. SL: 20.0 cm (8″). H: 1. S: 2. P: 2, 5, 6.

This strikingly marked species is known in Hawaaian as *humu humu umaumalei* ("the lei-wearing fish that fits things together"), because of the golden yellow cheek bars of some specimens. The whiteline trigger is an excellent beginner's choice because it is small by the standards of the family, and

*Sufflamen bursa,* the whiteline triggerfish.

Male (upper left) and female spotted boxfish, *Ostracion tuberculatus.*

quite peaceful towards other species. These attributes more than compensate for the fact this this species is less colorful than its more famous relative, the Picasso trigger.

Families Canthigasteridae, Diodontidae and Ostraciontidae –
Smooth Puffers, Porcupine Fish and Boxfish

Representatives of all three families, together with the triggerfishes, are representatives of the distinctive suborder Plectognathi. They share a number of anatomical features that allow them to efficiently exploit invertebrates as a food source, a fact that the marine aquarist should always take into account when selecting their tankmates. None of these fish are strong swimmers. As this precludes flight as a means of avoiding predation, all possess alternative defense mechanisms. Reference has already been made to the ability of triggerfish to lock themselves securely into a refuge by means of their stout first dorsal fin spines. As their common name suggests, puffers have the ability to increase their overall dimensions by inflating themselves with water until they are too large to be swallowed by potential predators. The closely related porcupine fish bear formidable spines that are erected during inflation, making them, if possible, an even less attractive prey item. Boxfish seem at first glance to be totally defenseless. However, many species are capable of secreting highly toxic mucus that

apparently makes them distasteful to predators in nature and can prove lethal to tankmates in a closed system.

The true puffers of the family Tetraodontidae are hardy, easily maintained aquarium residents, and many species are attractively colored in the bargain. However, the family's marine representatives grow too large to make entirely satisfactory aquarium residents. The smooth, or long-nosed puffers, on the other hand, contain many colorful species that do not exceed 15.0 cm (6″) in length. These hardy, easily maintained fish make excellent aquarium residents provided some forethought is given to the selection of their tankmates. Smooth puffers are sure death to crustaceans, molluscs and both fan and tube worms. They also have a tendency to nip the fins of larger, slow swimming fishes and will prey opportunistically on smaller fishes. Wrasses, damselfish, scats, tangs and triggerfish seem to hold their own successfully with smooth puffers. Angel and butterflyfish, grammas, dottybacks, batfish and such inoffensive bottom-dwellers as gobies and mandarin fish do not.

Smooth puffers are not particularly fond of flakes but soon learn to take tablets from between their keeper's fingers. They should be offered plenty of fresh seafood on a regular basis. The fused jaw teeth of both smooth puffers and porcupine fish grow constantly. Unless the fish are afforded the opportunity to wear them down, the resulting malocclusion can interfere seriously with a specimen's ability to eat and lead to death from starvation. Periodic offerings of un-shelled shrimp or small whole mussels pro-vide these fish with a pleasurable opportunity to keep their beaks in trim.

All the smooth puffers to date studied are gonochoristic. They live as either mono-gamous pairs or in a harem system. These fish do not appear to practice parental care as such. The demersal eggs are shed within a territory defended by both parents, or in the case of harem-dwelling species, by the female alone. The larvae are small and the larval interval persists for about a month, facts that do not augur well for efforts to breed these interesting fish in captivity.

Most of the forgoing observations apply equally to the porcupine fishes. These prickly relatives of the puffers also grow quite large – up to 60.0 cm (2°) in some instances. How-ever, aquarists are willing to put up with this inconvenience largely because of their out-going personality. Porcupine fish are *always* hungry and display an almost embarrasing enthusiasm at the appearance of their human meal ticket. Specimens will often take food from their keeper's fingers within a day of their purchase and quickly assume the status of a family pet.

Many aquarists succumb to the temptation of demonstrating the defensive behavior of puf-fers and porcupine fish by removing them from the water and gently stroking their ven-tral surface. This stimulation causes them to gulp air and swell to their full size. This prac-tice is not recommended, as it can lead to permanant swim bladder damage. A much safer way to demonstrate this behavior is to hold the fish fully submerged in a net and sti-mulate the swallowing response. The fish have much less difficulty expelling the water they have taken in and do not run any risk of irreversible injury.

Porcupine fish are also gonochoristic pair-spawners, but unlike smooth puffers, shed their pelagic eggs directly into the water column. There have been a number of spawnings reported in captivty, but no in-stances in which the larvae were successfully reared.

Boxfishes are small, inoffensive, boldly colored little fishes. They are such slow swimmers that divers can easily approach and study them in nature. They are among the easiest of all coral reef fishes to capture with a net. It is thus all the more ironic that many of the specimens available to North American aquarists are cyanide-poisoned fish from the Philippines. However, even net-caught specimens often do poorly in captivity. As these fish feed in part on live anthozoans in nature, it is likely their fragility is a matter of dietary deficiency, complicated by the fact that boxfish are such poor swimmers that they are easily outcompeted by other fishes at feeding time. Prospective boxfish or cow-fish keepers are more likely to enjoy success if they keep their pets in a mini-reef setup with relatively sedentary companions like gobies.

When stressed, boxfish secrete an extremely toxic mucus. There are well documented in-stances of such episodes causing mass mor-talities in shipping bags or holding boxes. Unequivocal accounts of the impact of such behavior on the inhabitants of a well filtered aquarium seem lacking. However, prudence dictates the regular use of a chemically active medium such as PolyFilter or ChemiPureà in a tank housing any member of the family Ostraciontidae.

All the boxfish to date studied are gono-

A male *Lactoria fornasini*, an attractive Indo-Pacific boxfish.

**The unusual shape of boxfishes such as these *Aracara ornata* makes them slow swimmers.**

choristic, harem-dwellers characterized in many instances by dramatic sexual color differences. Unlike many of the smaller coral reef fishes, they neither produce demersal eggs nor practice any sort of parental care. The pelagic eggs are shed into the water column as dusk. The larval period is less than a month long. This fact, taken with the ease with which most species can be sexed, suggests that boxfish might profitably engage the attentions of aquarists seriously interested in breeding marine fishes in captivity.

*Arothron nigropunctatus* – Dogface puffer. D: 4. SL: 40.0 cm (16″). H: 1. S: 3. P: 3, 5, 6.

Juveniles of this species are sometimes exported by Asian collectors. They make satisfactory aquarium residents, but often outgrow their welcome. *Arothron* species are often quite social in nature, but as is the case with many coral reef fishes, this tolerance of conspecifics does not carry over into captivity.

*Canthigaster jactator* – White-spotted Puffer. D: 3. SL: 7.5 cm (3″). H: 1. S: 2. P: 2, 5, 6.

This charming little fish is one of the smallest of the smooth puffers. It is routinely offered by Hawaiian exporters and is usually available at a reasonable price. Like all puffers, it will nip the fins of slow-moving tankmates, particularly if hungry. Otherwise, the white-spotted puffer is a satisfactory community tank risk.

*Canthigaster valentini* – Sharpnosed Puffer. D: 4. SL: 15.0 cm (6″). H: 1. S: 2. P: 2, 5, 6.

The larger adult size of the sharpnosed puffer must be taken into account when selecting its tankmates, as its potential to do them injury is proportionately greater than that of the white-spotted puffer. This species is in other respects an easily maintained aquarium resident that quickly becomes a real pet.

**The banded porcupine fish, *Diodon holocanthus* (left).**

**The spotted porcupine fish, *Diodon hystrix* (right).**

*Diodon holocanthus* – Barred porcupine fish. D: 7. SL: 25.0 cm (10″). H: 1. S: 2. P: 2, 5, 6.

*Diodon hystrix* – Spotted porcupine fish. D: 7. SL: 60.0 cm (24″). H: 1. S: 2. P: 2, 5. 6.

These two species differ only in details of their color pattern and adult size. Porcupine fish are really only suited to community living as juveniles. Aquarists who have purchased small specimens often end by setting setting up a separate aquarium for a now awkwardly large *Diodon* that has attained the status of a family pet! Specimens more than 15.0 cm (6″) long should be handled with great care, as their powerful jaws can deliver a serious bite.

**Female (above) and male (below) polka-dot boxfish, *Ostracion lentigenosum*.**

*Ostracion melagris* – Blue or polka dot boxfish. D: 3. SL: 15.0 cm (6″). H: 3. S: 6, but see below. P: 1.

The two common names this species bears reflect its dramatic sexual dimorphism. Females are deep blue with a uniform pattern of white spots over their entire body, hence polka dot boxfish. The aquarist who elects to keep these droll little fish in a group should take pains to avoid housing two males together. The blue boxfish's behavior towards other fishes is otherwise exemplary. As noted in the discussion of the family, this species should not be kept with aggressive or very active companions.

*Lactoria cornutus* – Long-horned Cowfish. D: 4. SL: 25.0 cm (10″). H: 3. S: 3. P: 1.

The Betty Boop eyes and droll movements of this species and the slightly smaller blue-spotted cowfish, *Lactoria fornasina* are all but irresistable to novice aquarists. Regretably, most specimens do not thrive under home aquarium conditions, possibly because they are denied access to the live coral that comprises part of their diet in nature. Specimens > 5.0 cm (2″) long have a better chance of adapting to aquarium conditions than do smaller specimens. However, keeping them in a mini-reef setup still offers the best hope of success with cowfish.

Family Muraenidae – Moray Eels.

The lurid reputation of moray eels reflects the overactive imaginations of the authors of adventure novels rather than objective reality. The characteristic gape-jaw appearance of a moray eel reflects the basic mechanics of respiration, not unrelenting aggression. Indeed, unless molested, morays ignore divers as well as any fishes too large to be con-veniently swallowed. Morays are hardy, easily maintained aquarium residents, but the large adult size of most species limits their suitability for home aquaria, their sedentary habits notwithstanding. The species included herein are considered small by the standards of the family, but the prospective moray keeper would do well to consider their ulti-mate disposition before making a purchase.

Morays must be furnished with a cave or similar shelter. A piece of CPVC pipe of a dia-meter slightly greater than the crosssection of the eel's body and just a bit longer is readily accepted and has the advantage of being easily camouflaged in the bargain. Many species like to intertwine their body among the branches of a coral head. No matter how inextricably a moray seems entangled, it can – and will – disentangle itself when it feels the need to do so. Well-meaning intervention by its keeper can result in injury to both parties. Morays do not appreciate handling of any sort and have the wherewithal to make their disapproval painfully clear.

Morays have a well-deserved reputation for wanderlust. It is absolutely essential to keep their tanks tightly covered. The ribbon eel in particular displays an almost preternatural ability to squeeze through minute openings. More conventionally configured morays can display an amazing turn of strength. It is thus prudent to keep their tank covers well weighted down.

Newly imported morays should initially be offered live food. Once they have started feeding, they can be easily taught to take thin strips of fish or shellfish from the end of of a pointed stick. Ever since the airing of tele-vision documentaries showing divers hand-feeding wild morays, attempts to emulate such behavior in captivity have become fashionable among some marine aquarists. **Hand-feeding captive morays is not recommended.** Their eyesight is not acute and they appear to rely heavily upon chemical cues to identify and locate prey. The liklihood that an overenthusiastic speci-men will mistake the fingers holding a morsel for the food itself is thus quite high. All morays have formidable dentition and even

The chain-link moray, *Echidna catenata.*

small specimens can do a great deal of damage. Furthermore, their teeth are invariably filthy, so a bite carries with it an excellent chance of a serious secondary infection.

With the exception of the ribbon eels, which are protandrous hermaphrodites, morays are gonochoristic. They spawn either as pairs, or in groups, a single large female being attended by a number of smaller males, depending upon species. The pelagic eggs are shed at dusk. The larval stage persists for 6–10 months. This fact, as much as the very large adult size of most moray eels, effectively precludes any liklihood of captive breeding.

*Echidna catenata* – Chain-link Moray. D: 1. SL: 1.3 m (4"). H: 1. S: 7. P: 3, 5.

While not as spectacularly marked as some of its IndoPacific relatives, this attractive Caribbean species is extremely hardy, generally available to North American aquarists and reasonably priced in the bargain. The chain-link moray is a good eater that quickly learns to take non-living prey in captivity.

*Echidna nebulosa* – Snowflake Moray. D: 3. SL: 1.0 m (3"). H: 1. S: 7. P: 3, 5.

Specimens of Hawaiian provenance are gratifyingly hardy and settle readily into captive life. Like the forgoing species, the snowflake moray feeds extensively upon crustaceans in nature, a fact reflected in its stouter jaw teeth. The only exceptions to this rule are

*Echidna nebulosa,* the snowflake moray.

the various cleaner shrimps, whose intimate presence is tolerated both in the reef and under aquarium conditions. Most *Echidna* species are good community risks, for they tend to disregard even relatively small tankmates as long as they are well-fed.

*Muraena pardalis* – Dragon Moray. D: 3. SL: 1.0 m (3″). H: 1. S: 7. P: 3, 5.

This spectacularly marked species has a reputation for snappishness that justifies very careful handling in captivity. It is also more markedly piscivorous than the preceding two species, which suggests that its companions must be both good-sized and well protected to avoid its attentions. Lionfish fit both requirements nicely and thus get along surprisingly well with moray eels, this species among them. Hawaiian specimens tend to be expensive, but are far more likely to settle into a long and uneventful existance than less costly fish from the Philippines.

*Rhinomuraena amboinensis* – Ribbon Eel. D: 4. SL: 1.0 m (3′). H: 4. S: 7. P: 3, 5.

This attractive eel has a distinct color pattern for each phase of its life. Juveniles are black in color, and were described as a distinct species, *R. quesita*. They then develop the blue coloration of mature males, and as they grow larger and change to functional fe-males, turn golden yellow! Ribbon eels have a reputation for delicacy that may reflect the fact that most specimens available to North American aquarists are of Philippine provenance. For whatever reason, it is often difficult to get specimens to feed in captivity, although once a specimen begins to take food, it subsequently displays a robust appetite. The narrow mouth and delicate teeth of the ribbon eel greatly limit its choice of prey. For this reason, it is undoubtedly the moray best suited to life in a community aquarium.

Other Desirable Marine Fishes

*Plotosus anguillaris* – Coral Catfish. D: 4. SL: 35.0 cm (13′). H: 2. S: 6. P: 2, 5.

This strikingly marked catfish is the most usually available member of the predominantly marine family Plotosidae. **It must be handled with extreme care.** Its sharp spines are highly poisonous and can deliver an excruciatingly painful wound. If due allowance is made for its large adult size, the coral catfish makes a satisfactory community resident. Solitary specimens tend to be extremely shy, but small groups swim actively about in the open spaces of their tank.

The ribbon eel, *Rhinomuraena amboinensis*.

Plotosus lineatus – Coral Catfish.
D: 4. SL: 35.0 cm (13'). H: 2. S: 6. P: 2, 5.

This pair-spawning gonochorist deposits its demersal eggs in a nest constructed of coral rubble. The male defends the spawn against predators until the fry hatch, 7 to 10 days later. The fry are large and do not have a planktonic phase. The coral catfish has been bred successfuly several times in captivity.

Monodactylus argenteus – Mono. D: 4. SL: 15.0 cm (6'). H: 1. S: 6, but see below. P: 2.

Both this species and the much deeper bodied Monodactylus sebae are inexpensive, hardy fishes often used to run in a newly set-up tank's biological filters. Highly social in nature, monos will display such behavior in captivity only if kept in large tanks in groups of 6 or more individuals. They are active, highspeed swimmers with voracious appetites. They thus make poor tankmates for shy or slow-moving fishes and are best housed with species sufficiently assertive to hold their own at feeding time.

Monos are gonochoristic pair-spawners that move into brackish water to shed their pelagic eggs. The larval period is extremely brief and the larvae themselves quite large compared to those of most coral reef fishes. Both species are regularly bred in captivity, and a substantial proportion of the juvenile specimens commercially available are actually tank-reared.

Platax orbicularis – Round Batfish. D: 4. SL: 40.0 cm (16'). H: 2. S: 7. P: 1.

Adult batfish tend to resemble large monos. They are common residents of the coral reef. Juveniles are typical inhabitants of mangrove swamps, where their highly developed finnage and rusty brown coloration afford them effective camouflage. Because their depth from dorsal to anal fin tip can exceed their standard length, juvenile batfish require very deep aquaria to do well in captivity.

Batfish have a reputation for being picky feeders, and newly imported specimens often refuse to eat. It is therefore unwise to purchase any batfish that has not demonstrated a healthy appetite in the dealer's tank. Individuals that do feed prove gratifyingly hardy

The mono, *Monodactylus argenteus.*

*Scatophagus argus* – Scat. D: 4. SL: 30.0 cm (12″). H: 1. S: 6, but see below. P: 2.

This hardy, gluttonous relative of the butterflyfish is another excellent starter fish for a newly set-up marine tank. Scats tend to be prone to skin parasites, but these are easily eliminated with recourse to freshwater baths which these fish tolerate extremely well. They should be handled with care, as their dorsal fin spines can inflict extremely painful wounds.

Though highly social in nature, they are apt to prove otherwise in captivity unless housed in very large aquaria with conspecifics the same size. Scats are strongly herbivorous and will graze a tank bare of *Caulerpa* or other macroalgae in record time. They do best on a diet built around prepared foods with a high vegetable content, such as Tetra Conditioning Food, and should be routinely offered fresh greens. Scats come on very strongly at feeding time and should not be housed with easily intimidated companions. They are otherwise perfectly acceptable community tank residents.

Surprisingly little is known of scat reproductive biology. They are thought to deposit demersal eggs on a pre-cleaned surface and provide some degree of parental care to the spawn. The resulting fry are extremely similar to the *Tholichthys* larvae of butterflyfish, and like them, spend a considerable time as part of the plankton. There are no reports of successful scat spawnings in captvity.

**A juvenile round batfish, *Platax orbicularis*. Adults lack the striking finnage of juveniles and look more like an angelfish or spadefish.**

and grow a good deal more rapidly that their owners might wish! These slow-moving, longfinned fish are very vulnerable to harrassment from faster, more aggressive tankmates. They do best in the company of small, relatively sedentary fishes such as gobies, mandarin fish and hawkfish.

Batfish have much the same reproductive pattern as monos. However, their larval period lasts longer. There are no reports of batfish spawning in captivity, a fact that may reflect the difficulties inherent in trying to breed such robust fishes under aquarium conditions.

# CHAPTER 13.

# Learning more about Marine Aquaristics

While presenting a number of workable approaches to marine aquarium keeping, this work is not intended as a comprehensive treatment of this very broad subject. We therefore feel obligated to introduce the reader to additional sources of information should he desire to pursue further pursue his interest in the natural history and husbandry of marine organisms.

One of the pleasures of fish keeping is the opportunity it affords to share experiences with other enthusiasts. The traditional avenue for such interactions is the local aquarium society. While it is always worth belonging to such an organization, regardless of one's particular area of specialization, many enthusiastic aquarists live in areas where such an option is denied them. Others feel frustrated because too few members of their local society share their interest in marine aquarium keeping. Membership in a regional or national marine specialty club is the simplest means of circumventing both difficulties. These organizations publish regular bulletins that provide a useful forum for the exchange of information and ideas, while their membership rosters are a useful means of tracking down like-minded persons living nearby.

The following is a partial list of organizations dedicated to promoting interest in marine aquaristics:

## British Marine Aquarists' Association

Dues:
£  9.00/yr (Domestic)
£ 15.00/yr (Overseas)
Contact:
Mr. G. E. Kay
10 Beeches Rd.
West Bromwich
West Midlands B70 6QB
UNITED KINGDOM

## Marine Aquarium Society of Toronto

Dues:
US $ 15.00/yr
Contact:
Mr. Ken Brown
P. O. Box 376, Station W
Toronto M6M 5C1
CANADA

## Marine Aquarium Society of Victoria

Dues:
US $5.00 one-time application fee
US $15.00/yr
Contact:
Membership Chairman
P. O. Box 286
Morabbin
Victoria 3189
AUSTRALIA

## Windows to the Sea Aquarium Society

Dues:
US $15.00 (Domestic)
US $20.00 (Foreign)
Contact:
Mr. Bob Denton
P. O. Box 374
Piscataway, NJ 08854
U.S.A.

An alternative to membership in a formally constituted society open to home computer owners whose equipment includes a MODEM is participation in FishNet, a forum for tropical fish enthusiasts offered by CompuServe, an electronic information service. Over 60% of FishNet's traffic is devoted to marine topics, and the nature of the forum makes it an excellent place to obtain information on current developments in such areas as filtration systems technology, nutrition and diagnosis and treatment of diseases. Access to FishNet is free to CompuServe subscribers. For information on FishNet, contact

Mr. John Benn
425 N. Court St.
Florence, AL 35630
U.S.A.

For subscription information on CompuServe, contact

CompuServe Information Service
5000 Arlington Center Blvd.
P. O. Box 20212
Columbus, OH 43220
Telephone: (800) 848-8199
In Ohio, (614) 457-0802

## Recommended Reading

The following selection of material, while hardly exhaustive, should serve to broaden the reader's knowledge of marine aquaristics. To simplify the task of locating particular references, we have broken this annotated bibliography down into the following subject areas:

### Theory and Practice of Marine Aquaristics

Brower, C. E. 1983. **The Basic Marine Aquarium**. Charles C. Thomas.

Brower, C. E., Turner, D. T. and S. Spotte. 1981. PH maintenance in closed seawater culture systems: limitations of calcareous filtrants. **Aquaculture 23** (1–4): 211–217.

Emmens, C. W. 1975. **The Marine Aquarium in Theory and Practice**. T.F.H. Publications.

Herwig, N. 1979. **Handbook of Drugs and Chemicals Used in the Treatment of Fish Diseases**. Charles C. Thomas. (The standard reference on the properties of the medications used to treat parasites and diseases of ornamental fish.)

Moe, M. A. 1982. **The Marine Aquarium Handbook: Beginner to Breeder**. Green Turtle Publications. (One of the few treatments of marine fish breeding techniques geared to a reader without a specialized background in commercial aquaculture.)

Spotte, S. 1973. **Marine Aquarium Keeping: The Science, Animals and Art**. John Wiley and Sons.

Spotte, S. 1979. **Fish and Invertebrate Culture. Water Management in Closed Systems**. John Wiley and Sons. (Somewhat technical, but unquestionably the best treatment of filtration theory published in English to date.)

Spotte, S. 1979. **Seawater Aquariums: The Captive Environment**. John Wiley and Sons.

### The Natural History of Coral Reefs and their Inhabitants

Carpenter, R. B. and B. C. Carpenter. 1981. **Fish Watching in Hawaii**. Natural World Press.

Freiberg, M. A. and J. G. Walls. 1984. **The World of Venomous Animals**. T. F. H. Publications. (Strongly recommended addition to the library of anyone intending to keep venomous marine organisms in his aquarium.)

Thresher, R. E. 1980. **Reef Fish: Behavior and Ecology on the Reef and in the Aquarium**. Palmetto Publishing Company.

Thresher, R. E. 1984. **Reproduction in Reef Fishes**. T. F. H. Publications. (The most thorough account available on the reproductive biology of coral reef fishes.)

Wilson, R. and J. Q. Wilson. 1985. **Watching Fishes: Life and Behavior on a Coral Reef**. Harper and Rowe.

Zann, L. P. 1980. **Living Together in the Sea**. T. F. H. Publications. (An excellent account of symbiosis between marine organisms.)

Zupanc, G. K .H. 1985. **Fish and their Behavior.** Tetra Press. (A readable and informative account of such phenomena as territoriality and behaviorally induced sex changes in coral reef fishes.)

### Identification, Natural History and Husbandry of Invertebrates

Colin, P. L. 1978. **Caribbean Reef Invertebrates and Plants**. T.F.H. Publications. (Particularly useful aid to the identification of *Caulerpa* species.)

Debelius, H. 1983. **Armored Knights of the Sea**. Reimar Hobbing Verlag. (Excellent treatment of the most popular coral reef crustaceans.)

Dunn, D. F. 1981. The clownfish sea anemones: Stichodactylidae (Coelenterata, Actinaria) and other sea anemones symbiotic with pomacentrid fishes. **Trans. Amer. Philosophical Soc. 71** (1): 1–115. (A very thorough scientific review of this group of anemones.)

Friese, U. E. 1973. **Marine Invertebrates in the Home Aquarium**. T.F.H. Publications. (Dated, but still a useful introduction to this area of marine aquaristics.)

George, D. and J. George. 1979. **Marine Life: An Illustrated Encyclopedia of Invertebrates in the Sea**. John Wiley and Sons. (A comprehensive, well-indexed treatment of the major groups of marine invertebrates, with emphasis on their classification and natural history. The quality of the numerous color illustrations does not match that of the text.)

Giwojma, P. 1978. **Marine Hermit Crabs**. T.F.H. Publications.

Herwig, N. 1979. **Starfish, Sea Urchins and their Kin**. F.A.M.A. Anrhology Library. (A useful introduction to the aquarium husbandry of echinoderms.)

Lippe, K. 1984. The care and feeding of Joubin's octopus. **F.A.M.A. 7**(10): 40–43. (A concise account of the aquarium management of this species including useful information on rearing the young that is applicable to other octopus species as well.)

National Research Council Committee on Marine Invertebrates. 1981. **Laboratory Animal Management: Marine Invertebrates.** National Academy Press. (A different but still useful perspective on the husbandry of marine invertebrates.)

Walls, J. G. 1979. **Cone Shells: A Synopsis of the Living Conidae**. T.F.H. Publications. (Strongly recommended reading for any aquarist seriously interested in maintaining these interesting but venomous predators.)

Walls, J. G. (Ed.) 1982. **The Encyclopedia of Marine Invertebrates**. T.F.H. Publications. (Comprehensively illustrated, but its disorganized layout and poor indexing severely limit its use as a reference work.)

Walls, J. G. and J. Taylor. 1975. **Cowries**. T.F.H. Publications. (Aquarists will find the chapter on the living cowry by Taylor particularly interesting.)

Wood, E. 1983. **Corals of the World**. T.F.H. Publications. (Primarily useful as a guide to the identification of corals.)

## Identification, Natural History and Husbandry of Reef Fishes

Allen, G. R. 1975. **Damselfishes**. T.F.H. Publications. (The generic level nomenclature used in this work is somewhat dated, but this does not distract seriously from its value as a reference work.)

Allen, G. R. 1980. **The Anemonefishes of the World**. Aquarium Systems. (Comprehensive treatment of these popular aquarium residents.)

Allen, G. R. and R. C. Steene 1987. **Reef Fishes of the Indian Ocean**. T. F. H. Publications. (Magnificently illustrated treatment of inshore fishes from the entire Indian Ocean region, inclusive of the Red Sea.

Bock, K. R. 1978. **A Guide to the Common Reef Fishes of the Western Indian Ocean**. Macmillan.

Burgess, W. 1978. **Butterflyfishes of the World**. T.F.H. Publications. (Well-illustrated treatment of the Chaetodontidae.)

Carcasson, R. H. 1977. **A Field Guide to the Coral Reef Fishes of the Indian and West Pacific Oceans**. Collins.

Chaplin, C. J. and P. M. Scott. 1979. **Fishwatcher's Guide to West Atlantic Coral Reefs**. Harrowoood Books.

Colin, P. 1976. **Neon Gobies**. T.F.H. Publications. (Contains much useful information on the captive breeding of these delightful little fishes.)

Debelius, H. 1986. **Colorful Little Reef Fishes**. Reimar Hobbing Verlag. (Concentrates on those species suited for life in the mini-reef aquarium.)

Kaplan, E. H. 1982. **A Field Guide to the Coral Reefs of the Caribbean and Florida**. Houghton-Mifflin.

Mills, D. 1985. **A Fishkeeper's Guide to Marine Fishes**. Arco Press. (A useful introduction to many of the more popular marine fishes.)

Randall, J. E. 1983. **Caribbean Reef Fishes**. T.F.H. Publications. (Indispensable guide to the identification of these widely available marine fishes.)

Randall, J. E. 1983. **Red Sea Reef Fishes**. IMMEL.

Randall, J. E. 1985. **Guide to Hawaiian Reef Fishes**. Harrowood Books. (Though aimed primarily at the recreational diver, aquarists will also find this well-illustrated book very useful.)

Smith, J. L. B. 1977. **Sea Fishes of Southern Africa**. Valiant Publishers. (The definitive treatment of the reef fishes of the Western Indian Ocean, this work will also prove useful to the aquarist seeking to identify fish from the Western Pacific as well.)

Steene, R. D., Allen, G. R. and H. A. Baensch. 1978. **Butterfly and Angelfishes of the World. Volume 1: Australia**. John Wiley and Sons.

Steene, R. D., G. R. Allen and H. A. Baensch. 1978. **Butterfly and Angelfishes of the World. Volume II: Atlantic Ocean, Caribbean Sea, Red Sea and the Indo-Pacific**. John Wiley and Sons. (Magnificently illustrated treatment of the families Chaetodontidae and Pomacanthidae.)

Stokes, J. F. 1984. **Divers' and Snorkelers' Guide to the Fishes and Sea Life of the Caribbean, Florida, the Bahamas and Bermuda**. The Academy of Natural Sciences of Philadelphia.

Thompson, D. A., Findley, L. T. and A. N. Kersitch. 1979. **Reef Fishes of the Sea of Cortez**. John Wiley amd Sons.

# Concordance of Common and Scientific Names

Butterflyfishes ........................................................................................................ Chaetodontidae
   Arabian Butterfly ...................................................................... *Chaetodon arabicus*
   Banded Butterfly ........................................................................... *Chaetodon striatus*
   Barberfish, Cortez Wimplefish .................................... *Johnrandallia nigrirostris*
   Bennett's Butterfly ..................................................................... *Chaetodon bennetti*
   Black-backed Butterfly ............................................................. *Chaetodon melonotus*
   Common Butterfly ........................................................................ *Chaetodon plebius*
   Copperband Butterfly .................................................................. *Chelmon rostratus*
   Four-eyed Butterfly ................................................................ *Chaetodon capistratus*
   Four-spot Butterfly ........................................................ *Chaetodon quadrimaculatus*
   Heni, Wimplefish ................................................................ *Heniochus acuminatus*
   Lemon Butterfly, Crochet Butterfly ............................................ *Chaetodon miliaris*
   Long-nosed Butterflyfish ................................. *Forcipiger flavissimus, F. longirostris*
   Meyer's Butterfly ......................................................................... *Chaetodon meyeri*
   Mirror Butterfly ....................................................................... *Chaetodon speculum*
   Ornate Butterfly ................................................................... *Chaetodon ornatissimus*
   Pakistani Butterfly, Red-tailed Butterfly ................................... *Chaetodon collare*
   Pearlscale Butterfly ................................................................. *Chaetodon xanthurus*
   Pyramid Butterfly ................................................................. *Hemitaurichthys zoster*
   Racoon Butterfly ......................................................................... *Chaetodon lunula*
   Reef Butterfly ....................................................................... *Chaetodon sedentarius*
   Saddleback Butterfly .............................................................. *Chaetodon ephippium*
   Teardrop Butterfly .............................................................. *Chaetodon unimaculatus*
   Threadfin Butterfly ...................................................................... *Chaetodon auriga*
   Tinker's Butterfly .......................................................................... *Roaops tinkeri*
   Vagabond Butterfly ................................................................. *Chaetodon vagabundus*
   Yellow Butterfly .................................................................... *Chaetodon semilarvatus*

Cardinalfishes ............................................................................................................. Apogonidae
   Candystripe Cardinalfish .......................................................... *Apogon cyanosoma*
   Flame Cardinalfis ....................................................................... *Apogon maculatus*
   Pyjama Cardinalfish .......................................................... *Sphaeramia nematoptera*
   Red Cardinalfish ......................................................................... *Apogon erythrinus*
Chambered Nautilus ............................................................................ *Nautilus macrophalus*
Cleaner Shrimps ........................................................................................ *Lysmata* spp.
   Cardinal Cleaner Shrimp, Scarlet Cleaner Shrimp ............................. *Lysmata debelius*
   Caribbean Cleaner Shrimp .................................................... *Lysmata wurdemanni*
   Caribbean White-stripped Cleaner Shrimp ............................... *Lysmata grabhami*
   Catalina Cleaner Shrimp ..................................................... *Lysmata californica*
   Monaco Cleaner Shrimp .................................................... *Lysmata seticaudata*
   White-stripped Cleaner Shrimp ............................................ *Lysmata amboinensis*
Clownfishes, Anemonefishes ...................................................... *Amphiprion* spp.
   Cardinal CLownfish, Saddle CLownfish ................................. *Amphiprion ephippium*
   Common Clownfish ............................................................. *Amphiprion ocellaris*
   Maroon Clownfish ................................................................. *Premnas biaculeatus*
   Orange Skunk Clownfish ................................................. *Amphiprion sandaracinos*
   Saddle-backed Clownfish .................................................... *Amphiprion polymnus*
   Sebae Clownfish ..................................................................... *Amphiprion sebae*
   Skunk Clownfish ............................................................. *Amphiprion perideraion*
   Tomato Clownfish ................................................................. *Amphiprion frenatus*
   Yellow-tailed Clownfish ............................................................ *Amphiprion clarkii*
Colonial Anemones ....................................................................................... Zoanthinaria
   Green Colonial Anemone ............................................................ *Zoanthus sociatus*

Dancing Shrimps, Camelback Shrimps .................................................................... *Rhynchocinetes* spp.
    Red Dancing Shrimp ................................................................................. *Rhynchocinetes ringens*
    Rosy Dancing Shrimp ................................................................................... *Rhynchocinetes uritai*
Dottybacks .................................................................................................................... Pseudochromidae
    Bicolor Dottyback ........................................................................... *Pseudochromis paccagnallae*
    Orchid Dottyback ............................................................................... *Pseudochromis fridmanni*
    Red-capped Dottyback ......................................................................... *Pseudochromis diadema*

Egg Shells ............................................................................................................................... Ovulidae
    Flamingo Tongue Snail ................................................................................. *Cyphoma gibbosum*

Featherduster Worms ............................................................................................................ Terebellida
    Peacock Featherduster Worm ............................................................ *Sabellastarte magnifica*
Foxface .................................................................................................................................. *Lo vulpinus*

Giant Clam .................................................................. *Tridacna* cf. *elegans, Tridacna maxima*
Gobies .......................................................................................................................................... Gobiidae
    Bicolor Neon Goby ............................................................................................ *Gobiosoma evelynae*
    Blue-banded Goby, Catalina Goby ................................................................ *Lythrypnus dalli*
    Firefish ............................................................................................. *Nemaptereleotris magnificus*
    Green-banded Goby ................................................................... *Gobiosoma multifasciatum*
    Neon Goby ....................................................................................................... *Gobiosoma oceanops*
    Red Clown Goby ..................................................................... *Gobiodon quinquestrigatus*
    White-stripped Eel Goby ....................................................... *Pholidichthys leucotaenia*
Gorgonians, Sea Fans .......................................................................................................... Gorgonacea
Grammas ..................................................................................................................................... Grammidae
    Black-capped Gramma ............................................................................. *Gramma melacara*
    Royal Gramma ............................................................................................... *Gramma loreto*
Groupers ..................................................................................................................................... Epinephilinae
    Argus Grouper, Blue-spotted Grouper ........................................... *Cephalopholis argus*
    Blue-stripped Grouper ............................................................... *Cephalopholis boenack*
    Goldline Grouper ......................................................................... *Grammistes sexlineatus*
    Panther Grouper ............................................................................. *Chromileptes altivelis*
    Red Argus Grouper ..................................................................... *Cephalopholis miniatus*
    Saddleback Grouper ................................................................. *Plectropomus maculatus*
    Snowy Grouper ............................................................................. *Epinephelus summana*

Harlequin Shrimp ..................................................................................................... *Hymenocera picta*
Hawkfishes ................................................................................................................................. Cirrhitidae
    Arc-eyed Hawkfish .......................................................................... *Paracirrhites arcuatus*
    Flame Hawkfish ................................................................................. *Neocirrhitus armatus*
    Long-nosed Hawkfish ........................................................................... *Oxycirrhites typus*
Hermit Crabs ........................................................................................................... *Dardanus* spp.
    Caribbean Hermit Crab ......................................................................... *Dardanus cadenati*
    Red Reef Hermit Crab ............................................................................. *Dardanus megistos*

Jawfishes ................................................................................................................... Opistognathidae
    Pearly Jawfish ..................................................................................... *Opistognathus aurifrons*

Lionfishes, Scorpionfishes ...................................................................................... Scorpaenidae
    Common Lionfish .................................................................................................... *Pterois volitans*
    Dwarf Lionfish ..................................................................... *Dendrocheirus brachypterus*
    Fu Manchu Lionfish .............................................................. *Dendrocheirus biocellatus*
    Hawaiian Lionfish ................................................................................................. *Pterois sphex*
    Zebra Lionfish ........................................................................................ *Dendrocheirus zebra*

# Index

A **boldface** entry indicates an illustration of the cited subject.

# About the autors

**Hans Albrecht Baensch** has been a dedicated aquarist since ha was eight years old. During his younger years he spent very many hours at streams and ponds near his home in Hanover. At the time, his father was the owner of a pet shop and a fish breeding farm for tropical fish. Almost every day Hans Baensch was busy with fish.

At the age of 18, Hans ended his 2½ year apprenticeship as a zoological wholesaler and then began his travells of the world. He worked in Canada and U.S.A. for one year, and in 1961 entered his father's company TetraWerke.

Hans A. Baensch visited practically all tropical fish waters and countries of the world, such as Singapore, Hong Kong, Japan, Australia, Mauritius, Seychelle Islands, South Africa, Kenya, and the Carribbean. The climax of all his travells was the Amazon basin and the capture of the red neon and discus fish species which are to be found there.

Hans A. Baensch became general manager for sales and advertising at TetraWerke in 1970.

His interest in seawater aquaria was awoken during a trip to Asia, as the author experienced the often sad conditions in the fish farms and export companies there. In Mauritius he captured some seawater fish and brought them home with him for his own seawater aquarium. With much trial and error came the burning ambition to successfully rear and care for seawater fish.

During the past five years the author set up to 10 seawater aquariums in his home, using the Tetra research department for further studies. The "Marine Aquarists Manual" is the result of his own observations during this period.

**Dr. Paul V. Loiselle** is an accomplished aquarist of over twenty years experience. The internationally published author of numerous articles on the care and breeding of aquarium fishes, he is a Contributing Editor for *Freshwater and Marine Aquarium*. Dr. Loiselle has his Master's degree from Occidental College in Los Angeles, and took his doctorate at the University of California at Berkeley. His professional background includes five years as a Peace Corps fisheries biologist in West Africa, where he carried out faunal and environmental impact surveys in Togo and Ghana. During the course of his career, Dr. Loiselle has had the opportunity to observe the behavior of cichlids in Lakes Victoria and Tanganyika, in Mexiko and in Central America. A founding member and Fellow of the American Cichlid Association, he currently serves the A.C.A. as Technical Editor of its journal, *Buntbarsche Bulletin*, and as Chairman of the Special Publications Committee.

# Photographs